SOLIDARITY DIVIDED

The publisher gratefully acknowledges the generous contribution to this book provided by the Valerie Barth and Peter Booth Wiley Endowment Fund in History of the University of California Press Foundation.

SOLIDARITY
DIVIDED

THE CRISIS IN ORGANIZED LABOR
AND A NEW PATH TOWARD
SOCIAL JUSTICE

Bill Fletcher, Jr.
Fernando Gapasin

UNIVERSITY OF CALIFORNIA PRESS
BERKELEY   LOS ANGELES   LONDON

University of California Press, one of the most distinguished university presses in the United States, enriches
lives around the world by advancing scholarship in the
humanities, social sciences, and natural sciences. Its
activities are supported by the UC Press Foundation
and by philanthropic contributions from individuals
and institutions. For more information, visit
www.ucpress.edu.

University of California Press
Berkeley and Los Angeles, California

University of California Press, Ltd.
London, England

Library of Congress Cataloging-in-Publication Data

Fletcher, Bill, Jr.
    Solidarity divided: the crisis in organized labor and
a new path toward social justice / Bill Fletcher Jr.,
Fernando Gapasin.
        p.   cm.
    Includes bibliographical references and index.
    ISBN: 978-0-520-25525-8 (cloth : alk. paper)
    1. AFL-CIO.   2. Labor movement—United States—
History.   I. Gapasin, Fernando, 1946–   II. Title.

HD8055.A5F54   2008
331.880973—dc22   2007033594

Manufactured in the United States of America

17 16 15 14 13 12 11 10 09 08
10 9 8 7 6 5 4 3 2 1

The paper used in this publication meets the minimum
requirements of ANSI/NISO Z39.48-1992 (R 1997)
(*Permanence of Paper*).

Fernando Gapasin dedicates this book to his uncle Philip Vera Cruz, former vice-president of the United Farm Workers, who taught him about working-class solidarity and socialism.

Bill Fletcher, Jr., dedicates this book to the veterans of the Charleston 5 Defense Campaign, who demonstrated what global and national trade unionism could really be—and that we could win!

CONTENTS

PREFACE
Revelations in South Africa

JOHANNESBURG, SOUTH AFRICA. In a hotel conference room in June 2001, a critical dialogue took place between leaders of the U.S.-based Service Employees International Union (SEIU) and the South African National Education, Health & Allied Workers Union (NEHAWU). Also in the room were representatives of the Congress of South African Trade Unions, with which NEHAWU is affiliated. The discussion, part of a several-day exchange between the two unions examining issues facing their respective movements, focused on political action. After an insightful presentation by NEHAWU, a free-flowing exchange unfolded. A young progressive SEIU local union leader from the West Coast, commenting on the role of the union in political action, noted what must have seemed obvious to him: that the role of a union is to represent the interests of its members. The representatives of NEHAWU offered a careful and diplomatic reply: "Comrades," they began, "the role of the union is to represent the interests of the working class. There are times when the interests of the working class conflict with the interests of the members of our respective unions." Silence descended on the room. The SEIU leaders said nothing. Time seemed to have stopped. The discussion proceeded, but no one commented on the statement by the NEHAWU leaders.

In many respects, this book concerns that exchange, or at least the difference in vision and politics it dramatized. In that room in South Africa, we heard two approaches to trade unionism represented by unions and leaders who could all be defined as progressive. The contradiction that became evident spoke to the difference between the paradigm that has existed in the United States and the one that grew in South Africa over the years of struggle against apartheid. This book examines that paradigm in the context of the explosive developments rocking the U.S. trade union movement over the past decade.

The U.S. trade union movement finds itself on a global battlefield filled with land mines and littered with the remains of various social movements. It is engaged in a war for which it was entirely unprepared, having convinced itself that it had secured a permanent seat at the table of national authority because of its loyalty to the state during the Cold War and to the interests of U.S. capitalism. Though at its high point the U.S. trade union movement had gained representation for only slightly more than one-third of the workforce, that foothold gave the union movement significant power within the political and economic establishment of the capitalist United States.

As of the writing of this book, approximately 12 percent of the U.S. workforce is represented by unions. The National Labor Relations Act (NLRA), passed in the 1930s in the midst of a worker insurgency and a broad progressive movement, was poisoned by the Taft-Hartley amendments in the 1940s and, particularly as a result of judicial decisions, is largely archaic today.[1] Worse than archaic, the NLRA in practice serves the interests of employers in restricting the ability of workers not only to organize but also to bargain effectively against enormous employers who can mobilize massive resources.

Under permanent assault by capital, the union movement has increasingly been pushed onto the defensive. At each point, however, its leaders have wished to believe that the worst was behind them and that a new regime of labor-management peace could be secured. That peace has not come. Nor can these leaders, or anyone else, identify any sector of corporate America that intends to establish a new social compact with labor.

In the face of this frustration, struggles broke out in the AFL-CIO (American Federation of Labor and Congress of Industrial Organization) in the 1990s and early 2000s over the direction the union movement should take. The 1995 reform movement that brought John Sweeney, Richard Trumka, and Linda Chavez-Thompson to office also brought the *possibility* for labor renewal. Despite various initiatives, however, both in the AFL-CIO and among several of the affiliates, union representation continued to decline as a percentage of the workforce. Ultimately, frustration, personal ambition, and desperation resulted in a challenge to the Sweeney administration, first from Sweeney's own union—the Service Employees International Union—and later from several other big unions, which formed a coalition, Change to Win (CTW), to challenge Sweeney's leadership.

However, instead of setting off a great debate on the future of the labor movement, this challenge treated union members and their allies to months of sparring between opposing leaders in which secondary issues, such as the structure of the AFL-CIO and the amount of per capita rebates, became the charged discussion points. Big-picture questions about the global economy, the evolution of U.S. political structure, and the changing nature of the workforce were mostly ignored. The discussions not only ignored these key issues but also largely excluded those who matter most: union members. Except for opinion polls, Web news, and PowerPoint presentations, members remained largely out of the loop about what was transpiring in the clouds.

Even now, at the local central labor council (CLC, the local analogue to the national AFL-CIO) level, members and local union leaders are asking, "Did something happen? If it did, nobody included me in the discussion." In local areas where unions work together, there remain a commitment and a need to do so. Understanding this fact, the AFL-CIO and the Change to Win Federation have negotiated "Solidarity Charters." These charters allow local CTW unions to rejoin their local central labor councils and state federations. CTW unions will pay a national-level tax for their locals to participate at the local and state levels of the AFL-CIO. In local central labor councils, CTW members are saying, "I'm not sure what is going on, but maybe something good will happen." One thing is clear: the real issues facing U.S. workers are not being discussed. If somebody doesn't begin to make sense of this confusion, the union movement will continue to weaken—fast.

This situation was the impetus for our decision to offer another point of view—one that would challenge *both sides* and their respective frameworks. Between the two of us, we have decades of work in the union movement, at various levels and in more than a dozen unions, including experience as rank-and-file member, officer, and staff. In addition, as activists of color who have also been involved in the Chicano and the Black Freedom movements, respectively, we bring a unique viewpoint to a discussion of the future of the union movement. We do so in part because the perspectives of people of color are largely ignored in discussions about the future of the labor movement, except and only insofar as someone is addressing race. We do not accept such pigeonholing. Instead, we believe our experiences give us the opportunity and vantage point to look at the problems facing the U.S. trade union movement in a slightly different way.

This book is not an autobiography. Instead, we are participant observers in the social and historical process that has created today's U.S. union movement. Besides firsthand experience, our research is grounded in the study of original documents, historical analysis, and the review of scholarly literature, and we use critical ecological, institutional, and political perspectives to interpret this information. In the following pages, we examine the influences of the political, economic, and social environment on the union movement; formal and informal union systems; and the interaction of conflicting political ideologies and their effect on the union movement. After thus describing the current state of the union movement, we analyze the need and prospects for transformation and call for a critical reexamination of the ideological and structural underpinnings of today's union movement. We then look at the crisis in the U.S. trade union movement as it has developed over the past generation, ultimately examining the struggle that unfolded in the AFL-CIO and resulted in an unjustified split.

We contend that labor renewal in the United States depends on the adoption of a different theory and practice of trade unionism than has prevailed until now. Such an approach must understand the neoliberal global environment, reexamine who should be in the labor movement (and who is currently excluded), and redefine the role of the union movement in a process of social transformation. We are not interested in perpetuating illusions: the reality is that, absent an alternative, transformative trade unionism, the United States will see no labor renewal. Rebuilding the AFL-CIO, or even creating a new federation, will have been an exercise in futility unless we get to the roots of the problems facing organized labor.

We begin our narrative with the July 2005 boycott by the Change to Win coalition of the AFL-CIO Convention in Chicago. In Part I we examine the historical and ideological roots of U.S. trade unionism. Part II discusses the union movement after George Meany, the changing international situation, and the confluence of domestic social movements and the union movement. Part III examines "the crisis" in U.S. unionism that led to the election of the New Voice slate in 1995. Part IV looks at some of the roads not taken by the Sweeney administration and the implications of these lost opportunities. Part V outlines a transformative model for the union movement and discusses some key tasks necessary to create a union movement dedicated to social justice.

For fans of science fiction, we offer the following metaphor. In 1984 John Carpenter produced a film called *They Live* in which aliens had secretly taken over the Earth and transformed it into a neocolony. In doing so, the aliens had the cooperation of many Terrans. The aliens had a machine that masked their appearance to make them look like the rich denizens of whatever country they were in. A resistance group emerged who discovered that wearing a certain kind of sunglasses could help them identify who was actually an alien and who was human.

We are asking you, the reader, to take a deep breath and, yes, put on the sunglasses.

Fernando Gapasin
Bill Fletcher, Jr.

CHANGE TO WIN AND THE SPLIT IN THE AFL-CIO

JULY 2005, CHICAGO, ILLINOIS. Until the Sunday preceding the Monday (July 25) opening of the AFL-CIO Convention, many insiders, despite the heated rhetoric reflected in the media, believed that the two key factions would broker a deal to prevent a split in the AFL-CIO. Though the language had become increasingly incendiary over the previous eighteen months, backroom discussions had been taking place to construct an acceptable, face-saving rapprochement between the forces aligned with AFL-CIO president John Sweeney and those leading the newly formed Change to Win coalition—which included the Service Employees International Union, the International Brotherhood of Teamsters, UNITE HERE!, United Food and Commercial Workers (UFCW), Laborers International Union of North America (LIUNA), the United Farm Workers (UFW), and the United Brotherhood of Carpenters and Joiners of America (hereafter the Carpenters).

The existence of backroom discussions should have been a surprise to no one. Although many media commentators maintained that the clash within the AFL-CIO mirrored the 1930s clash in the old American Federation of Labor—which resulted in the formation of first the Committee on Industrial Organization and later the Congress of Industrial Organizations—those at the top of U.S. organized labor knew otherwise. Though views on the nature of a labor federation differed, the divergence between the two camps was far from antagonistic—or at least it should have been.

1

What did heighten tensions, however, was the way in which the evolving clash had been personalized by both sides, which seemed to many outsiders to be playing a gigantic game of "chicken," approaching each other at maximum speed. Neither side seemed to be prepared to brake, even though both groups knew they could avoid a collision by mutual action.

Individual members of the Change to Win coalition (later Federation)—with the apparent exception of at least the Service Employees International Union—undertook discussions with the Sweeney team to resolve the confrontation. In each discussion, they reportedly conveyed an interest in settling matters in a way that would avoid a split.

Despite suggestions that a deal was in the making, CTW held a Sunday afternoon press conference to announce that four of its six unions would boycott the convention. That press conference was noteworthy for three reasons: one, the CTW's evasiveness about why a boycott was necessary; two, the contradiction between the Change to Win coalition's submission of resolutions and amendments for consideration by the AFL-CIO and the fact that four of the six CTW unions would not be in the house to argue for them; and, three, the upbeat nature of these announcements. In discussing the last, veteran labor activist Jerry Tucker, reporting on the entire convention, contrasted the enthusiasm at the CTW press conference with the dismal atmosphere at the AFL-CIO rally taking place at the same time.[1]

The boycott demonstrates one of the most bizarre tactical approaches taken by the Change to Win coalition leading up to the split in the AFL-CIO. In preparation for the convention, the CTW coalition submitted fifteen amendments and resolutions under the collective title of "Amendments and Resolutions to Change the Federation to Win Better Lives for Workers and Their Families through Organizing and Maintaining Contract Standards" (dated July 2, 2005).[2] These amendments and resolutions, while in some cases suggesting significant changes in the AFL-CIO, were consistent with proposals that had been on the table during the prior two years of discussions. They were not fundamentally inconsistent with anything proposed by the Sweeney team. Thus, most observers were perplexed by the fact that CTW made little effort to win broad support either for the collective proposal or for individual measures. Further, the convention floor would have been an optimal venue for the Change to Win coalition to gain a national, indeed an international, hearing for its views. The much-desired debate on the future course of the labor movement, which had been so lacking in substance over the prior two years, could have actually taken place.

The unions that chose not to boycott the AFL-CIO Convention—LIUNA and the UFW—would not accept nomination and would not participate in the leadership of the AFL-CIO following the convention. This approach was interesting and curious, and, at least in the case of the UFW, it infuriated the Sweeney team. Essentially, these two unions chose to sit as observers at the convention, a course of action seen by many outsiders as fence-sitting while their leaders tried to decide whether to exit the AFL-CIO entirely.

The special fury generated by the UFW's position had historical roots. As columnist Nathan Newman noted in his July 23, 2005, blog, the UFW's defection to CTW must be set against the significant support, including a national march in 1997, that the Sweeney-led AFL-CIO offered to the UFW in its failed strawberry campaign in the mid-1990s. This action, combined with the history of antagonism between the UFW and the Teamsters in the California fields in the 1970s, when the AFL-CIO offered support to the UFW, made the UFW's decision to join CTW (which included the Teamsters) that much more difficult to take. The resulting bitterness in the Sweeney camp would have ramifications later in the year during discussions about CTW unions' affiliating with state and central labor bodies.[3]

The Change to Win unions have never explained why a boycott was necessary. The coalition's inability to clarify the differences between it and the AFL-CIO leadership pointed to one of two troubling possibilities. One possibility is a lack of cohesion within the CTW coalition and a lack of agreement on this tactic: the leaders were simply unable to explain the decision to boycott the convention without looking like fools. A separate—and more ominous—possibility is that a decision had already been made either to cripple or to destroy the AFL-CIO and to pick up the pieces from the shattered federation. Few other explanations are possible, given that the leaders of the CTW unions were, of course, familiar with bargaining strategy and unlikely to have been so incompetent as to back into a boycott followed by a split.

Further reason exists to question the tactical approach and the motives of those who first boycotted the convention and later left the AFL-CIO: the implications of a split for the state federations and central labor councils. Every state, as well as the Commonwealth of Puerto Rico, has a state federation (or, in the case of Puerto Rico, a commonwealth federation) of labor—that is, a state body representing AFL-CIO–affiliated unions. And hundreds of cities of varying sizes have central labor councils in which AFL-CIO–affiliated unions can participate. These bodies exist largely to facilitate union coordination, particularly in the areas of politics, legislation, and mutual support. At the leadership level of the national and international unions, the implications of a split for the state federations and labor councils received little discussion before the AFL-CIO Convention. Leaders of state and central labor councils were horrified at the possibility, yet CTW leaders largely ignored their voices until the very last minute—even though the possibility is remote that CTW conducted its discussions without considering all the potential impacts of a split.

The announcement of the boycott of the AFL-CIO Convention was followed the next day by the exit of the SEIU and Teamsters from the AFL-CIO. As with the earlier announcement, the enthusiasm sharply contrasted with the lack of substance. Change to Win was now off and running, with the exit from the AFL-CIO of UNITE HERE!, LIUNA, UFCW, and the UFW to follow in the next few months.[4] The formal establishment of the CTW Federation took place in September 2005 in St. Louis. The title of Jerry Tucker's analysis of the CTW convention summarizes an ongoing theme at the time—and to some a problem: "If Enthusiasm on Display Were Substance, CTW Could Claim a Good Start."[5]

The split in the AFL-CIO thus seemed to defy explanation. The existence of a crisis, one that included, but was not limited to, the declining percentage of the workforce in unions, was beyond argument. Nevertheless, when the split finally took place, many commentators were left scratching their heads. Though some in organized labor and its allies hoped the split might result in a renewal of the labor movement, the failure to embark on a substantive debate—as well as the lack of a dramatic transformation on either side—suggested that the struggle had been about personalities, egos, turf, and money. In our opinion, although all these factors contributed, the ultimate motivations behind the split were two: (1) money: some unions were seeking a way to reduce costs, which they did by ceasing to make payments to the AFL-CIO; and (2) insulation against globalization: those unions believing they could carve out a section of the workforce less affected by globalization (particularly job relocation) clashed with those unions affected more directly by these forces. Those remaining in the AFL-CIO represented a mix of unions very directly affected by globalization, such as the United Steelworkers of America, and those not, such as the majority of the building trades. CTW was constituted by unions believing themselves to be relatively free of the threat. The irony, of course, is that all workers are affected to varying degrees by globalization

Three years after the split, we can identify very little significant change in organized labor. Plans have been advanced and some projects undertaken, but even champions of the CTW Federation have found little to excite either supporters or would-be supporters. We must therefore ask some tough questions:

- What actually led to the split in the AFL-CIO?
- What lies beneath the crisis of U.S. trade unionism?
- Did either side advance an analysis of the situation facing workers globally and domestically that could be translated into a new and possibly winning strategy?

To answer these and many other key questions, we must dig behind the headlines. The crisis facing organized labor—indeed the crisis facing the entire U.S. working class—originated generations before the arrival on the scene of all the major and minor players in the AFL-CIO split. It is this story to which we turn our attention in the following pages.

PART ONE

CHALLENGES FACING
THE U.S. LABOR MOVEMENT

Workers of the world awaken.
Break your chains, demand your rights.
All the wealth you make is taken,
By exploiting parasites.
Shall you kneel in deep submission
From your cradle to your grave.
Is the height of your ambition to be
A good and willing slave?

Joe Hill,
"Workers of the World,"
1910

CHAPTER 1

DUKIN' IT OUT

Building the Labor Movement

Today's U.S. union movement is the product of relentless struggle between workers and employers. The strategies that the capitalist class has adopted to rid itself of the union movement have changed over time, but never the ultimate goal of leaving the working class unionless and defenseless.

When we think about capitalism, we usually think about competition between businesses, with one corporation trying to take market share and profits from the others. But capitalism also creates another form of competition: competition between workers to win and keep jobs and to secure other resources. Because of the fundamental imbalance in power and wealth within capitalist societies, workers are played against one another by employers, always to the employers' benefit. Labor unions came into existence in response to this problem facing working people. They formed because of the workers' need to develop a common front against employers rather than deal with employers on an individual basis.

The trade union movement appeared on the U.S. scene in the 1820s to 1840s, during the early Industrial Revolution. This period saw the emergence of Jacksonian Democracy, the rise of trade unions, the appearance of the first labor parties, and demands for a shorter work-week. It also saw the rise of the abolitionist movement.[1]

We must make a critical distinction here. Though this period witnessed the emergence of trade unions in the United States, it was not the beginning of a *labor movement*. If we understand a labor movement as an effort by workers to improve their conditions and strengthen their power against the forces of capital by organizing, then the actual labor movement in the United States started during the colonial period with the introduction of indentured servants—from Europe, Africa, and the First Nations—onto North American soil. Organizations existed among indentured servants and later slaves, and among artisans, sailors, and other workers, and these evolved into what we would consider unions in the nineteenth century.

Capitalism, wherever it is found, promotes competition within the workforce generally and the working class in particular. Yet in the United States, that competition took a particular form: beginning in the 1600s, ruling elites, as a matter of ensuring social control over the workforce, used racist oppression as a means of driving a wedge between workers. By constructing a relative—though critically important—differential between workers who would later be classified as "white" and those who would be characterized as Black and Red (Indians), colonial elites—planters, merchants, and manufacturers—were able to set groups of working people at odds with one another.[2]

In North America, the competition that capitalism engenders played itself out not just in pitting worker against worker, but increasingly in setting white workers against African, Indian, and later Asian and Latino workers, who were both demonized and subjugated, always defined as an "Other" to be expelled or as an irrelevant population to be used. Regardless of whether actual competition existed between white workers and workers of color, the notion that all "white people" shared certain things in contrast with the Other thus identified the latter as a threat to all those eventually classified as white. The net effect of this structure of social control was to create a white front crossing class lines and thereby blurring class distinctions (and class struggle) between and among those of European American heritage and people of color. It also eliminated the idea that common class interests crossed the legal and social boundaries separating workers of different "races."

In the developing labor movement, the color line became the main division within the working class, although other divisions—by religion, ethnicity or nationality, and gender—played important roles as well. In that sense, the fight over inclusion versus exclusion, which is a theme of this book, has always had racial implications.[3]

Indeed, the racial implications of exclusion and inclusion in effect crippled the U.S. labor movement from its birth. One can argue that the United States has never had a true labor movement, only a segmented struggle of workers. The establishment of essentially a white labor movement in the United States ensured that the character of the movement would depend on who, at any one moment, was determined to be "white"(a determination rooted in the orientation of the Euro-American ruling elites beginning in the 1600s). This situation prevailed until well into the 1930s. For instance, clauses in union constitutions limiting union membership to "white men of high moral standing" obviously excluded people of color and women but also excluded any group deemed to be unacceptable, including immigrants who had not yet "become white."[4] The inability of the white labor movement to break from the exclusionary (and largely racial) paradigm made labor vulnerable to constant challenges and caused it to deal with questions of immigration in reactive, if not reactionary, ways. Insofar as the U.S. white-dominated labor movement considered immigrants—first those from eastern and southern Europe and later those from the Global South—to be outsiders or competitors, it was unable to embrace these new sectors.[5] The history of labor-supported, cross-class efforts to exclude immigrants is legendary. And such efforts flowed directly from the racial construction of the United States.

With the formation of unions came a schism within the working class that would define the movement—and that continues to exist today. The central question was how to address the competition within the working class that capitalism engenders and exploits. One orientation was that of exclusion: the desire to increase the relative value of each worker by narrowing the number of workers with the skills needed by a particular employer. The other was that of inclusion: the desire to organize as many workers as possible to narrow the opportunity for employers to play off one worker against another. The resulting clash between exclusion and inclusion strategies took organizational forms both before and after the U.S. Civil War. In the pre–Civil War period, the trade union movement was white and largely male. Reflecting the controversy within the society as a whole, the labor movement was divided over the question of slavery, with some trade unionists supporting slavery (because they feared competition in the labor market from freed Africans); some opposing it (because they recognized that free labor can never compete successfully against slave labor); and some believing that slavery was not a "union issue" and was therefore divisive. The pre–Civil War union movement was never able to resolve these divisions.

In the period following the Civil War, a new union movement began to emerge, starting with William H. Sylvis's establishment of the

National Labor Union (NLU).[6] This movement, too, divided along the axis of race, with white workers tending to form unions, such as the NLU, that might fiercely oppose capitalism yet compromise completely on matters of race, often supporting the exclusion of African Americans, Asians, Latinos, and the First Nations.[7] And at each juncture in its struggle to unite workers and win concessions from employers, the union movement was divided over the question of exclusion. The great strikes of 1877, for instance, broke out in response to wage cuts and paralyzed much of the country's railroads for weeks. This bitter struggle took place at the same time that Reconstruction was being abandoned in the South, yet white labor did not see the course of Reconstruction as central to the future of the working class. The Knights of Labor, a dramatic effort to build a national labor federation during the 1880s, which at one point had seven hundred thousand members, openly welcomed African American and Mexicano/Chicano workers, yet shunned the Chinese!

In the early 1880s, the formation of the organization that eventually became the American Federation of Labor (AFL) marked the development of a relatively stable national labor federation on U.S. soil. Though rhetorically committed to organizing all workers regardless of race, creed, and gender, the AFL advanced craft organization as the key to the future of organized labor.[8] Ignoring the racial and ethnic cleansing taking place in the skilled trades and on the railroads of the U.S. South, where employers were removing African Americans from positions they had long held and replacing them with whites, the AFL welcomed into its ranks white-supremacist unions that often had clear racial-exclusion clauses in their membership requirements. Though the AFL did include certain industrial unions such as the United Mine Workers of America,[9] these groups were a minority of the unions in the federation, and the mind-set of the craft unions dominated the AFL. In time, the craft-based narrowness of the AFL expanded and merged into racial and gender narrowness. Workers of color were either excluded outright from the movement or restricted to second-class organizations, either within unions or within the AFL. Women, with the notable exception of the formation of the International Ladies Garment Workers Union and later the Hotel Employees and Restaurant Employees Union, were for the most part ignored.

Labor leaders staked out various positions along the spectrum from inclusion to exclusion as they sought to carve out a working-class movement in the United States. Eugene Debs and Samuel Gompers, for example, often took contradictory positions. By exploring their views, we can gain an understanding of the clashing visions that drove the U.S. working-class movement in general and organized labor in particular.

As the twentieth century unfolded, technological advances changed the methods of production. The advent of giant, integrated production centers and assembly-line processes transformed the nature of work and influenced the debate about the structure of the union movement.[10] One of the most articulate advocates for inclusionism within labor was Eugene V. Debs, a leftist president of the American Railway Union, founding delegate of the Industrial Workers of the World (IWW), and four times the Socialist Party's candidate for president. Debs opposed capitalism and argued for applying democratic political traditions to this economic system that subjugated workers in their daily lives. He was a powerful advocate of industrial unionism and criticized the American Federation of Labor's exclusionary craft policies. In 1918, as an expression of his radicalism, he wrote, "The Russian Revolution is the soul of the new-born world,"[11] and in June 1918, he delivered a series of speeches criticizing U.S. involvement in World War I. He spoke out against the idea that citizenship requires Americans to wrap themselves in the flag and pledge loyalty to these military adventures and exhorted workers to be free men and women instead of industrial slaves. Debs concluded that socialists have a duty to build the new nation and the free republic, and he called upon people to draw on their "manhood and womanhood to join us and do your part . . . to proclaim the emancipation of the working class and brotherhood of all mankind."[12] Debs was arrested for his speech under the Espionage Act of 1917 and sentenced to ten years in federal prison. In 1920, Debs, though still a federal prisoner, received one million votes in his last run for the presidency. Debs was representative of a political tendency within the labor movement that held industrial unionism—one union for one industry—not only as an essential part of unionism but as something close to a calling. This advocacy of industrial unionism overlapped with that of inclusionism, with proponents generally recognizing that industries could not be organized by labor groups that were divided along racial and ethnic lines.[13]

Debs and his allies realized that the structure of the U.S. economy was changing and that new forms of organization would be essential if the working class were to develop any power. Though Debs was a socialist, he was not sectarian and was quite prepared to ally himself with non-socialists. Moreover, though Debs and many other industrial unionists recognized the dire implications of racial exclusion, they did not quite "get" the question of race or understand the special oppression suffered by peoples of color. For example, Debs, while seeking the inclusion of African Americans into the American Railway Union, did not seem to appreciate the need for U.S. organized labor to address, first, the counterrevolution against Reconstruction and, later, the birth of Jim Crow segregation.

Debs was constantly at odds with traditionalist Samuel Gompers, who was president of the AFL from 1886 to 1924 and who had, originally and ironically, been a socialist. By the early 1900s, all sense of Gompers as a man of the Left had vanished. Speaking at the 1903 AFL convention, for instance, Gompers denounced any belief in class struggle as the basis of working-class trade union organization. Taking a position counter to Debs's orientation, he told socialist delegates, "Economically, you are unsound; socially you are wrong; industrially, you are an impossibility."[14]

With this attack on the left wing of the trade union movement, Gompers broke with the then-prevalent political position in the United States and Europe: that the working class should have its own political party. He believed that the role of the trade union was to fight in the interests of workers in the workplace. However, the trade union movement should accept the existence of capitalism and take no steps to oppose the system itself, instead working for its fuller development and evolution.[15] In repudiating socialism, Gompers declared that he no longer opposed the capitalist system: as he told a House of Representatives investigating committee, "It is our duty to live out our lives as workers in the society in which we live."

Gompers's view, which became known as "bread-and-butter" or "job-conscious" trade unionism, emphasized a formally nonideological approach.[16] In the political realm, this stance meant that organized labor would not, to paraphrase Gompers, have permanent friends or enemies but permanent interests. Though this view might appear to be class conscious, Gompers was not speaking about the entirety of the working class: he was speaking only of its organized sector. When Gompers spoke of political action, he was thinking of lobbying rather than the political mobilization of the working class. Gompers's view was thus an early version of today's so-called interest-group politics.

Gompers's trade unionism grew out of his view of class, the state, and, by implication, issues of race, gender, and U.S. foreign policy. His views evolved (or devolved) from his original adherence to socialism in two important respects. First, his renunciation of socialism and the elimination of a compelling anticapitalist view of the future are critical in understanding Gompers the man as well as what we term the *Gompersian framework*. The role of trade unionism was simply to improve the lives of those who were fortunate enough to be union members. Gompers embraced a form of trickle-down thinking in his belief that the victories of trade unions might at some point improve the lives of unorganized workers. Yet the unorganized sector was not Gompers's concern. In his opinion, if unorganized workers wanted a better life, they should join or form unions.

This belief reflected the exclusionary tendency within the U.S. trade union movement. In the late 1800s and early 1900s, the AFL excluded the bulk of unskilled workers, as well as the mass of workers of color and female workers. This pragmatist pursuit of narrowly defined self-interest by most organized labor demonstrated the concept's inherent racism and sexism.[17] The pursuit of "what works" in the immediate term, and in the absence of a larger conceptual framework that questioned the structure of existing social relationships, resulted in capitulation to white supremacy and male supremacy. Regardless of rhetoric such as "an injury to one is an injury to all," the evolution of the Gompers-led AFL reveals a blind spot, even a wall, to issues of race, gender, and ethnicity, which organizers saw as divisive.

In addition, Gompers came to view government as essentially an empty vessel that could be filled by any sort of politics or political or economic influence. Thus, he believed the trade union movement's purpose was to pressure government to act on issues facing organized labor specifically and workers in general. In his view, the working class need not challenge the capitalists for state power. In simplistic terms, the state was open to influence by either organized labor or big business, so organized labor's job was to gain the greater influence. Gompers thus abandoned the notion that the state has a class character.[18] As we will see, assuming that the government is a neutral force in society ignores the reality of the government's bureaucracy and its influence, the pressures that lead to pro-business legislation, and the factors that encourage the suppression of independent working-class activity of any sort.

These precepts influenced the political practice of Gompers and the trade union movement he led. In embracing pragmatism, Gompers also slowly but steadily abandoned any earlier concerns about matters of race and gender. After the great 1892 general strike in New Orleans, the question of race lost importance for him. By the early 1900s, Gompers's advocacy of a form of racially inclusive unionism had given way, first, to agnosticism on matters of race and, ultimately, to open promulgation of white supremacism.

One significant aspect of Gompers's views on the state and class was his reading of the relationship of unions to business and matters of foreign policy. Having repudiated the notion of class struggle, Gompers believed that labor and capital have a unity of interest in improving the economic climate that justifies their cooperation. His policy of rewarding friends and punishing enemies, according to a sympathetic biographer, flowed from his need to be accepted by the "leaders" of society, not from the power of the broad masses of working people.[19] In the realm of foreign policy, this view took a particularly rabid form, for Gompers believed that organized labor should support U.S. foreign policy almost unconditionally.[20] Perhaps the most dramatic step in this direction was his unqualified support for U.S. entry into World War I and his support of the suppression of opponents of the war. In his view, the interests of organized labor lay with strengthening capitalism and ensuring the success of U.S. foreign policy, regardless of the impact on workers in other countries. The flag of imperialist patriotism was to be the banner of the AFL.

Gompers's political views (which we would call traditionalist) translated into a narrow political direction for organized labor, reflecting positions that would continue to benefit, in the main, the privileged white workers who made up most of the AFL. Gompers supported the government's Asian exclusionary policies and personally denied membership to Japanese workers when they and their Mexican brothers sought affiliation with the AFL. In 1903, after a hard-fought struggle for fair wages, Japanese and Mexican workers created the Japanese-Mexican Labor Association (JMLA) and, with their seven hundred members, applied for a charter with the AFL. In response, Gompers wrote, "It is . . . understood that in issuing this charter to your union, it will under no circumstance accept membership of any Chinese or Japanese. The laws of our country prohibit Chinese workmen or laborers from entering the United States, and propositions for the extension of the exclusion laws to the Japanese have been made on several occasions [by organized labor]."[21] The JMLA refused the charter under these racist conditions. The Mexican members of the JMLA leadership, in rejecting Gompers's proposal, proclaimed their solidarity with their Japanese brothers, explaining that they had stuck together through the harshest of times and would not be divided now: "We would be false to them and to ourselves if we accepted privileges for ourselves which are not accorded to them."[22] The terms set by Gompers and the failure of the AFL to accept the Japanese into the federation set the stage for the ultimate demise of the JMLA.

The protection of craft jobs, rather than the idea of organizing workers and developing the AFL as a class movement, was the credo of the AFL. This emphasis placed Gompers at odds both with the masses of workers of color (particularly, but not solely, Black workers who were seeking admission to unions) and with the growing demand for industrial unionism.

Gompers presided over the expansion and consolidation of an exclusivist federation, one that was quite comfortable—at least at the leadership level—in suppressing internal and external opposition (the most notable external opposition coming from the Industrial Workers of the World). The AFL was, for Gompers, a partner with U.S. capital and the U.S. state in their program of world expansion. That this partnership with capital put the AFL in direct opposition to the interests of the mass of workers in the United States, as well as to those of workers around the world, did not concern Samuel Gompers.

CHAPTER 2

THE NEW DEAL

The labor movement of Samuel Gompers and Eugene Debs at the end of the nineteenth century confronted employers who were transforming the economy from a laissez-faire operation to one dominated by trusts and monopolies. Business interests were moving away from the rail-road "pools" of Jay Gould to John D. Rockefeller's Standard Oil and Andrew Carnegie's U.S. Steel. In response to the abuses of these power-ful new national corporations, Populism developed in the 1890s out of farmers' alliances and farmer-worker alliances in the Midwest, West, and South. Populists advocated an increase in the money supply, greater government regulation of business, and other reforms to enhance the political voice of voters and improve the lives of farmers and workers. In 1889 and 1890, radical farmers formed the People's Party, usually called the Populist Party. Socialism and Populism were widely seen as political alternatives to the traditional two-party system and had a sig-nificant influence on electoral politics during the early part of the twen-tieth century.[1]

Both the socialist and populist movements called for social and eco-nomic justice and spread the idea that government intervention was needed to alleviate the misery caused by the unpredictable swings of a capitalist economy and the manipulations of markets by powerful cap-italists. These ideas, in diluted form, helped fuel Progressive Era reforms, from Theodore Roosevelt's Square Deal of 1904 to Woodrow Wilson's New Freedom of 1913.

During the 1912 presidential campaign, for example, the platforms of the Socialist, Progressive, and Democratic Parties contained reforms that required the state to intervene on behalf of working people, including social insurance, the eight-hour workday, restrictions on child labor, minimum-wage legislation, and safety and health standards. Democrat Woodrow Wilson, influenced by the "People's Lawyer," Louis D. Brandeis, called for labor's unequivocal right to organize, citing it as a key aspect of his New Freedom.[2]

Whereas the Socialist, Bull Moose, and Democratic Parties argued that the state should play a positive role in industrial society, Gompers stood in opposition to progressive reforms. In hearings before the 1914 Industrial Relations Commission, Gompers emphatically expressed the AFL's opposition to minimum-wage legislation for men and state insurance for the unemployed: "For a mess of pottage, under the pretense of compulsory social insurance, let us not voluntarily surrender the fundamental principles of liberty and freedom, the hope of the United States, the leader and teacher to the world of the significance of this great anthem chorus of humanity, liberty."[3]

World War I brought an end to the Progressive Era, with the labor movement and Socialists and other leftists split on whether to support U.S. intervention in the war. Opposition to the war led to government prosecution and purges of antiwar leftists. Moreover, the defeat of a series of strikes, from the 1919 steel strike led by future communist William Z. Foster to the bitter coal and railway strikes of the early 1920s, broke attempts by labor radicals to unite skilled and immigrant labor. A postwar employers' offensive rolled back labor's wartime gains and nearly halved the AFL membership during the 1920s.

William Green was selected by the AFL Executive Council to succeed Samuel Gompers as president of the AFL in 1924 after the latter's death. Green accepted the position only after getting the approval of his boss, John L. Lewis, president of the United Mine Workers of America (UMWA). Green, a traditionalist, was in favor of industrial unionism but continued to maintain the narrow policies of the dominant craft unions. He strongly opposed communists and radicals generally. He railed against strikes and militant mass action by workers and embraced a religiously inspired apparition of labor-management cooperation. At the 1929 AFL convention, delegates voted unanimously to engage all the affiliated unions in a massive campaign to organize textile mills in the South. Southern workers demanded a militant approach to organizing, but as the AFL opened its campaign at a conference in Charlotte, North

Carolina, on January 6, 1930, Green devoted most of his speech to attacking the methods of Communists and advocating the "constructive" and Christian mission of the AFL.[4] Appealing to all kinds of social and civic groups, Green assured the South that the AFL was not composed of godless radicals and troublemakers and that the AFL's organizing work was "paralleling the work of the Church."[5] But union organizers met only stiff resistance, and not a single textile mill heeded Green's message of Christian charity. Despite continuous failures, Green persisted in his message of labor-management cooperation.

The 1920s, a decade that combined deep attacks on workers with myriad proposals for collaboration between the working and capitalist classes, gave way to the Great Depression in October 1929; by 1933, one of three U.S. workers was jobless. Looking for relief, U.S. unions backed the election of Democrat Franklin Roosevelt in 1932. Roosevelt's New Deal adopted Keynesian economic strategies that expanded government intervention into all aspects of the economy, including labor-management relations.[6] With the National Labor Relations Act in 1935, government created a vehicle to mediate the conflict between capital and the growing insurgency of the U.S. working class and its unions.[7] Pragmatist union leaders such as John L. Lewis of the United Mine Workers and Sidney Hillman of the Amalgamated Clothing Workers of America (ACWA) appeared to understand that the social conditions spawned by the Great Depression and the interventionist strategy of Roosevelt's New Deal had created an opportunity to accelerate social democratic politics and industrial organizing.[8] Pragmatist leaders of this period also understood that if they did not take the initiative to advocate a corporatist model, they could lose their ability to maintain a union movement within the context of capitalism.[9] Leftist unionists had played a vital role in building the momentum for industrial unionism, linking industrial unionism with the broader struggle to expand democracy. They were the most disciplined, dedicated, and active union organizers and were a major force within what evolved from the Committee on Industrial Organization to the Congress of Industrial Organizations (CIO). Lewis and Hillman, by contrast, were staunch defenders of capitalism. Though they were leaders in the AFL, their unions, the UMWA and ACWA, were already industrial unions. While the majority of the AFL leaders had become complacent in the face of changes in U.S. capitalism (as well as changes in the political situation) and were willing to abandon the larger interests of the U.S. working class in order to maintain their jurisdictional claims, pragmatist leaders like Lewis and Hillman understood that unless they made the structural adjustment to broad-scale industrial organizing and included women and workers of color within their ranks, they would have no union movement to lead.[10] Lewis and Hillman hinged their success on their unequivocal support for Roosevelt.[11] And Lewis, although he was an anticommunist who voted Republican most of the time, employed many communists and socialists as the leading organizers for the CIO because he understood that he had to build a strong rank-and-file movement if he was to maintain the mass base to leverage Democratic Party support. Lewis also understood that, at that historical moment, he and the Left had overlapping though not identical agendas.

The notion of overlapping but not identical agendas is critically important for understanding the developments of the 1930s, including the confusion that arose within the Left at certain periods. Paul Buhle, in discussing Hillman, puts the pieces together in a useful way:

> Communists usually found common ground with Sydney Hillman of the new Amalgamated Clothing Workers of America (ACWA), who more successfully rode the waves of militancy, modulating the challenges by embracing or coopting erstwhile leftists (including Communists) who saw the successful mobilization of labor as the great possibility of the time. But the problem was never simply one of flexible and inflexible leaders. By the 1930s, the Jewish-led unions, especially the ILGWU [International Ladies Garment Workers Union] and ACWA, had the requisite strength and energy to establish a framework for the emerging industrial labor movement. Located in the regions somewhere between liberalism (or the liberal socialism of the "mixed economy," a phrase invented by an ILGWU educational director) and conservatism (including quiet acceptance of a prevalent racism), this style of unionism placed heavy emphasis upon maintaining the support of government allies—first in Albany, then in Washington. These two unions, the ILGWU in particular, had played no small role in isolating the Industrial Workers of the World, before the decisive federal government crackdowns on the Wobblies. The ACWA would play a very large role in strategizing a CIO path mediated with government functionaries and political leaders, sans the participation of ordinary workers or systematic regard (rhetoric apart) for the fate of racial minorities and others left out of the compact.[12]

Roosevelt's support contributed to the success of the historic United Auto Workers (UAW) sit-down strike in Flint during the winter of 1936–37, when neither he nor the Democratic governor of Michigan would use the National Guard or the army to evict the striking autoworkers.[13] But the decisive factor in the UAW victory was Lewis's alliance with assorted leftists in the UAW, including Wyndham Mortimer,

Bob Travis, Nat Ganley, Kermit Johnson, Genora Johnson (Dollinger), and Victor Reuther.

The Roosevelt administration continued to construct a social safety net and helped create a political and social environment conducive to notions of social justice, through reforms like the Fair Labor Standards Act, social security, welfare, unemployment insurance, and widespread public-works projects. Direct assistance to militant workers, as in the Flint sit-down strike, began to decline almost immediately as opposition from conservatives increased; the Little Steel Strike of 1937 was defeated when Ohio's governor used troops to break it up, and Chicago police killed ten workers at a Memorial Day demonstration in support of the strike.

After the victories in auto and big steel, John L. Lewis gained national fame and popularity. Lewis was, however, always an *enigmatic* pragmatist labor leader. Sidney Hillman was the classic pragmatist labor leader. He was committed to reason, progress, and science and desired to change traditional cultures, but he was uninhibited by ideology in his pursuit of power. He viewed unionism as a method of taming the anarchy of laissez-faire capitalism. Probably more than any other union leader, he forged the corporatist model in an attempt to tie together the conflicting interests of government, business, and unions. He created the CIO's Labor Non-Partisan League to mobilize support for Roosevelt.[14] He later helped found a CIO political action committee (known after the merger of the AFL and the CIO in 1955 as the AFL-CIO Committee on Political Education) to funnel support to the Democratic Party. Hillman worked secretly with Roosevelt to undermine Lewis after Lewis attacked the administration for failing to aid unions more actively. Just before the 1940 CIO convention, Hillman attempted to obtain a blanket endorsement from the convention for all of Roosevelt's domestic and foreign policies. Roosevelt rewarded him with appointment as associate director of the Office of Production Management later that year. Unfortunately for the union movement, Hillman's sycophantic relationship with Roosevelt forced him to take positions against the interests of unions—for example, his support of Roosevelt's decision to use federal troops to break a wildcat strike by the UAW against North American Aviation.[15] Hillman's relationship with Roosevelt made him lose sight of his independent base in the union movement and his real power as a labor statesman. Instead, he lived out his life as a minion for the Democratic Party.[16]

In focusing on these individuals and their views, we have an opportunity to look at the contending ideological orientations of the time, particularly along the spectrum from exclusion to inclusion, as well as the demands of different social bases. As white men, the leaders we discuss here represented the dominant, if not exclusive, strain of leadership in organized labor. Their status as white male labor bureaucrats influenced to a great degree their practical and theoretical interpretation of the categories we explore in the next chapter: leftists, pragmatists, and traditionalists.

Although the union movement in the United States has always had a Left tendency or segment—including the Industrial Workers of the World, Mexicans affiliated with both the IWW and the revolutionary Partido Liberal Mexicano in the U.S. Southwest, the Syndicalist League of North America, and the International Working People's Association—the left wing of today's union movement was originally shaped by its experiences between 1919 and 1947.[17] During that period, capitalism was being challenged by the social experiment of socialism. In the wake of the Russian Revolution, amid the horrors of World War I, people throughout the world began to believe that another world was possible and that through a revolutionary socialist movement, the working class and other oppressed peoples could liberate themselves. Socialism has existed in many forms, with the main current rooted in the theories of Karl Marx and Frederick Engels. From there, variations developed, several of which took shape in the first socialist state, the Union of Soviet Socialist Republics (USSR). The two main variations were evident in the split between Bolshevism (which evolved into Stalinism) and Trotskyism.[18] U.S. socialism also had indigenous roots in U.S. populism and anarcho-syndicalism.[19] During the period of union formation in the early twentieth century, socialist parties, such as the Socialist Party of America, the Communist Party (CP), and later the Socialist Workers Party, had many common roots.[20] Many other leftist groups and individuals participated in the U.S. union movement as well. They shared several basic beliefs: that class struggle exists; that the purpose of unions is to organize workers in their self-interest; and that through the day-to-day fights for their economic interests, workers could come to understand the true nature of capitalist society and eventually organize to end capitalism.[21] To varying degrees, forces on the left believed that unions had to look beyond the immediate economic interests of the workers in one or another workplace and become vehicles for making socialist principles a reality in the workplace and transmitting this program to the rest of society.

Leftist organizations, especially the Communist Party, the Socialist Party, and later the Socialist Workers Party, put their beliefs into practice through political positions or "lines" that, if adopted, could be translated into organizational bylaws and collective-bargaining demands by unions.[22] The organizational Left thus had the capacity to push similar positions or lines in a variety of workplaces simultaneously, positions that reflected the social aspirations and economic concerns of working people.[23] In general, leftist parties and groupings were essential players in developing a class-conscious militant core within a variety of unions.[24] These militants included many members of the most dedicated and committed union cadre of this period, and they were essential to the early success of the CIO during labor's upsurge during the strike wave in 1936 and 1937.[25] The CIO union movement thus became an instrument for asserting the hopes of many workers.

At the apex of its influence within the U.S. trade union movement during World War II, the Communist Party, the largest party of the organized Left, made a policy decision to liquidate its independent presence within the trade unions and adopt a position of nearly unconditional unity within the movement, despite the sharp differences within the movement about the direction forward. Earl Browder, the principal leader of the CP during the 1930s and through most of World War II, took the ultimate step of liquidating the CP as a political party in 1944 and declared that monopoly capital in the United States was being domesticated and that the contradictions between labor and capital were no longer antagonistic.[26] This position was influenced by the position of the international communist movement, which advocated building a united front against the Axis during World War II. Browder and his allies in the U.S. Communist Party believed that the Yalta agreements between the major antifascist allies signaled the arrival of long-term peace, not only between the Soviet Union and the West but also between those who advocated socialism and those, like Roosevelt, who seemed to advocate a more "humane" capitalism. The CP's position weakened the Left's position in the CIO, particularly in the UAW, because it undermined the Left's reputation for militancy and its ability to act independently within the trade unions.[27]

Despite constant attacks, communists and other leftists continued to build strong unions and to strengthen the CIO throughout the 1930s and 1940s. Research, particularly by Judith Stepan-Norris and Maurice Zeitlin, shows that unions built by leftists were statistically more democratic, allowing different factions of workers to shape union policy, than were non-Left-led unions. In addition, contracts negotiated by Left-led unions, which advocated workplace democracy and vigorously fought management prerogatives, tended to be more prolabor than those negotiated by their rightist critics. The studies show that leftists also negotiated far more contracts that maintained the right to strike and contained grievance procedures, with much shorter time spans for resolution. This line of research, supported by our experience, contradicts the conventional wisdom that rests on the work of Robert Michels and Seymour Martin Lipset.[28] Michels's *The Iron Law of Oligarchy* points to the alleged natural tendency of bureaucracies to maintain themselves and their leaders. Lipset asserts that Communists have a corrosive effect on democracy in unions.[29] In the real world, however, leftists tend to create more democratic procedures, if for no other reason than to ensure that they have a voice in institutions and societies that otherwise restrict their point of view. This research suggests that the road to oligarchy or democracy is the result of political struggle and choice. Unions led by leftists have a significantly larger chance of moving along the path of democracy.[30] Indeed, the effectiveness of the Left in championing U.S. democracy and social reform, with a strong base in the CIO and other unions, is precisely why it became a target of the Cold War witch hunts of the late 1940s and early 1950s.

CHAPTER 3

THE COLD WAR ON LABOR

Following World War II, the architects of U.S. policy resolved that the wartime alliance with the Soviet Union had to end and that the political Left and progressive movements had to be rolled back domestically. The Cold War became the instrument for carrying out this program, but it is worth noting—particularly in light of the neoliberal offensive beginning in the 1970s—that the attack on the Left and progressive movements was largely a political attack rather than an economic one. The living standard of the average U.S. worker continued to rise even while many of the vanguard forces fighting for social justice were themselves under assault.

This "golden age" of the post–World War II era created illusions about the fundamental nature of capitalism and helped lay the basis for organized labor's continued suppression of the Left. The prosperity of the postwar years seemed to promise workers that their lives, and their children's, would improve without any need for radical initiatives. Much of the U.S. labor movement became convinced that labor must continue to follow the strategic direction set by American Federation of Labor founder Samuel Gompers. This path was one of unapologetic acceptance and support of U.S. capitalism and loyalty to the U.S. capitalist state in its Cold War struggle with the Soviet Union—a Faustian bargain that would, millions of workers believed, ensure stability, prosperity, and social harmony.

This postwar "social contract" or "social accord" with capital played itself out in all the advanced capitalist countries to one degree or another, but in the United States it had particular elements worth noting.[1] Cold War competition between the United States and the Soviet Union quickly followed defeat of the Axis powers in 1945. In Western Europe and Japan, both heavily damaged by the war, the competition between the two antagonists was heavily influenced by forces on the political Left. These forces included, but were not limited to, pro-Soviet communist parties as well as other parties and organizations on the socialist and revolutionary Left. In Western Europe, the combination of these factors, together with fear of a renewal of the Great Depression of the 1930s, led to broad acceptance of the notion of a welfare state, though the process of winning the welfare state had actually started in the 1930s in response to both the Great Depression and the danger of fascism.[2]

With the end of the Cold War and the opening of many files and archives, we can now see that the Cold War was largely about containing the Soviet Union and squeezing the political Left in the advanced capitalist world. Little evidence exists that the Soviets had any postwar plans to invade Western Europe; indeed, their primary interest seemed to be in securing what they understood to be their sphere of influence (which the Western allies appeared to recognize in the Yalta agreements in early 1945).[3]

The so-called Red Scare purges of the U.S. union movement that occurred throughout the 1940s and the 1950s were the result of several factors: the general Cold War assault on the Left, both domestically and internationally; weak leadership in the union movement that was prone to surrendering real working-class power to maintain the semblance of labor-management cooperation; and poor strategic decisions by leftists themselves, in particular by the Communist Party.

As the tension between the USSR and the United States increased, so did the anticommunist tenor of U.S. public life—providing an opportunity for conservative forces to roll back New Deal reforms. The Taft-Hartley amendments to the National Labor Relations Act, for instance, not only moved against the political Left in the union movement but also straitjacketed the movement by limiting the tactics it could use to organize workers and bargain with employers. These attacks on the unions proceeded under the guise of leveling the playing field between labor and capital while ridding the union movement of communist trouble-makers. A drumbeat of anticommunist attacks in the media blamed militant strikes, like the 1946 Allis-Chambers strike in Milwaukee, on communist leadership in the CIO and set the stage for congressional conservatives to force through the Taft-Hartley Act in 1947 over the veto of President Truman. In addition to its so-called right-to-work (for less) provision and its limits on secondary boycotts, the Taft-Hartley Act required unionists to sign an affidavit affirming that they did not support the Communist Party.[4]

Leaders of the CIO like Philip Murray and John L. Lewis opposed the affidavit requirement up to 1949.[5] By contrast, Walter Reuther took advantage of the tools handed him by the Taft-Hartley Act to consolidate his control of the UAW. Aligning himself with the rabidly anticommunist Alliance of Catholic Trade Unionists (ACTU) and anticommunist socialists, he defeated the Communists and their allies at the 1947 UAW convention and consolidated his faction's hold over the UAW. His move in the UAW paved the way for the CIO's surrender on the anticommunist affidavit issue in 1949.

For the CIO and the U.S. union movement, the loss was devastating. Left-led unions had about 1.4 million members, and in 1949–50, the CIO expelled eleven of these unions for refusing to sign the anticommunist affidavit; eventually sixteen unions left the CIO. These unions still constituted a formidable force, but in large part because of the CP's decision to emphasize labor unity, they formed no alternative federation. The CP leadership had concluded that creating an alternative or third labor federation would further fuel anticommunism and increase the isolation of the Left. Instead, the Left decided to attempt to influence the CIO—principally—and the AFL secondarily from the inside. The CP tried to convince members of Left-led unions such as the United Electrical Workers to join AFL or CIO unions rather than establish their own coalitions, thus further undermining the most militant sector of the U.S. union movement.[6]

Despite Taft-Hartley, the mainstream union movement did not sense itself to be under a full-scale assault by capital and its right-wing political allies.[7] Yet with the purge of the political Left, the overall strategy of the union movement underwent significant changes. Pragmatists like Reuther aligned themselves with traditionalists in opposing the Left's class-struggle approach to the labor movement. In doing so, they ushered in a version of trade unionism that assured an increase in the standard of living for the unionized section of the working class while accepting tight restrictions on the exercise of union power.[8] This postwar social accord with capital was symbolized by the so-called Treaty of Detroit in 1950, in which corporate America bought back managerial initiative and control of the shop floor in exchange for cost-of-living raises, employer-sponsored health care, and pension plans.[9] The price was abandonment of class struggle against corporate America and further bureaucratization of the union movement.[10] Grievance and arbitration procedures replaced the right to strike. "Professional" labor-relations representatives replaced rank-and-file shop stewards as the primary representatives of the unions. Grievance procedures became more complicated and legalistic. Collective bargaining came to be almost entirely limited to economic issues, and struggles for control of the work process were almost completely abandoned. The process of collective bargaining itself became an insular firm-or site-based process that only rarely became a forum for broad social or political engagement.[11] Thus, over time, the NLRA (as amended by the Taft-Hartley Act and interpreted by the courts) became a legal mechanism to thwart organizing efforts and restrict union actions.

And the unions affiliated with the CIO, which had tended to be more progressive on racial matters, backed away from any thoroughgoing commitment to racial justice. The CIO's Operation Dixie, an attempt to organize the South between 1947 and 1953, collapsed, with a contributing factor being the purge of the Left.[12] By the early 1950s, for example, African American workers found themselves at odds with both employers and union leaders, necessitating independent forms of organization, such as the short-lived National Negro Labor Council (1951–55). Except for receiving support from Left-led unions, Chicanos in the Southwest were also largely abandoned by the union movement.[13]

Ironically, the formation of the AFL-CIO in 1955 coincided with the high point of unionization in the United States: thereafter, the percentage of the workforce represented by unions began a slow decline (though the absolute number of union members remained relatively steady over the decades). Coming slightly more than five years after the purge of the Left-led unions, the merger signified the surrender of the much-weakened CIO to the AFL and the renunciation of any effort to build an alternative trade unionism by the pragmatist leaders of organized labor. Thus, even before the end of the so-called golden era of postwar capitalism in the early 1970s, the union movement in the United States had hit an impasse.

The ascension to the leadership of the AFL-CIO in 1955 of a consummate union bureaucrat clearly indicated the future direction of the federation. George Meany, a quintessential traditionalist, had become a union plumber in 1916, been elected to his local's executive board in 1920, and in an effort to avoid seasonal work, had become his local's business manager in 1922. From that time until he retired from the AFL-CIO in 1979, he was never off the union payroll. Meany was a narrow craft unionist straight out of the tradition of Samuel Gompers, and he bragged about never having been on strike or walking a picket line. He believed that the function of unions was not to organize unorganized workers but rather to preserve the privilege of union membership for a stratum of already organized skilled workers. Meany built his career as a bureaucrat on his encyclopedic knowledge of union jurisdictions, contracts, and work classifications. When he confronted nonunion workers, his goal was not to organize them but to take their jobs away: "We didn't want the people . . . ; we merely wanted the work. So far as the people who were on the work were concerned, for our part they could drop dead."[14]

Meany was a virulent anticommunist who believed that the fight against communism should take precedence over the welfare of the trade union movement.[15] The AFL-CIO barred Communists from membership.[16] It also set up, with U.S. government funding, international institutes to train trade unionists from around the world and promote what it euphemistically called "free-trade unionism" but which is more aptly described as "anticommunist" or "anti–left-wing" trade unionism. One such institute was the American Institute for Free Labor Development, which came to be associated with anticommunist activity in the Western Hemisphere, including, but not limited to, efforts to oust the prime minister of British Guiana (currently Guyana), Cheddi Jagan, in 1964 and Chile's president Salvador Allende in 1973.[17] Meany staunchly supported the Vietnam War and worked diligently to influence state federations and local central labor bodies to do the same. One of the main jobs of AFL-CIO field staff became the policing of AFL-CIO bodies to prevent infiltration by leftist organizations. Meany was thus constantly at odds with radicals and militants inside and outside the union movement. The AFL-CIO supported the passage of the Civil Rights Act of 1964, but Meany vehemently opposed Black militancy in any form. Under Meany, an extremely narrow version of bureaucratic business unionism became entrenched in the culture of the U.S. union movement.[18]

Many people saw the UAW's Walter Reuther as a progressive in contrast to Meany. However, Reuther underwent his own evolution, rapidly changing from a social visionary who advocated the redistribution of wealth through collective bargaining to a pragmatist who crushed the ideological core of militancy in the union movement and created a model for the modern bureaucratization of union activism. Reuther's model for unions set in motion the trend toward narrow service unionism and contributed to the current decline of the U.S. union movement. Even now, when a quick review of the *Wall Street Journal*'s editorial page makes it clear that the capitalist class has abandoned the postwar compromises typified by the Treaty of Detroit, union pragmatists still hope to reform the system to create a new version of the postwar social accord.

CHAPTER 4

THE CIVIL RIGHTS MOVEMENTS,
THE LEFT, AND LABOR

The post-1955 period is often mischaracterized as a dormant period for labor organizing. Contrary to a view that gained some prominence during the early 1990s, organizing continued after the merger that created the AFL-CIO. It was different from the organizing of the 1930s and the Left-led organizing following World War II largely in its scale and character. Post-1955 organizing generally lacked the dynamism, strategic focus, and social movement "feel" of the earlier period, in no small part because efforts in the 1950s lacked the leadership and energy of the Left.[1]

Despite the crushing defeat of the Left and the dominance of "business unionism" during the Meany years, important organizing did occur. The most significant, from our perspective, was the success of the United Farm Workers union, whose leader at that time, César Chávez, gained renown as a major leader of the Chicano Movement and of the struggle for both civil rights and economic justice. After decades of organizing by numerous farmworker organizations, the community-based unionism of the National Farmworkers Association, inspired by Saul Alinsky–trained organizers and implemented by Mexican and Filipino farmworkers, succeeded in securing collective bargaining for more than seventy thousand farmworkers. To win union recognition, workers struck and orchestrated an international boycott for five years, turning their struggle into a spearhead of the Chicano/Mexicano Movement and a rallying point for advocates of social justice. The UFW also withstood a major raid by the Teamsters Union, largely inspired by then-president Richard Nixon, a friend of agribusiness, and implemented by Nixon's close ally Teamsters president Frank Fitzsimmons.[2] Fitzsimmons said, "As far as I'm concerned, as a trade unionist for 47 years, César Chávez is not a trade unionist. I wouldn't even let him be a janitor in a trade union office."[3]

The UFW strike was led by the Mexican and Filipino union leaders and was largely supported by the United Auto Workers and by the AFL-CIO organizing director, Bill Kircher, a former UAW organizer. On several occasions, the UFW and Meany were in conflict about the scope of the boycotts, primarily because of the impact on the Retail Clerks International Union (now United Food and Commercial Workers) and the amount of money spent on the effort. Tension also existed between the UFW and the AFL-CIO because of the UFW's left-wing staffers and the broader Left's support for the UFW.[4] Meany, commenting on Chávez, made his own outlook clear: "I admire César Chávez. He's consistent and I think he's dedicated. I think he's an idealist. I think he's a bit of a dreamer. . . . He's fighting not only the ranch owners and the Teamsters, he's fighting the Bank of America and the State of California. He's got a hell of a problem."[5]

The UFW's legacy of 1960s organizing tactics and strategies inspired the Sweeney/New Voice administration of the AFL-CIO to the extent that many thought that the 1997 Watsonville demonstration of more than thirty thousand people in support of the campaign by UFW strawberry workers was the coming-out party of the New Voice AFL-CIO. Despite the magnitude of the demonstration, however, it was not matched by the emergence of a new broad-based farmworkers' *movement*.

The Meany years were also the time that the Teamsters, after being purged from the AFL-CIO for corruption, organized themselves into the largest amalgamated union in the United States, with nearly two million members. The strategies that the Teamsters used then and that the SEIU uses today are not new. In the 1860s, William H. Sylvis (founder of the National Labor Union, the first attempt to create a national labor center) used similar techniques in an effort to control specific labor markets. The goal was to control wages and thereby reduce or eliminate competition between companies in the same industry. "Leverage" strategies, developed by socialist Farrell Dobbs, were responsible for the meteoric growth of the International Brotherhood of Teamsters (IBT) during the late 1950s and 1960s.[6] IBT grew rapidly under the pragmatist and often controversial leadership of James Hoffa, Sr. Leverage campaigns, or what SEIU calls "pressure" campaigns, require broad-based organizing aimed at unionizing large sections of a particular labor market and finding economic, social, or political circumstances that will pressure companies within that labor market to acquiesce to unionization. Leverage or pressure campaigns may eschew NLRB secret-ballot elections and challenges when companies offer neutrality or voluntary recognition or enter into card-check agreements (in which they agree to acknowledge a union if a majority of employees sign cards verifying their union membership). Strategically, such campaigns can also move far more rapidly toward a first contract than traditional organizing approaches can.

The importance of such strategies is clear because they offer an alternative to organizing one workplace at a time in an industry, which is a tremendous resource drain and can fail more broadly if individual companies either gain the support of other nonunion firms or cannot compete with nonunion firms. If industry-wide pressure campaigns are part of a strategy for social and economic justice, the workers' desire for unionization can align with broader social justice forces, expanding progressive conditions and the potential for building political power.

THE SIXTIES: THE LEFT, CIVIL RIGHTS, AND UNIONS

The Left and progressive movements launched critiques of organized labor in the early to mid-1960s that focused largely on the racial politics of labor and labor's general approach to social issues. By the late 1960s and early 1970s, the critiques intensified, taking two directions: one strain of criticism charged that unions as presently constructed could never bring about fundamental social change and therefore needed to be replaced by alternative organizations; the other held that unions suffered from ossified leadership, so replacing those leaders would open the path for dramatic change.

The slow decline of organized labor was not particularly noticeable until late in the 1960s. More noticeable was the evaporation of any sense of a movement almost the moment that the Left-led unions were purged from the CIO in the late 1940s. Black trade unionists began challenging the CIO in the early 1950s with the formation of the National Negro Labor Council. By the late 1950s, A. Philip Randolph was openly challenging the newly formed AFL-CIO from the inside on its inconsistency and frequent racism, resulting in his decision to take the lead in the formation of the Negro American Labor Council.[7] Internal and external challenges to racism in organized labor, particularly the battles to desegregate the building trades, revealed the alienation of organized labor from other progressive social movements.

Though historians often cite the infamous attack on anti–Vietnam War demonstrators by some New York construction workers as an example of the antipathy between organized labor and the progressive movements,[8] the attitude of organized labor toward internal racism and the dynamic Black Freedom Movement was a more telling indicator of the larger problem. Organized labor, as a whole, had failed to grasp the strategic significance of the growing civil rights movement in the 1950s and early 1960s. Operation Dixie was dying at the point that the civil rights movement was being born. Only a few unions, such as District 65 of the Distributive Workers of America and Local 1199 of the National Union of Health and Hospital Workers, fully appreciated the importance of building a bloc with the Black Freedom Movement. Some other unions, such as the United Auto Workers, supplied financial aid and some political support but had internal practices that were not compatible with the objectives of the Black Freedom Movement. The national AFL-CIO supported legislative initiatives in favor of civil rights but avoided linking itself to the movement.[9]

The radical caucus movement represented an insurgent challenge to organized labor. Though the League of Revolutionary Black Workers (and its founding organization, the Dodge Revolutionary Union Movement) was certainly the leading force in this movement, the caucus movement was very diverse, running the gamut from ad hoc groupings against the Vietnam War to union democracy movements, campaigns for racial justice aimed at both employers and unions, and semisyndicalist formations that sought either to replace existing unions or to transform them.[10]

The caucus movement, being largely an outgrowth of the civil rights/Black Power movements and the anti–Vietnam War movement, was affected by the decline of those movements as well as by the 1973–74 recession. At this point, the caucus movement evolved in two different directions. The semisyndicalist efforts, such as the League of Revolutionary Black Workers, went into a steep decline and disappeared, with some its members moving on to form Marxist-Leninist organizations. At the same time, certain union-reform efforts began to emerge, such as the Miners for Democracy and Teamsters for a Democratic Union (TDU). The Miners for Democracy helped rid the UMWA of corruption and lay the foundation for a renovated organization. TDU helped jump-start the process of change and democratization in the Teamsters and remains an important force in that union to this day. The critiques by the caucus movement never entirely disappeared and continued to influence developments both within the union movement and in the so-called workers' center movement.

THREE IDEOLOGICAL TRENDS

In the preceding chapters on labor's development and consolidation up to the eve of the 1970s neoliberal assault, we identified Eugene Debs as a leftist, Samuel Gompers as a traditionalist, and John L. Lewis and Walter Reuther as pragmatists. Despite continual attempts to ensure a "safe" and ideologically monolithic labor movement (for example, the purges of the so-called Red or Left-led unions in the late 1940s), contention among these three ideological stances continues to exist within labor. Today the dominant coalition of traditionalist and pragmatist union leaders continues to shape union culture, whereas leftists get co-opted or marginalized. This situation limits the union movement's scope of struggle and narrows unions' political and social impact.

Though some might argue that other theories about the labor movement influenced these changes, we find three ideological perspectives to be most relevant: we call these positions *leftist, pragmatist,* and *traditionalist,* recognizing that each contains a range of views.[11] Each of these perspectives has its own way of answering three key questions:

1. What are the constituencies of the union movement?

2. Who are the friends, allies, and enemies of the union movement?

3. What is the geographic scope of our concern for the working class?

Labor activists' answers to these questions, laid out in the sections below, help place them in one of the three categories.

The Labor Movement's Constituencies

Pragmatist and traditional unionists consider the primary constituency of the labor movement to be union members. Leftists like Eugene Debs, Wyndham Mortimer, Nat Ganley, Rose Schneiderman, A. Philip Randolph, William Z. Foster, Miranda Smith, and Bert Corona defined that constituency more broadly to include all members of the working class.

The AFL-CIO's decision to admit undocumented immigrant workers provides a recent example of pragmatist unionists' broadening their view of labor's constituency. Before 1999, the AFL-CIO supported the employer sanctions provision of the 1986 Immigration Reform and Control Act, and most union leaders opposed the inclusion, or practiced the exclusion, of immigrant groups in U.S. unions. Leftists in the union movement helped bring about the AFL-CIO's dramatic shift, prompting the organization to call for repealing employer sanctions, demand full amnesty for undocumented immigrant workers, and promote equality with U.S. workers under existing labor laws. The shift occurred mostly because of the increasing number of immigrant workers in sectors of the economy that the union movement wants to organize. Thus, pragmatic concerns drove some trade union leaders to change their stance on organizing immigrant, especially undocumented, workers.

Allies and Enemies

Traditionalist unionists like Samuel Gompers, William Green, Philip Murray, and George Meany considered "good capitalists" and some politicians to be their allies. Sidney Hillman's relationship with Franklin Roosevelt illustrates how pragmatists and traditionalists rely on alliances with important figures in the U.S. business and political establishment. Traditionalists in particular see communists, socialists, and leftists generally as the enemy: George Meany's fear of leftists marked every decision he made about the domestic and foreign policy of the AFL-CIO.[12]

Leftists tend to define allies and friends as those who favor a range of reforms that aim to enhance the power and welfare of working-class people. In a strategic sense, allies are participants in social movements whose struggles objectively weaken imperialism. Leftists usually view pragmatist unionists as potential allies. Enemies for the Left include transnational corporations, the International Monetary Fund, the World Bank, and government elements that support antiworker or antipeople policies. Most leftists also see traditionalist unionists as enemies, largely because the traditionalists are normally on a continual search-and-destroy mission against progressives and leftists inside and outside the union movement. Although segments of the Left have often been at war with one another in fits of sectarianism, such conflicts turn upside down leftists' typical definitions of strategic allies and enemies. The period of the so-called Popular Front—from 1935 to 1939 and later between 1941 and 1946—was an interesting effort to forge Left unity.[13]

Pragmatists generally define friends and allies in the same way that traditionalist unionists do. However, they view leftists, communists, and socialists less as enemies than as potential (but disposable) allies they can call on if they need dedicated and disciplined ground troops—for example, when organizing is a priority for the union movement. John L. Lewis's reliance on communist organizers in building the CIO during the 1930s is the classic example of this view; César Chávez, whose alliance with leftists combined political and personal relations, is a more recent example. Anyone who threatens the power or institutional leadership of pragmatist union leaders is an enemy. For example, longtime leader of the United Auto Workers Walter Reuther, although he had been influenced by both communists and socialists in the 1930s, engaged in a ruthless factional battle against Communist Party–aligned members of the United Auto Workers in his drive for supremacy. Once in control, he worked to stamp out opposition to his "one-party rule" in the UAW. This action contradicted his attacks on the alleged antidemocratic policies of the Communist Party and other leftists (domestically and internationally). Reuther also had an ambiguous relationship with labor traditionalists and sought to distinguish himself from them. For example, he supported the civil rights movement while presiding over a segregated UAW bureaucracy.

Geographic Scope

Leftists are concerned about workers around the world and seek to unite with them in their struggles against oppression. Pragmatists are more interested in how cooperation with workers around the world can help preserve U.S. unions. In contrast, traditionalist unionists (such as Samuel Gompers, Philip Murray, and George Meany) tend to support U.S. international policies and the policies of companies employing their members, because they consider their interests to be tied directly to the success of U.S. corporations.

As we'll see in the following chapters, however, U.S. corporations, which had been willing to buy peace with labor in the Treaty of Detroit, changed their tune during the 1970s. At that point, they decided that their own interests were no longer tied to participation in a social compact with labor.

PART TWO

THE REVOLUTION WILL
NOT BE TELEVISED

When you get too old to produce anymore,
They hand you your hat and they show you the door.
Too old to work, too old to work,
When you're too old to work and you're
too young to die.
Who will take care of you, how'll you get by
When you're too old to work and you're
too young to die?

Joe Glazer,
"Too Old to Work," 1956

CHAPTER 5

WHOSE WELFARE
MATTERS, ANYWAY?

NEOLIBERAL GLOBALIZATION

To make sense of the crisis that faced trade unionism in the Global North beginning in the 1970s, we must understand the economic shift that undermined the welfare state in the advanced capitalist West.[1] The economic stagnation that afflicted the United States by the early 1970s was the result of many factors, including the cyclical end of the long postwar boom, the Vietnam War, competition from other capitalist states like West Germany and Japan, and domestic class struggle that put pressure on corporate profits. Within Western Europe, the verdict on capitalism was far from clear. Britain had gone into a downward spiral almost immediately after World War II and was facing the implications of the end of its empire. Other capitalist states, such as West Germany, Sweden, and Japan, were faring much better in competition with the United States, having integrated themselves into the U.S.-dominated global capitalist system and, in the case of Germany and Japan, having rebuilt from the ashes of the war. As many commentators have pointed out, this integration was both peculiar and particular in that the advanced capitalist states surrendered a significant degree of their foreign policy to the United States in the name of fighting the Cold War. The United States offered these nations military "protection," and as a result they did not have to divert their resources into defense spending and could instead invest in rebuilding more modern, competitive industries.[2]

Ironically, the Soviet bloc and much of the West entered almost simultaneously into a period of economic stagnation, which the welfare states of the West (Japan, Western Europe, the United States, and Canada) were unable to accommodate. In the United States, in response to the Vietnam War and the demands of progressive social movements (such as the Black Freedom Movement), President Lyndon Johnson tried to buy maneuvering room through a policy of "guns and butter" that combined deficit financing of a major war with domestic social reform programs. His successors during the 1970s tried to deal with a combination of radical social movements and economic stagnation and inflation by increasing the tax burden on the middle-income sectors, including sections of the working class, small businesses, and professionals and managers, rather than on the corporations and wealthy. By the late 1970s, this strategy for coping with the growing crisis had prompted many people to identify the welfare state as the primary problem in society.[3] This factor made the middle strata particularly susceptible to reactionary antitax messages and movements.

Right-wing populist demagogues in the 1970s, who were set on rolling back various domestic reforms, aimed to stop social and economic reform by cutting off the oxygen to the public sector through attacks on the tax structure. Building an unstated but objective alliance between the wealthy and the middle-income segments, they sought tax relief by cutting or eliminating key taxes and making the system more retrogressive. Thus, rather than making the system more progressive, lawmakers responded by increasing taxes in indirect ways (by instituting fees, for example) for lower- and middle-income taxpayers. Essential revenue for government programs dried up, creating a vicious cycle of shrinking government and popular frustration with the government's inability to deliver needed services. California's Proposition 13 in 1978, which froze property taxes at existing levels, was the opening salvo in this offensive against the public sector, public service, and, indeed, the working class.

Though President Nixon had declared in 1971 "we are all Keynesians," the reality is that ruling circles in the United States and other capitalist countries were searching for new economic models. The 1970s saw adoption of new, post-Keynesian models that promised to break the hold of stagnation and inflation and restore corporate power and profits. Central to these strategies was the imposition of discipline on the working class, which meant—from the standpoint of the working class—wrecking their organizations and diminishing their hopes and expectations. Working-class people in the advanced capitalist world, and particularly in the United States, would no longer be able to expect continuing improvement in their standard of living. Federal Reserve chairman Paul Volcker gave the following official summary of the program in a report to Congress in 1979: "The standard of living of the average American has to decline."[4] In optimistic and misleading terms, the architects of the program advocated reinforcing the ethos of "sacrifice" and "coping" among the people, but particularly among those within the working-class and lower-middle strata. They wanted to reorient these citizens to focus on themselves as individuals and, perhaps, as family units, but to give up the notion that "struggle pays," at least in any collective sense.

The assault on the U.S. working class during the 1970s was linked to, though not identical with, the counterattack that began against other progressive social movements. The decade witnessed the rise of the anti-choice (antiabortion) movement, which not only sought to eliminate a woman's right to choose but also aimed to reinforce patriarchy more generally. And the 1970s began with the often-deadly repression of the social movements of people of color.

In fact, the assault on the U.S. working class was successful precisely because the opening round targeted people of color, who could thus be blamed for the growing woes of the working class as a whole (but particularly the white working class). The idea was that this focus would minimize resistance.

This scenario played out at both the local and the national levels, with the leadership of organized labor—again—unprepared both ideologically and practically to resist the assault. For example, in the late 1970s, General Dynamics, which was among the most reactionary of employers, chose to introduce a new management philosophy at the Quincy Shipbuilding Division in Quincy, Massachusetts. One of the first steps was to smash the 1977 strike led by Local 5 of the Industrial Union of Marine & Shipbuilding Workers of America.[5] Defeating the union was not difficult, and in many respects, this workplace-focused action was emblematic of developments in organized labor nationally. The very conservative leadership of Local 5 had expected a more or less traditional employer-union bargaining scenario. With little preparation, on a warm July day, the leadership called for the strike, and the members voted their approval. Hundreds of workers took to the streets on the first day, but a court order quickly limited the number of picketers, and the Local 5 leadership had no follow-up strategy in place. After three months, the Local 5 leadership settled the dispute, largely on management's terms, and the workers returned to work. The returning workers, however, were demoralized and angry, and the leadership offered little direction.

Over the next two years, conditions at the shipyard became more repressive. For example, the company unilaterally decided to ban napping during the third shift (11:00 P.M.–7:00 A.M.), which had been allowed as long as workers had completed their assigned jobs and were unobtrusive. General Dynamics first targeted Black and Latino workers for immediate termination if they were found sleeping. Management's assumption was actually quite brilliant: given the conservative and predominantly white nature of the Local 5 leadership, the company could expect nothing more than formal resistance to such actions because, after all, Blacks and Latinos were the only ones losing their jobs.[6]

Many national leaders of organized labor in the United States fell prey to similar strategies. The nearly complete disconnect between organized labor and the progressive social movements of the 1950s and 1960s, plus the open opposition of organized labor to aspects of those movements, left the national leaders of the union movement with the illusion that—despite all the warning signs—they were on high ground and could ignore the approaching tsunami.

An additional complication for the leadership of organized labor was the growing resistance among the working-class members of organized labor. Inspired by other progressive movements, these members had launched a caucus movement. Although the most famous caucus was probably the one that spurred the formation of the League of Revolutionary Black Workers, other movements, including the Miners for Democracy and smaller insurgencies in the telephone industry and other sectors, rattled labor's leadership. These insurgencies had various objectives, some related to workplace problems and others related to developments within the union. A new leadership was emerging from these struggles that threatened conventional business unionism.

The 1973–74 recession was the first and probably most dramatic form of discipline meted out against the working class in the new era.[7] The shock of the oil squeeze, layoffs, and the beginning of large-scale plant closings placed the working class in jeopardy.[8] This period in effect ushered in the phenomenon that came to be called "deindustrialization," though a better description is "deurbanization of industry," in the context of capitalist restructuring.[9] This period also followed an extremely repressive period aimed at eliminating the more left-wing leaders of the progressive social movements of color.[10]

Neoliberalism, the common term for the economic model emerging at the time, was thus not a conspiracy hatched in a small room but the result of experimentation and struggle within the ruling circles. Introduced in the 1970s by British prime minister Margaret Thatcher and later U.S. president Ronald Reagan, the notion first took shape in the economic approach of the Chilean military dictatorship that overthrew democratically elected President Salvador Allende in 1973. The dictatorship made no attempt to buy off the working class; instead it moved to eliminate its organizations and atomize its existence as a class. The Chilean rulers dismantled public social benefits and saw privatization as the key to economic development. One of the most notorious examples of this policy in action, one that is relevant to the U.S. debate on the future of the social security system, was General Pinochet's privatization of Chile's pension system.[11]

Neoliberalism was thus not simply an approach to domestic economics. Rather, it became the philosophical underpinning for the reorganization of global capitalism, the process generally referred to as "globalization." Its five main characteristics are privatization, deregulation, casualization of the workforce (use of casual workers to avoid committing to full-time contracts), deunionization, and free trade. We examine neoliberalism in greater detail later in the book.

THE STORM BREAKS: LANE KIRKLAND
AND THE PATCO STRIKE

The social accord ushered in by Reuther's postwar Treaty of Detroit came to a dramatic end with the 1981 strike of the Professional Air Traffic Controllers Organization (PATCO).[12] When President Reagan fired the air traffic controllers, the immediate response of Lane Kirkland, Meany's handpicked successor, was to appeal to Reagan's decency and remind him of his tenure as president of a union, the Screen Actors Guild (AFL-CIO). Kirkland believed that such an appeal would be the best way to restore the jobs of the thirteen thousand fired controllers. Three possibilities might explain Reagan's refusal to back down: Reagan could not remember his past, he had no decency, or the AFL-CIO lacked power. Many people then thought that Reagan would ultimately back down if organized labor barked loudly enough and long enough. Kirkland, under pressure from both pragmatist and leftist unionists, agreed to sponsor a public display of unity for the fired air controllers. The Solidarity Day March and national demonstrations in the fall of 1981 attracted an impressive number of protesters, but these events were one-shot deals. Kirkland and the leadership of the AFL-CIO cooled growing militancy by ruling out coordinated work stoppages by AFL-CIO unions for fear that the unions would be penalized via the no-strike clauses in many contracts.[13] The Taft-Hartley restrictions aimed at preventing general strikes and the contractual bars to striking were indeed formidable obstacles. In any case, the AFL-CIO leaders could have entertained and implemented other forms of activity but did nothing else.

Organized labor was both technically and theoretically unprepared for Reagan's assault. While acknowledging Reagan to be a political conservative, they clearly expected someone much more like Richard Nixon—that is, a Republican who was prepared to make peace with organized labor, at least at a price. Reagan, much like Margaret Thatcher in Britain, had a different agenda. And organized labor, having thought itself immune to the repression of progressive social movements during the 1970s, was unable to conceptualize, never mind generate, the social force necessary to resist Reagan's new conception of labor relations.

The AFL-CIO did not grasp that the growing right-wing movement in the United States was not only amenable to attacking the social movements of people of color and women but also to neutralizing progressive efforts generally and gutting the power of even the most conservative sectors of labor. Carrying out this strategy called for changing the overall political climate, including raising hostility, particularly among middle-income whites, toward social programs and collective demands by workers. The late 1970s and early 1980s marked the beginning of the "greed is good" era, typified by George Gilder's best seller *Wealth and Poverty* (not surprisingly, according to Gilder, the best way to help the poor was to make the rich richer). Reagan popularized such notions by suggesting that the time for social movements had ended and that the country now needed greater stability. Stability really meant less resistance by the oppressed. In the wake of President Carter's firing of postal workers after the 1978 wildcat strike and then the dramatic firing of the PATCO workers by President Reagan, organized labor had no sense of how to build a massive social movement that was anything more than a lobbying effort. Organized labor made excuses for its inaction rather than reflectively and self-critically acknowledging that labor's "Pearl

Harbor" had taken place and that a new form of class warfare was unfolding on a national level.[14]

FROM CRISIS TO COLLAPSE

AFL-CIO president Lane Kirkland clearly realized that organized labor had a problem, but he had no framework for addressing it. He made special efforts to reunite within the AFL-CIO key unions that were outside the federation, including the United Auto Workers, the International Longshore and Warehouse Union, and the Teamsters. He also appointed AFL-CIO secretary-treasurer Thomas Donahue to oversee a new effort known as the Committee on the Evolution of Work. This committee produced a report in 1984 that received a great deal of attention because of its suggestions for reorganizing the union movement.[15] However, most of its recommendations were ignored.

But Kirkland had another side: he was an unapologetic Cold War trade unionist. In fact, by the 1990s, Kirkland's fixation on international affairs was unnerving many leaders of the affiliated unions. His obsession with overthrowing Soviet-bloc regimes and attempting to undermine communist and Left-led movements, such as the South African anti-apartheid movement and the Central American anti-imperialist movements, led him to align the AFL-CIO with Reagan's foreign policy at the same time that Reagan's domestic economic and political policies were undermining working-class people and their unions. Kirkland never drew the connection, or if he did, he chose to ignore the implications. In the late 1980s, several unions—most prominently, the United Auto Workers—finally broke openly with Kirkland on foreign-policy issues, publicly condemning U.S. intervention in Central America and forthrightly supporting the antiapartheid movement in South Africa. These unions joined with others to sponsor, in 1987, a major rally in Washington, D.C., against U.S. policy in Central America and South Africa.

With the end of the Cold War and the collapse of the USSR, any remaining tolerance that affiliate presidents had for Kirkland's approach dissipated. Although Kirkland believed in organizing, he wanted to build U.S. labor into a reliable partner of U.S. capital and a supporter of U.S. foreign policy, a goal that was entirely consistent with Gompers's vision of the role of the U.S. union movement. In this regard, he was a true traditionalist. He also focused his attention on the Washington Beltway, cultivating relationships with the White House and congressional leaders. Three debacles brought home to many in the AFL-CIO the failure of his leadership: the passage of the North American Free Trade Agreement, the collapse of Bill Clinton's health-care initiative, and the 1994 congressional victories handing control of the House of Representatives to Newt Gingrich and the Republicans. With these events, frustration with Kirkland turned into a mutiny.

CHAPTER 6

WHAT'S LEFT FOR US?

Elements of the Old Left and the New Left, from a variety of traditions, participated in the caucus movements of the late 1960s and 1970s. Without the institutional base the Left had enjoyed before the purges of the late 1940s, it lacked power. But in some unions, the Left was able to maintain a presence. In the UAW, with its history of caucuses, some thirty or more leftist or left-leaning caucuses functioned in plants throughout the United States. At the UAW conventions in the 1970s, Left-influenced delegates numbered between two hundred and three hundred. In 1977, a coalition of pragmatists and leftists was briefly able to slow down the concession movement led by the UAW International. Later, many UAW members active in the caucus movement formed the New Directions caucus, which challenged the Leadership Administration caucus of the UAW with a progressive slate of reforms for the UAW and for the U.S. union movement.[1] Yet the overall reform movement stumbled.

Contending views emerged within the reconstituted left wing of labor about how to assess the depth and scope of the crisis facing the union movement. The following sections outline this clash of views.

UNIONS CAN NEVER BE REFORMED

The view that unions were immune to reform became very popular in the late 1960s and early 1970s and led to the formation of alternative unions and unionlike organizations. In the wake of the experience of the

League of Revolutionary Black Workers, the Young Lords Party (a revolutionary Puerto Rican organization largely based on the East Coast) helped form the Health Revolutionary Unity Movement (HRUM).[2] This group attempted to navigate the ground between being an independent union and being an independent, revolutionary workers' organization. Similar organizations appeared across the country, such as the Transfusion organization (a Boston-area group of radical health-care workers) and, in the construction industry, predominantly organizations of workers of color, including Harlem Fightback, the Boston-based United Community Construction Workers (UCCW), and later the Third World Workers Association.

These organizations were either explicitly left wing or clearly led by people on the left. They showed the influence of radicalism in the workers' movement and the impact of the freedom movements of people of color, and several of them were able to attract significant support among workers. UCCW is an interesting case. As Philip Foner noted:

> Leo Fletcher, formerly of the Boston Urban League, convinced the black construction workers in the Boston area that they needed a separate organization to represent the minority work force in the area. The group formed the UCCW and, in a "Black Construction Workers Manifesto," declared that it did not have faith in the commitment of the established union of construction workers or the political power structure "to secure and maintain the rights of minority group workers in the Roxbury, Dorchester, and South End Community, and that this organization will make policies and organize to enforce those policies." The UCCW pledged to move against "every contractor that practices racism and discrimination against our people and who is depriving us of our rights as Americans, depriving us of economic stability for ourselves and our families."[3]

However, these movements or initiatives faced some dilemmas. Given the National Labor Relations Act and the codification of exclusive rights to collective bargaining to one union at a time, these radical workers' organizations could not compete with the existing unions for representation.[4] This situation led to a major identity crisis. The UCCW, and later its progeny the Third World Workers Association (TWWA), could not determine whether to define itself as a union, though in many respects it acted as if it were. Yet the UCCW and TWWA held no collective-bargaining agreements with contractors, and often—along with the Harlem Fightback and Black Economic Survival in New York—they found themselves at war with the building trades unions *and* contractors. To retain an institutional existence, TWWA formed the Third World Jobs

Clearing House, which helped construction workers of color obtain employment. In time, however, a debate emerged as to whether Third World Jobs Clearing House should be placing workers in nonunion construction or whether it should be more directly confronting the racist practices of most of the Boston building trades.

Groups like HRUM in New York faced another type of dilemma. Was HRUM independent of Local 1199 of the National Union of Health and Hospital Workers, or was it a rival to it, a radical caucus within it, or something else? This identity crisis appears to have inhibited the organization's growth and to impede its ability to decide how and where it should grow. When some workers from the public hospital in Mount Vernon, New York, approached HRUM organizers in the early 1970s, for example, the organizers seemed paralyzed on how to proceed, going so far as to say that the Mount Vernon workers needed to meet with them at the HRUM office in the South Bronx before anything would be done to help them organize.

With time, the more radical independent unions or unionlike organizations dissolved, with many of their members becoming active in the official union for that sector (if there was a union in that sector). In the early 1980s, however, a new round of independent unions and quasi-union organizations formed to address the needs of workers from the lower strata of the working class. Discussed in detail by Vanessa Tait in her excellent book *Poor Workers' Unions,* these efforts attempted to model a sort of trade unionism different from that of the official union movement, albeit less radical than formations like the League of Revolutionary Black Workers.[5]

The critique of the union as unreformable had a key element that was later lost: the question of the purpose of trade unionism and whether the trade union could rise above its current practice to play a different social role. The debate about the reformability of existing unions lost coherence amid the practical difficulties of establishing new organizations. Nevertheless, with the more recent emergence of the workers' center movement, this question has come full circle.

UNION "MISLEADERS"

Beginning in the early 1970s, the critique of U.S. trade unionism began to take a new direction, suggesting that the union movement was unable to fulfill its historic destiny because of a crop of alleged misleaders running the movement. These misleaders, according to the theory, needed to be exposed and ultimately replaced if the unions were to be able to reorient themselves to engage the class struggle. Once the misleaders were exposed for the bankrupt idiots they were, the workers would rally to the cause of militant class-struggle unionism.

This approach, while often emotionally satisfying, was far too simplistic. Drawing dogmatically on syndicalist and semisyndicalist critiques of organized labor from the early decades of the twentieth century, it evaded the question of where these misleaders had come from. Had they simply been anointed or beamed into office?

The leadership of organized labor reflects, at least in part, a social base within the union movement. Though many unions are certainly afflicted by corruption and lack of democracy, these elements alone do not explain the resilience of a conservative echelon of leaders. Instead, we need to look to the nature of the social base and the expectations within this base and others in the ranks of organized labor.

A union, by definition, is a united front. It is not an ideologically consolidated organization. Virtually all worldviews are represented within its ranks and, except in so-called right-to-work states or in unions that participate in agency shop agreements, an employee automatically becomes a member of the union after a period of time.[6] Unions normally do not require members to attend meetings or to vote in union elections. Participation in the activities of the union is voluntary. Members are generally most active at contract time—when a collective-bargaining agreement is about to expire.

Thus, a relatively small group can dominate the activities of any union, particularly if the group is well organized.[7] So-called apathy, or disengagement, can result in very low voter turnouts for union elections.[8] Members who consider the union to be relevant only to a portion of their lives or who feel that they have little influence or control are likely to allow the leadership clique to rule until and unless its actions conflict with the immediate material interests of the average member.

The "misleaders," then, are not akin to seaweed, floating forever on the ocean with no roots. They are more like crabgrass, which is deeply rooted and durable. These leaders' roots are not just in one section of the base but in the overall culture and practice of the organization. The ruling group thus understands the culture of trade unionism and the nuances of collective bargaining. Replacing these leaders is therefore not as simple as removing them from office, because the next ruling group will emerge from the same day-to-day workplace realities of capitalism and the practice of Gompers-style trade unionism and may not differ fundamentally from the one it follows.

What conclusions can we draw from these realities of union culture? In the capitalist workplace, workers compete for limited or declining resources. The union forms to address this competition by unifying the employer's workforce. With the possibility that nonunion workers will replace those represented by the union, unions and union leaders feel pressure to defend what they have against any perceived threats. Thinking and acting beyond the workplace (or in some cases beyond the industry) call for a leap beyond established trade unionism, in which the initiative is generally in the hands of the employer. Thus, the union is almost by definition continually on the defensive, responding to the actions of the employer rather than planning and carrying out its own course of action.

In turn, the unionism of Gompers and his followers privileged workers who were already in unions. For many members and leaders, union membership is a source of identity; it encourages them to see themselves in opposition to outsiders, or at least to focus on their own struggles while giving little attention to those of workers on the outside. Though this mind-set is understandable, it sometimes counterposes the interests of those already organized to those in the working class who wish to or need to be organized.

The operations of capitalism reproduce the conditions under which Gompers-style trade unionism reemerges. Only through an active counterprocess can unions resist, if not overcome, the tendencies to embrace the Gompers method.

In the 1970s, many of us on the left spoke of "in-office opportunists" and "out-of-office opportunists" to distinguish between the people in power guarding their privileged position and the people out of power wanting to gain such a position. Though the terminology was new, the situation was not. And the "in" and "out" distinction did not fully represent the complex power dynamics within unions. For example, a reform group can emerge that has no ties to any segment of the ruling group (or the aspiring ruling group), but once in office, it can succumb to the force of habit or subtle corruption. This form of corruption is not as easy to peg as traditional corruption because it is largely not about money in the usual sense, instead stemming from continued adherence to the Gompers paradigm.

Thus, as the following example indicates, union reform can be exceedingly difficult if the reformers focus simply on replacing the leadership and don't look to the overall culture. In 1989, the members of the National Postal Mail Handlers Union (hereafter Mail Handlers Union, or MHU), an affiliate of the Laborers International Union of North America (LIUNA), elected a reform slate. Under the banner "Team for Democracy," a young African American leader, Glenn Berrien, became the new president. One issue at stake was whether the MHU should establish autonomy, if not separate outright, from LIUNA. In any case, the Team for Democracy challenged the alleged corruption of LIUNA. The leaders of this new team were actually presidents of Mail Handlers Union locals who wished to gain distance from LIUNA. Their reasons were not entirely noble, but among them were the desires to gain full control of the health insurance plan (the largest at that time in the federal system and the source of an enormous amount of revenue); take charge of the contract administration system, which would give them greater authority in the workplace; and distance themselves from LIUNA, which was reputedly "mobbed up." In some ways, the situation was reminiscent of English barons' fight with King John in the thirteenth century. Though the barons forced the king to sign the Magna Charta, they were not true proponents of democracy. They instead wanted a change in the terms of the relationship. So it was for many of the local union leaders who signed onto Team for Democracy.

The MHU's new leadership team had neither a coherent view of change nor a clear vision of the union's future. The principal issue was the relationship with LIUNA. Berrien was not particularly ideological, though he had some good progressive instincts. Nevertheless, he ran into several traps, outlined in the following sections, that have also tripped up other trade union reform leaders.

Tradition

Tradition is simply another way of saying "the way that things have been done." For the new leadership of the Mail Handlers Union, the most graphic example of adherence to tradition was the contract negotiations with the U.S. Postal Service (USPS). The union had never launched a member mobilization at contract time, but in 1990, the new leadership authorized a comprehensive contract campaign: a wide-ranging effort to mobilize members and isolate the employer and pressure it to agree to a good contract. Contract campaigns normally involve, in addition to membership mobilization, the formation of alliances with other unions and community-based organizations. This type of activity was completely new to the Mail Handlers Union. Although the MHU was and is the smallest of the postal unions, it proved to be the most visible and activist in the 1990 round of contract negotiations. Nevertheless, resistance to member mobilization was a problem in many MHU locals. Berrien, who supported—at least in principle—the idea of a contract campaign, was not himself a strong enough force to fight for it, let alone insist upon it. Implementation was inconsistent, and the leadership faced near-endless sniping by the more conservative local union leaders, who would rather spend the union's money on preparations for binding arbitration (the method of resolving stalled contract negotiations) than on member mobilization and activism.

Tradition also influenced the manner in which funds were spent. For example, most unions hold conferences and gatherings at fancy hotels, and Berrien did not break from this practice. In line with expectations, he sought to entertain the local union leaders and treat them to the life to which many of them had become accustomed. One interesting challenge was members' expectation that they would be paid for anything they did for the union; the union had no spirit of volunteerism. Members who attended a training program expected to receive compensation, as did those who participated in a rally. In building the contract campaign, the MHU leadership (nationally and locally) was inconsistent in its responses to this challenge. Thus, some local unions did not participate, either because they could not get volunteers or because they would not receive financial compensation for the activities. Such a practice reinforces the notion that the union is separate and apart from the struggle of the workers for justice.

Organizational Resistance to Change

Resistance to change is the essence of conservatism. The MHU contract campaign and the response to it demonstrated the hold of the historical conservative pattern within the union. Embarking on a contract campaign, by definition, called for changing the manner in which the union operated. Local union leaders were deeply fearful that the contract campaign would veer out of their control and therefore outside of their comfort zone. In anticipating some of this fear, the leadership offered training for contract campaigns at a Presidents' Council meeting (an annual gathering of local union presidents) to familiarize them with the process. Another common fear was that the MHU would start organizing nonunion workers at subcontracted postal facilities. (During the contract campaigns, the union discovered a plan by the USPS to begin subcontracting its work.) In response, MHU leaders held discussions about the feasibility of organizing nonunion mail-processing facilities. The union had never undertaken this type of organizing, and the thought of organizing this sector was simply scary. Anxiety ran rampant, with local leaders worrying about where the resources for such organizing would come from, how much such a program would cost and where the funds would come from, whether the Mail Handlers Union had the skill to pull off such a campaign, how much time this organizing would take, whether the organizing effort would take away from other national or local union activities, and what the implications were for current MHU members.

The base also resisted in various ways. The hiring of staff from outside the union provoked resentment, despite the fact that the Mail Handlers Union had no staff familiar with organizing contract campaigns.[9] Postal unions tend to be insular, and employment of outside staff is not a common practice. Various worries arose when "outsiders" were brought in, including concern about the advisers' lack of familiarity with the USPS generally and mail handling in particular, fear that the outside staff would take away opportunities from mail handlers, and worry that outsiders would gain sway in the union. This unease also prevented some members from participating in the contract campaign, though it was not the dominant reason. As painful as this resistance was, it often hid other issues that had nothing to do with the staff—specifically, a desire for the union to remain in the comfort zone familiar to many of its leaders and members. Implicitly, the introduction of outsiders spoke to the need for the union to change its ways. Some workers and leaders took this action personally.

Resistance also existed to handling grievances through struggle. Members had accustomed themselves to an extremely cumbersome and bureaucratic process that led to the expectation at the base that grievances would not be handled through struggle but through the "process." The bureaucracy had created an echelon and a thinking that mirrored that of lawyers rather than that of workplace advocates and organizers. In fact, leaders and staff in the MHU often took great pride in their grievance-handling ability, dismissing the notion that grievances could or should be handled any other way.

Entitlement: "How I Am Supposed to Be Treated?"

Handling feelings of entitlement is one of the most significant challenges in union reform. Over the years, union leaders and members alike have formed an opinion about what a union leader should look like, dress like, and act like, and the expectation is that anyone who rises to a leadership role occupies a privileged position. In the Mail Handlers Union, the president typically received a house and a virtually unlimited expense account; he dressed impeccably, could travel almost anywhere with no accountability, was entitled to fancy hotel rooms, and had staff available to fill every need and indulge any whim. The list of perks goes on from there. Moreover, as in most organizations, a "leadership bubble"—a specially cultivated culture and practice—typically formed around the MHU leader and key staff members. The purpose of the "bubble" in any organization is to keep bad news from the leader, thus "protecting" him (or her). Ultimately, the people around the leader keep not just bad news from him or her but also the conveyors of bad news. The results are disastrous for the union.

In the Mail Handlers Union, Berrien bought into these expectations of privilege and engaged in significant questionable conduct that caused him to lose support at the base and ultimately led to his downfall. The problem was not his alone, however. Berrien surrounded himself with individuals who supported his lifestyle and manner of operating. As the situation deteriorated (with the president disappearing for long periods), individuals in Berrien's circle complained and worried but, by and large, refused to take action to remedy the problem. Instead, they enabled him to the point of undermining efforts that would have at least controlled the damage. Though the MHU is an extreme example of the culture of subtle corruption in business unionism and of the challenges of changing that culture, other, simpler practices can also perpetuate the prevailing culture of conservatism in a union.

In union reform movements, one pattern emerges time and again: in the absence of an ideological framework to place reform in a broader context of social transformation, the reformers tend to fall backward.[10] The MHU experience is a perfect example of this scenario.

Central to the perpetuation of the culture of subtle corruption and conservatism is the seduction of respectability. Working-class people in the United States are, by and large, regularly disrespected in their everyday lives. Their views are largely ignored, and they are treated as ignoramuses. Upon rising through the ranks of the union and reaching the top, they must interact with the employer group in a new way, which their earlier status did not allow. They may now be invited to lunch or dinner. They may be invited to play golf at a country club to conduct "business." They are, in effect, treated as colleagues, now rating address by their title or first name, and themselves being able to address employers by *their* first names.

Many people crave this sort of respectability, even though it is often satirized. This sort of respectful treatment confers a form of legitimacy in a class society that most working-class people do not receive. The prospect of losing this respectability and legitimacy is not only frightening in its own right but also opens up the fallen leader to punishment. Even reformers like Berrien are not immune to enjoying the sense of elevation in becoming president of the union: not only do they now hold an elevated title or have new authority, but their elevation marks the beginning of a transition from one class to another. Class tension results from the changing position of the individual both in his or her work and in his or her relationship to other workers.

The example of the Mail Handlers Union highlights some of the challenges that confront any reform movement. Though personality issues always play a role, the struggle within the Mail Handlers Union was about more than defects in Berrien's personality or psychological makeup. Removing "misleaders" and replacing them with reformers does not necessarily change a situation.

A platform and long-term strategy for effecting cultural change, ones that do not rely on the vision, charisma, or activity of one leader, are essential to defeat business unionism and the union traditionalists and pragmatists who uphold it. The defeat of business unionism is key to the notion of union transformation. But the question we must answer next is, transformation to what?

CHAPTER 7

ORGANIZING TO ORGANIZE
THE UNORGANIZED

In the main, the reform movements that developed in unions dissipated in the late 1970s and 1980s as a result of internal union repression and the restructuring of U.S. corporations, particularly the deconstruction of U.S. industrial centers in auto, steel, and related industries. Movements that had been largely supported by this industrial base of workers, such as the Black Freedom Movement and the Chicano Movement, were also weakened.

As jobs in high-wage manufacturing were downsized, relocated to nonunion locations, or shipped overseas and as the U.S. economy shifted toward service and low-paying jobs, many leftists were eliminated from the industrial workplace. Some thirty years after the McCarthyite purges of the Left within the unions in the 1940s, leftists were again being separated from their industrial base. Many leftists who were college educated moved into the public sector or health-care sector, obtained staff jobs in unions or community-based organizations, or retreated to academia. A few who were able to stay on their jobs or obtain other union jobs began to gravitate toward other local or regional union structures like the AFL-CIO's local adjunct, the central labor councils (CLCs). Because the Meany and Kirkland administrations lacked the vision to build a union movement grounded in local communities, the national AFL-CIO had done little to invigorate any of the 602 central labor councils that were the base of the AFL-CIO. Until the election of the Sweeney administration in 1995, most CLCs had never had direct contact with the national

AFL-CIO. Most active CLCs functioned because local unions supported their electoral political efforts, mainly backing local Democratic Party candidates. Less than a dozen consciously sought to link unions with vibrant local social movements.[1]

This neglect of the central labor councils left an opening for an early effort to address the growing crisis of organized labor: Jobs with Justice (JwJ), which was founded in 1987. JwJ was an alliance of unions and community groups modeled to a great extent on the Boston-based Massachusetts Labor Support Project, which had organized progressive labor activities in the early through mid-1980s. Like the Massachusetts Labor Support Project, JwJ reflected a nontraditional vision of the role of labor organizations. As its mission statement indicates, JwJ intended to speak to issues of workers' rights within the larger context of economic and social justice.[2] JwJ became a means for labor activists to connect to struggles outside of the normal parameters of the union movement. As such, it became an interesting experiment, serving both as a mass organization for individuals who wanted to be active but had been blocked by the bureaucracy of their unions and as a means of expanding the notion of workers' rights. JwJ also was able to attract many younger activists at a time when the bulk of organized labor was in the hands of a previous generation.

Despite the promise of its approach, JwJ received limited support within the union movement, with many union leaders viewing it with a certain amount of suspicion as a home for radicals. While the Communications Workers of America and the Service Employees International Union invested time, money, and other resources to help build JwJ, the organization was successfully ignored (and in some cases "blockaded") by most sections of the labor movement regardless of its contributions.

By the late 1980s and early 1990s, a critique of organized labor began to develop that caught on like wildfire. Known as the organizing model and popularized in various publications, including the now-defunct *Labor Research Review,* this critique sought an alternative to the bureaucratic methods that dominated the trade union movement.[3] The proponents of the model called for developing a new culture within the union movement that promoted activism in addressing grievances or other forms of workplace injustice. This activism entailed organizing members around the issues rather than relying on grievance procedures. As Cornell University labor studies professor Richard Hurd and others have pointed out, the organizing model eventually came to define a general behavior or

approach that favored organizing and mobilizing (internally and externally) over more passive and legalistic responses to injustice.[4]

Yet the organizing model critique of the trade union crisis has a
weakness that we and many other labor leftists failed to publicly
acknowledge at the time. Though the model was a step forward for
reformers, it was based on a superficial (or, at best, partial) diagnosis of
the larger problems facing the union movement, perhaps because of
self-censorship by the left wing of the union movement to avoid being
Red-baited. This problem becomes evident when we examine some of
the propositions later developed by Service Employees International
Union that were central to its rationale for splitting with the AFL-CIO.

Rather than using potentially inflammatory terms like *class-struggle
unionism*—and to influence the tactics of liberal-to-progressive labor
leaders—the proponents of the organizing model suggested that the
existing movement take significant, though limited, steps to promote
real change. Thus, reformers began to worship member mobilization
and activism, certainly a component of a vibrant trade unionism, without much discussion of who should do the mobilizing, what the objectives should be, and what methods were appropriate.

Proponents of the organizing model focused, for either tactical or
ideological reasons, on the symptoms of the larger problem—lack of
organizing and the corresponding union decline—rather than on the
problem itself: the existing structure and function of U.S. trade unionism and its Gompers-based ideology, which continues to be pervasive
even today.

Although the organizing model suggested that the members take more
responsibility for resolving the issues they faced, in practice, the organizing model tended to be staff driven. Relying on full-time staff to move
campaigns rather than promoting self-organization and membership
activity generally fails to create sustained organizational or institutional
change. Staff efforts were necessary to break the inertia of the union
bureaucracy, but in many cases, the staff became the be-all and end-all of
organizational change. This approach, at least in part, reflected the internal paralysis and toxic culture of so many unions. To address the depth
of the problem and to transform members' relationship to the union,
which was largely not the focus of most union leaders, reformers needed
a combination of staff organizing, internal education, planning, and
reorganization. Rarely did they connect these elements, and even when
they did, they tended to seek quick fixes rather than thoroughgoing
transformation.

Although the organizing model morphed somewhat to cover all forms of organizing—for example, by emphasizing that unions must organize both internally and externally—proponents soon discovered that no immediate correlation existed between *internal* organizing and *external* growth. This disjuncture prompted two different responses, as graphically illustrated in the reform efforts of the Service Employees International Union from the late 1980s to 1996.

The first response was to give priority to external organizing. Though most people within SEIU agreed that external organizing had to be at the cutting edge, they had different views about how to proceed. The framework that came to dominate the union, particularly after Andrew Stern took over in 1996, included the clear commitment of resources from the budget (up to 30 percent) for organizing at the local level; provision for each local union to pick an organizing director, plus staff dedicated to organizing new workers into the union; and a plan. The Justice for Janitors (JfJ) campaign, in which the International Union played a major role, had become the prototype for organizing.[5] In that campaign, the International Union ran the organizing program, hired skilled and dedicated organizers, and took on high visibility, making shrewd use of the media.

The other response was one that had little appeal to the SEIU organizing program: "local union transformation" (LUT). Proponents of this approach held that the growth of the union movement, including but not limited to local unions, required a transformation in the way unions did their work. This transformation required a major commitment to organizing but also had to include the development of an educational program to serve the growth of the union, the creation of a strategic plan, and the training and reorientation of staff and officers to meet the needs of a new labor movement. In SEIU, the proponents for LUT were largely in the Field Services Department (now dissolved) and the Education Department, though some elements of the two organizing departments also supported this thrust.

The organizing program that the SEIU eventually adopted rested on the following assumptions:

- Local unions must be forced to grow.
- Transformation of a local union, if it needs to happen at all, will happen with a quantitative change in the union: with growth will come transformation.
- If local unions do not move to grow, they should be taken over, one way or another.

- The 1930s demonstrated that the union movement must allocate significant resources to organizing if it is to see substantive change.

The emphasis of the program, which became clear after the change in the SEIU's leadership in April 1996, was on quantitative results and measurements. Leadership development programs and other educational mechanisms that did not have a quantitative outcome were de-emphasized, if not simply ignored and deconstructed.

Depending on which of the two approaches they favored, people within SEIU, and within other sections of the union movement, had vastly different views of the highly controversial trusteeship of SEIU Local 399 in Los Angeles in September 1995.[6] Local 399 was a multi-jurisdictional (amalgamated) local that included janitorial, health-care, and racetrack workers. It was led by Jim Zellers, a close political ally of John Sweeney, and it had been the home local of Sweeney's predecessor at SEIU, George Hardy. In the 1980s, the janitorial industry changed in its fundamentals, not only in Los Angeles but also in many other major metropolitan areas. Before this shift, janitors had been employees of a building and could retain these positions as a career. In the 1980s, the building services industry restructured, such that building owners no longer employed janitors directly but used contractors who would employ the janitors. Almost overnight, the heavily unionized, largely African American workforce transformed into a largely nonunion and overwhelmingly Latino workforce. The impact of this shift on African Americans is a story in itself, which goes beyond the scope of this book.

This new situation demanded an entirely different approach to unionization. Here, the brilliant and innovative work of SEIU's Stephen Lerner (first building services organizing director and later building services director) and the creation of the Justice for Janitors campaign made a remarkable difference. In Los Angeles, Local 399 president Jim Zellers essentially came to an arrangement with John Sweeney giving the International organization a role in moving the JfJ campaign into and through the local union. The campaign was highly successful in organizing new workers and winning back a market that had, for all intents and purposes, been lost to unionization.

After a period of highly successful organizing, some of which is dramatized in Ken Loach's commercial film *Bread and Roses* (2000), problems began to occur. Zellers, though at first appearance a mild-mannered, easy-to-get-along-with leader, was in fact cut from the old school. He was prepared to cooperate with Sweeney, but he was not prepared to make many fundamental changes in his local. Thus, JfJ became something of an outpost within Local 399; relations with the rest of the local became complicated (to the point that some people felt that Local 399 had actually split into two locals with different attitudes, cultures, and composition).

A second problem was that with the success of organizing, a "reform" group, the "Reformistas," emerged in the building service (janitorial) division of Local 399 and allied with another reform group coming out of the health-care division. The alliance put together a slate to run for executive board positions (but the reformers chose not to run anyone against Zellers himself) in the 1995 elections.

Much of what passes for a history of Local 399 and the crisis of the summer of 1995 is actually myth. For example, though many leftists and progressives have portrayed the merged reform group (technically known as the Multi-Racial Alliance though known collectively as the Reformistas) that ultimately swept the executive board as righteous rebels fighting against corruption and the old guard, the truth is far more complicated. Ironically, many of the workers organized by JfJ wanted Local 399 to put *fewer* resources into new organizing and more resources into servicing the new and existing members of the local. This position seemed almost counterintuitive given that these workers were the beneficiaries of the JfJ organizing campaign. In addition, members of the Reformistas had a broad spectrum of views about the future of the local, ranging from positioning for staff jobs within the local union for certain individuals to those who truly wished to transform the local.

In either case, Zellers, who was reelected without opposition, was furious about the Reformistas' sweep of the board, which he saw as a humiliating loss. The Reformistas, for their part, wanted to use their win to bring about changes in the local, including changes in staff. Zellers refused to go along with this program, arguing that the constitution of the local gave him the power to hire and fire staff. Thus, a stalemate ensued.

Panic quickly spread throughout the International Union, with the Building Service division concerned that the Reformistas would do something, either directly or indirectly, that would undermine the collective-bargaining agreements the union had won in Los Angeles. The Reformistas indirectly contacted SEIU headquarters in Washington, D.C., to indicate that they had no issue with the International leaders and were open to talking. John Sweeney, still president of SEIU at the time (though running for the presidency of the AFL-CIO), was open to discussions and refused some advisers' suggestion that he immediately move in and put the local into trusteeship. As a result, a staff person and an SEIU local union leader, with the agreement of Jim Zellers, began negotiations to resolve the crisis. The first round of negotiations broke down, largely because the Reformistas, after coming close to an agreement, decided at the last minute to up the ante. Every appeal to them to reconsider their regressive bargaining failed. A second round of negotiations took place with a different SEIU local union leader and with more direct discussions with Zellers and the Reformistas.[7] By this point, Zellers wanted the International to take over Local 399, and he made no moves to compromise. The Reformistas, although they knew that failure to compromise would mean a trusteeship, refused any effort to come to an agreement. Ultimately, the International leadership put the local into trusteeship and eventually broke it up.

The larger problem facing Local 399 was that it was stuck in an old model of organization and led by a local union leader who was willing to change only enough to ensure that he remained in office. Zellers had little appreciation of the value of building Local 399 into a major political force in Los Angeles, particularly given the expanding Latino community. Organizing new workers into Local 399 presented a challenge, not only because it forced a rethinking of the union itself but also because, as became clear, organizing was not enough. Paradoxically, new members entering the union under the most militant of circumstances were nonetheless prepared to insist upon an old model of servicing![8]

For some in the International—and this view came to dominate after Andrew Stern assumed office—change can come about only by blowing up a situation. The idea is rooted in a theory of corporate change that found favor with many within SEIU around 1995. A prominent article in the *Harvard Business Review* on the question of organizational change made its rounds within SEIU, with recommendations for how a CEO should handle problems of change.[9] One of the article's key points is that change is easiest to pull off during a crisis. It then suggests that if no crisis exists, the CEO should create one.

This *Harvard Business Review* article, along with a certain semi-anarchist tradition within a section of SEIU, combined to suggest the theory that the way to engender change was to create a crisis.[10] In the context of SEIU, a crisis could range from making an overly provocative statement in a debate to squeezing a situation until it explodes. Once the crisis is unleashed, according to this theory, the job of the national or international union (in this case, SEIU) is to pick up the pieces and rebuild the structure in the image that the national or international leaders deem appropriate. These actions should serve the interest of the members—at least so went the theory. In Local 399, for instance, the view was that an attempt to conduct transformative work with the local would be futile because (1) Zellers would not permit it, and (2) one should let things blow up and then pick up the pieces.

The first argument has a great deal of merit. Zellers was not interested in transforming the local, though we can't know whether his political ally Sweeney might have been able to compel him to make certain major concessions. But more important, the failure to link the organizing effort with an innovative educational and representational program that was itself transformational seemed to place organizing and representation at odds.[11] It also took the future of the local, at least for a while, out of the hands of the members.[12] Certainly, the union had other alternatives. In Washington, D.C., for instance, SEIU established a temporary "organizing local union" specifically because the local union in place was unwilling to do what needed to be done. And the leadership let ethnic tensions simmer without resolution. The organizing local took charge of organizing the new workforce, and only later did the organizing local and the established one merge. A similar approach would have been possible in Los Angeles in light of Zellers's attitude and practice.

The danger in "blowing up" the local, for lack of a better term, is that one cannot predict what will be left after the explosion and what unintended consequences might ensue. In the case of Local 399, a major ethnic clash could well have erupted between African Americans and Latinos, for example.[13] There could also have been a major decertification out of protest. If, however, the leadership had identified the local as a *transformative project,* it could have spurred creative thinking about organizing, representation, local electoral politics, education, and planning as a package. It could have stimulated reform by asking key questions: (1) What is Local 399's goal? (2) How can Local 399 build political and economic power for its members? (3) How can members become subjects in their own future rather than objects of manipulation? Implicit in this approach is the idea that the members must be won over to reconstructing their own union and be active participants in the change process rather than recipients of someone else's work, even if that work is conducted on their behalf.

The difference in these approaches within SEIU was symptomatic of a far deeper problem that became apparent after John Sweeney left the union and became president of the AFL-CIO: How should we understand the lessons of the labor movement's periods of growth, including and especially the 1930s, and what sort of movement do we want to (re)build?

PART THREE

SWEENEY'S GRAND GESTURE

CHAPTER 8

THE NEW VOICE COALITION
TAKES OFFICE

1995 AND THE SWEENEY COALITION

The 1994 Republican congressional victories were the final straw for many of the affiliate presidents within the AFL-CIO. Had the Cold War not ended a few years earlier, the affiliates' frustration might not have resulted in an insurgency. Nevertheless, the AFL-CIO showed no indication that it was prepared to face the realities of the deteriorating political and economic situation for organized labor and to project a new message, let alone a new practice.

Amid this frustration, a demand for change arose from various affiliates. SEIU president John Sweeney emerged as the leader and chief spokesperson for this initiative. Many people have described the 1995 Sweeney challenge as a "palace coup." We think this notion is inaccurate and unhelpful. A *palace coup* is normally a challenge from the inside that attempts to address an impending crisis before a popular mass movement does.[1] Thus, it aims to prevent more widespread change than the coup's perpetrators are prepared to accept. It may or may not represent a significant departure from the regime that preceded it.

The events of 1995 did not conform to this model, though a struggle was indeed taking place within the bureaucracy of organized labor. Though segments of the base were agitating for change, no coherent, organized movement existed independent of the AFL-CIO leadership to press for change. Certainly, critics were suggesting alternative paths, but the AFL-CIO was not on the verge of being swept away by the Left. Thus, we prefer to define the Sweeney effort as a reform movement that had sincere objectives for change within the existing paradigm of U.S. trade unionism. The Sweeney challenge was not a revolution, but neither was it a simple replacement of one bureaucrat with another.

THE NEW VOICE SLATE

The election of the New Voice slate (John Sweeney, the UMWA's Richard Trumka, and Linda Chavez-Thompson of the American Federation of State, County, and Municipal Employees) to leadership of the AFL-CIO in October 1995 created hope. Union activists all over the world hoped that the U.S. union movement would re-create itself and become a vehicle for social justice. And the U.S. union movement did change, a little. Though the New Voice agenda has remained clearly within the traditions of Gompers's "pure and simple unionism," it has prompted the AFL-CIO to give issues like race and gender more visibility, change its stance on immigrant workers, and take positions opposing some aspects of U.S. foreign policy.

However, the New Voice slate never clearly established a few key understandings. First, what role should the AFL-CIO play in organizing and bargaining? Although the New Voice slate emphasized the need for a new approach to organizing and political action, it was not clear what the affiliates would allow the AFL-CIO as an institution to undertake once the new leadership team was in office. Second, what role should the officers of the AFL-CIO play, and how should they lead? It became clear that the leaders had very different visions of what it meant to be second and third to John Sweeney, including questions about these officers' proper role in the day-to-day operations of the AFL-CIO. Third, how should the AFL-CIO and its staff interact with the affiliates? Answering these questions was critical in determining the affiliates' expectations and their attitude.

Despite high expectations of the New Voice slate by union leaders and activists, support was uneven from the beginning. On the positive side, former AFL-CIO secretary-treasurer (and briefly president) Thomas Donahue's supporters adopted a rather cooperative, or at least neutral, attitude toward Sweeney. Douglas McCarron, the newly elected president of the Carpenters Union, was a noticeable exception to this attitude. McCarron had swiftly begun his own restructuring of the Carpenters Union and wanted very little to do with the AFL-CIO. To his credit, he made clear from the beginning that he wanted a minimalist AFL-CIO that stayed out of his way. He wanted the AFL-CIO to limit its activities to politics and organizing, thereby further narrowing the scope of the union movement. This position may sound familiar to those who watched events unfold during the 2005 AFL-CIO Convention and remember the proposals of Change to Win to scale back the AFL-CIO.

Also on the positive side, the Sweeney administration made significant advances in the political realm. Sweeney brought on Steve Rosenthal as the political director. Originally from the Communications Workers of America, Rosenthal is both an excellent campaigner and something of a bull in a china shop. Never one to receive an award for diplomacy, Rosenthal nevertheless oversaw the reorganization of the AFL-CIO's political operation and its relationships with the political operations of the affiliates. Sweeney received high marks for this work.

On a lesser scale, Sweeney gained the support of the Executive Council in creating a member-focused economics education program. "Common Sense Economics," created by the affiliates, allies, and the AFL-CIO Education Department, was conceived as a means of speaking with the members about capitalism, class, and ultimately, the importance of new organizing and new trade unionism. Piloted in 1997, it received rave reviews; since then, however, insufficient usage and engagement by the affiliates and the national AFL-CIO have undermined the achievement of the original objectives.[2]

Like pragmatist leaders of the past, John Sweeney also invited participation by leftists, and they played a role in his victory and several of the New Voice programs. As a result of the purges of the Left in the 1940s and 1950s and the errors of the organizational Left, leftists have few institutional bases in the U.S. union movement. Thus, both old leftists, active from before the founding of the AFL-CIO, and new leftists, rooted in the union movement and active primarily in local unions and central labor councils, participated.[3] Leftists helped develop and direct major organizing campaigns and contract battles; assisted in developing education programs like the Common Sense Economics program, which provided economic reasons for organizing and engaging in political action via a dialogue about capitalism; helped formulate the Union Cities, Workers Voice, and New Alliance programs, which aimed at reorganizing the central labor councils and state federations of labor; and acted as the ground troops in moving the immigrant question forward, laying the foundation for the historic change in the AFL-CIO's position on immigration and immigrants. In coalition with other antiwar activists in unions and with no involvement by the Sweeney administration, the left-wing labor activists also helped create U.S. Labor Against the War (USLAW), which was pivotal in moving the AFL-CIO to adopt a position opposing the war in Iraq.

Sweeney introduced other important changes in the AFL-CIO, including the establishment of a Working Women's Department led by "9-to-5" founder Karen Nussbaum, and, noted throughout much of the world, moved to end the Cold War trade unionism for which the AFL-CIO was notorious. In fact, in international affairs, the AFL-CIO began a process of building or rebuilding relationships with labor movements with which it had either had no relationship or that it had attempted to destroy in the past.[4]

The AFL-CIO's Union Cities program provided a window of opportunity for local union movements to revitalize their alliances with prounion social movements and to create political agendas that improved the quality of life for all workers.[5] Most of all, the New Voice slate promised to focus on organizing the unorganized. Only 131 of 602 labor councils signed on to Union Cities, and very few of these made the transition to a "union city." The best labor councils created local labor movements by developing strategic political community alliances, which in turn created more favorable conditions for organizing.

The new leadership coalition ran into difficulties, however, during the first three years of Sweeney's administration. Immediately upon assuming office—in fact, before the end of the October 1995 AFL-CIO Convention—Sweeney had to deal with a campaign at A. E. Staley Manufacturing Co. and a nearly three-year-long management lockout of the workers. Workers at the Decatur, Illinois, facility had been embroiled in an intense contract struggle over the company's insistence on twelve-hour rotating shifts every six days. Management resorted to a lockout, and the workers, represented by Local 7837 of the United Paperworkers International Union, attempted to nationalize the struggle. The drama intensified when one of the local's bargaining committeemen, Dan Lane, began a hunger strike to raise awareness of the struggle at Staley within the union movement's top leadership. Lane addressed the 1995 AFL-CIO Convention in an emotional oration.

The Staley workers attending the AFL-CIO Convention were greeted as heroes, and enthusiasm grew for making the Staley issue a cause celebre of the union movement. Newly elected AFL-CIO president John Sweeney announced he had "promised Dan that a special 12-member AFL-CIO task force would begin meeting immediately to form and carry out strategies aimed at escalating our Pepsi campaign and ending our more than three-year dispute with Staley/Tate & Lyle."[6]

The convention discussions of the Staley situation led Jerry Tucker, the former regional director of the United Auto Workers, to propose a "strategically organized mobilization to convince Pepsi-Cola, a primary Staley customer, not to renew its corn syrup supplier contract . . . with Staley for 1996."[7] Tucker, who had been working with the union, developed a vision of a national-level campaign that went beyond the scope of actions at the time.

Despite attendees' enthusiasm for the Staley workers' cause and the commitments they made at the convention, the leadership established no national task force and offered no reason publicly for failing to do so. Ultimately, the Staley workers were forced to capitulate. Speculation abounded that the United Paperworkers president, Wayne Glenn, may have had something to do with the AFL-CIO's failure to act; he seemed to take a different approach to the Staley struggle, which excluded the notion of launching a national, multiunion, and community-based campaign to pressure Pepsi. This stalemate signaled a deep problem that has haunted the AFL-CIO and still haunts both the AFL-CIO and the Change to Win Federation: no one knows what the actual authority of a national labor center should be. Sweeney was probably sincere in making his commitment to the Staley workers, but opposition from the national/international union representing those workers placed the mandate of the AFL-CIO in question. The New Voice leaders did not discuss this problem publicly or take it to the affiliates as a fundamental strategic and structural challenge for a national labor movement.

Additional difficulties plagued the Sweeney administration. Three major Sweeney supporters—the United Auto Workers, the United Steelworkers, and the Machinists Union—had announced in 1995 a historic plan to merge and form a metalworkers union. This plan was highly symbolic of the sort of change that Sweeney wanted to see take place—namely, a greater concentration on industry-based organizing and initiative. Nevertheless, in 1997, Machinists Union president George Kourpias stepped down and was replaced by Thomas Buffenbarger, who was cut from different political cloth. Buffenbarger's political leaning was hard to pin down, and he saw himself as a maverick. In any case, Sweeney lost a key ally in Kourpias, and ultimately the plans for the merger were shelved. Why this project fell apart has been a source of speculation for years. Whether the failure was because of the reported unwillingness of certain unions to reveal their membership numbers or the desire of certain leaders to remain in office has not been confirmed. Clearly, however, since the collapse of the merger talks, none of the three unions has been able to develop a winning strategy for organizing metalworkers—on a large scale—in the United States. This failure is a serious blow to U.S. labor.[8]

Also in 1997, the AFL-CIO mobilized major support for the United Farm Workers' effort to organize strawberry workers. The AFL-CIO's Department of Field Mobilization viewed the strawberry campaign as the coming-out party for the New Voice. Modeling a nationwide campaign after the "Great Grape Boycott" of the 1960s, the AFL-CIO succeeded in pressuring grocery chains across the country to support the working standards established by the UFW for strawberry workers. These grocery chains, which included Kroeger, Safeway, and Lucky, pledged not to purchase strawberries from growers that violated the standards. The AFL-CIO devoted considerable staff to the effort—including Arlene Holt-Baker, then executive assistant to the executive vice president, and staff from the Organizing Department—because the Sweeney administration saw it as an opportunity to demonstrate the commitment of the new AFL-CIO to organizing, particularly to organizing lower-sector workers. Holt-Baker took a delegation of affiliate presidents to Watsonville, California, immediately before an AFL-CIO Executive Council meeting to observe the conditions faced by the workers. This visit helped build support for a massive march and rally of thirty thousand people in Watsonville later that year.

Despite enthusiasm, this effort unraveled. Why? The primary problem was one of strategy. The initial strategy emphasized the boycott potential and organizing opportunities at the shipping points, or "coolers." The UFW also believed that evoking the name of César Chávez would rally workers. However, the workers were organized in large part by the growers, in hometown groupings of smaller units of production. Each grower typically hired people from a particular location in Mexico, establishing a field boss from that area who then hired selected people or families from his hometown.[9] With the emergence of an independent union that intervened in the "recognition election," the importance of these hometown groups became clear, as they controlled the nodes of communication among the workers. Initially, the UFW was not able to influence opinion effectively in the fields. The tactic of announcing that the UFW was the union of César Chávez had little impact on these groups of immigrant workers, who thought the reference was to a famous Mexican boxer named César Julio Chávez. Also contributing to the initial defeat was the diminished internal capacity of the UFW, which was a shadow of what it had been in the 1970s. The union's infrastructure was weak, and it desperately needed assistance from outside. Yet the legacy of the César Chávez purges of the 1970s, when Chávez eliminated many of his left-leaning supporters, leaders, and staff, including numerous *veteranos* who had led previous UFW campaigns, haunted the UFW even in the late 1990s. This legacy was a deep problem.[10]

Another problem was the long-term commitment necessary to organize the strawberry workers. Uncertainty existed about the commitment of the AFL-CIO to such an effort, not to mention about whether affiliates would devote any of their own resources to assist the UFW in a campaign that was essentially a major rebuilding effort.

In addition, throughout this entire period of the late 1990s, the farmworkers' cause did not gel as a social movement. The UFW hit the national and international stage in the 1960s under the charismatic leadership of César Chávez, who made the cause of the farmworker the cause of all who believed in social justice. The farmworker movement became an expression of the Chicano national movement and secondarily of the Filipino movement, as well as an expression of a form of unionism committed to a broader sense of social justice. The UFW sought allies for the farmworkers everywhere in the late 1960s and early 1970s. Boycott committees enlisted younger and older activists committed to social and economic justice. In 1997, however, this sense of commitment to a larger cause, and even this sort of strategic orientation, was missing. The union positioned the strawberry workers' struggle as a large-scale organizing campaign rather than as a front in the struggle for social justice. Over a matter of months, the nationwide movement to unionize strawberry workers seemed to disintegrate, though the UFW had limited success in the strawberry fields later.

The year 1997 also marked the implosion of the Ron Carey administration in the Teamsters Union. Carey had been a close ally of Sweeney's, and, regardless of the problems in his administration, he had served as a beacon for union reform efforts. The manner in which the Carey administration collapsed, with a scandal implicating several of his subordinates in redirecting union money into his reelection campaign, was a major blow to labor progressives. It also came on the heels of the Teamsters' outstanding campaign and strike against United Parcel Service and in many ways neutralized the positive impact of this effort. The Teamsters had turned that contract battle into a battle for full-time work. As such, it garnered widespread support outside the union movement. The Carey implosion took the wind from the sails of that effort.

Yet another problem with the New Voice's reign was the affiliates' perception that Sweeney was running the AFL-CIO as if it were a union rather than a federation of unions. Despite clear, public rhetoric about the fact that the AFL-CIO was a federation, the staff's management practices, as well as its way of interacting with the affiliates, led to major tension between the AFL-CIO and the affiliates. Many of the affiliated unions believed that everything was staff driven and scripted. Thus, little genuine discussion could take place at the Executive Council; most discussions took place in informal settings. Truth be told, this scenario was standard operating procedure for most of the union movement, but the practice nevertheless rankled the affiliate leaders who were not running the show.

When the Sweeney administration took office in 1995, even people in his camp did not agree about the nature of the mandate they had received for a new AFL-CIO. Though the administration did institute a program, it lacked consensus on the role of and expectations for a national labor center. This topic should have been a priority in the first series of discussions with affiliate leaders—collectively—in late 1995 and early 1996. Instead, discussions were largely one-on-one. Although the new team undoubtedly had a sincere interest in gaining the opinion of the affiliate leaders, its approach did not draw on the ability to solve problems collectively. Thus, the affiliates themselves had no clear consensus about what they wanted, a fact that contributed to major tensions.

Internal and external pressures came to a head in a bizarre incident at the end of organizing director Richard Bensinger's tenure with the AFL-CIO. Bensinger, formerly with the AFL-CIO's Organizing Institute (and originally from the Amalgamated Clothing and Textile Workers Union [one of the predecessors of UNITE HERE!]), had been in charge of the newly formed Organizing Department of the AFL-CIO. A creative and outspoken rebel, Bensinger was deeply committed to moving the union movement into organizing mode. He was not above calling situations as he saw them, and he spoke his mind regularly, both inside and outside the organization. However, Bensinger had a reputation as a poor manager of his department, and he himself acknowledged the problem. He was more interested in the work of the department than in its management. In addition, he made little effort to strengthen his relationships with many other departments within the AFL-CIO. Over time, these two problems combined, leading the president's office to propose that he assume the role of assistant to the president for organizing. The theory, at least, was that Bensinger, as a charismatic figure, would be in charge of the broader campaign to win back the right of workers to join or organize unions (eventually known as the Voice @ Work Campaign). In his place would be an organizing director who was a better manager and would be able to work more closely with other departments.

Bensinger rejected this proposal, seeing it as a promotion out of the organization—a transition to elimination—and decided to leave. Once word got out that Bensinger was no longer organizing director, a battle ensued over how to spin the story of his departure. Some people assumed that Bensinger had alienated affiliate presidents and had therefore been bounced.[11] Bensinger probably did alienate several affiliate presidents, but he was actually caught in a much larger problem.

Bensinger, on behalf of Sweeney, had been prodding the affiliates to step up their organizing efforts. In addition, he had been advancing proposals, such as the notion of carrying out geographic organizing via central labor councils.[12] The geographic-organizing proposal and the fairly hostile response it received from the national affiliates (though local unions tended to support the idea) were signs of the larger problem of defining the role of the AFL-CIO in organizing. Ironically, some of the unions that eventually formed the Change to Win Federation, who currently insist on a greater AFL-CIO commitment to organizing, were vocally opposed to expanding the AFL-CIO's role in organizing efforts, such as its role in Bensinger's proposal. In fact, at the organizing directors' meeting at the AFL-CIO Executive Council meeting in February 1998, shortly before the end of his tenure, Bensinger encountered great resistance to his proposal from some of his key affiliate allies.

By 1998, the reform effort seemed to be running out of steam. Sweeney did not replicate the exciting first months of his tenure when the AFL-CIO championed its America Needs a Raise campaign (complete with a book by Sweeney) to address the declining living standard of U.S. workers. Instead, Sweeney fell back into his consensus-building mode, a style with which he seemed most comfortable. And he missed important opportunities.

On the political front, the Sweeney administration was reluctant to do anything potentially embarrassing to the Clinton administration. For example, it had a mild response to the 1996 repeal of welfare and the establishment of Temporary Assistance for Needy Families (TANF), Clinton's "end of welfare as we know it," which have had a devastating impact on the working poor. Much of the impact of these measures was hidden at first, both because of the time delay in cutting off funds for recipients and because of the better economic conditions during the dot-com boom through roughly 2000 and 2001. But despite protests by community-based organizations and organizations of welfare recipients, the AFL-CIO did next to nothing in response to this attack on one of the poorest sections of the working class. Though the AFL-CIO issued a press statement expressing its disagreement with President Clinton, the leadership made no attempt to explain to union members the potential impact of welfare repeal on welfare recipients *and* on members of unions (including the introduction of TANF workers into the workplace who would not be covered by collective-bargaining agreements). The AFL-CIO leadership never explained its silence, except for vague statements that the federation had never received feedback from welfare rights organizations about how to respond.

Why the AFL-CIO would need to wait for the welfare rights organizations (and other poor people's organizations) to address the repeal of welfare is of course unclear. Compelling welfare recipients (now TANF recipients) to accept often-unsuitable working situations would have a direct material impact on union members. Leaving aside the fact that welfare recipients should be considered part of a class-based labor movement, TANF recipients were often placed into work situations next to workers from the formal workforce, including but not limited to union members. This practice had an impact on job conditions as well as on worker-to-worker relations.

The only reasonable conclusion is that, as in the earlier national health-care reform debate, the AFL-CIO had a deep fear of embarrassing the Clinton administration. The view of the leadership of most of the union movement, including officers within the AFL-CIO, was that Clinton was a friend of "working families" (a term that has come to replace "the working class" and "working people" in the lingo of many union leaders). The repeal of welfare was a de facto Republican initiative and should have been attacked for what it represented. Instead, the AFL-CIO took a pass.

The "Battle of Seattle"—the demonstrations against the World Trade Organization (WTO) in November 1999—was yet another example of the AFL-CIO's ambivalence about crossing President Clinton. Inside the AFL-CIO, the organization was slowly gearing up to support the demonstrations. Joe Uehlein, formerly of the Industrial Union Department and then part of the Field Mobilization Department, was charged with overseeing AFL-CIO preparations. This support was, on the one hand, historic because it signaled that the AFL-CIO was willing to ally, even tactically, with sections of the global justice movement.[13] On the other hand, many within the organization greeted the prospect of working with sections of the global justice movement with reluctance bordering on embarrassment. Tensions came to a head in the fall of 1999, shortly before the demonstrations. Two different approaches toward the WTO were at work. The bulk of the global justice movement was uniting around the notion that the WTO was a menace that needed to "sink or shrink" (be eliminated or drastically reduce its jurisdiction). In contrast, the AFL-CIO, in keeping with its alliance with the Clinton administration, took the position that the WTO could and should be reformed. To paraphrase the words of a top staff person, a need existed to regulate trade, so how could the AFL-CIO call for the outright elimination of the WTO? This point of view, which was the dominant one in the AFL-CIO, nevertheless created controversy. The AFL-CIO leadership essentially ended the debate by fiat rather than pursue consensus. Affiliates' attitudes remained ambiguous, influenced by contending views on trade, the positions of allies, and attitudes toward the Clinton administration.[14]

Missing from this internal decision making was an analysis that would promote a clearer and more accurate understanding of the WTO as an organization.[15] To the demonstrators and many other advocates of social justice, the WTO is more than a regulatory body; it is a major player in a process seeking to reorganize global capitalism. It has not been a neutral or democratic body in any respect, instead advancing policies and programs that have undermined national sovereignty and forced countries to take economic paths that are largely to the advantage of the Global North. In that sense, the WTO is poison to many people.

The AFL-CIO kept tensions under wraps, however, and along with many affiliates, participated in the so-called Battle of Seattle. The AFL-CIO–led demonstrations paralleled and sometimes overlapped those of the broader global justice movement. For many people, the interaction of organized labor with the global justice movement was a historic advance. The frequent references to "turtles and Teamsters" working together signified hope that a progressive bloc was developing around issues of global trade (and perhaps even globalization). Certain affiliates, such as the United Steelworkers, played a major role in the mobilization, in part to dramatize the impact of neoliberal globalization on their industries. The results, however, were far more mixed than the rhetoric suggested. While some top staff people within the AFL-CIO lauded this initiative, others were deeply fearful that organized labor had somehow been tainted by the alleged anarchy of the global justice movement. This latter interpretation later played itself out in the inability of organized labor and global justice groups to engage in significant joint initiatives targeting the International Monetary Fund and World Bank. It also lay behind a politically reactionary effort to label China the source of U.S. workers' problems. Such campaigns are classic examples of moving one step forward, two steps back.

Yet even if the top officers and staff of the AFL-CIO had accepted a global justice analysis, acting upon it would have raised significant questions about the relationship of the AFL-CIO to President Clinton and the Democratic Party. The AFL-CIO did not want to do anything to undermine President Clinton at a point when the political Right had him in their sights, especially when the Monica Lewinsky sex scandal came to light and the political Right took it up as a weapon against Clinton. This caution became a reason, some would say excuse, for the failure of the AFL-CIO to offer badly needed criticisms of the economic policies of the administration.

Another example of this ambivalence was the AFL-CIO's response to Clinton's so-called race initiative of 1997, which aimed to launch a national dialogue on race. The president appointed the National Commission on Race, chaired by the distinguished historian John Hope Franklin, which included the AFL-CIO's executive vice president, Linda Chavez-Thompson. A great deal of fanfare surrounded the creation of this commission, and an equal amount of fanfare took place within the AFL-CIO. The AFL-CIO held a major staff meeting to discuss the Race Commission and distributed some statistics on the continued racial differential in the United States. Yet nothing of substance happened. The creation of this commission overlapped the beginnings of the Monica Lewinsky scandal, thus undermining Clinton's moral authority. Even in the absence of the scandal, however, it is far from clear what the commission could have accomplished. In any case, the AFL-CIO took no initiative to support the Race Commission. Here was an opportunity to take the lead in a national discussion of race and racism—a step that would have had special impact coming from organized labor—yet nothing happened. Excuses about lack of available staff seemed superficial. Indeed, the organization allocated few resources to the initiative, despite general excitement about Chavez-Thompson's appointment. However, no agreement existed within the AFL-CIO on the role of such a commission and how the AFL-CIO could use it to advance working people's interests. Instead of waiting for the Clinton commission to act, the AFL-

CIO could have held hearings around the United States in union halls and in community centers to look at issues of race facing the working class (for example, job discrimination, immigration, housing discrimination, and inadequate health care).[16] No such events occurred. The failure to take advantage of this situation was actually compounded some years later in the buildup to the 2001 United Nations World Conference Against Racism in Durban, South Africa. The AFL-CIO played a minimal role, sending over a small delegation led by William Lucy, secretary-treasurer of the American Federation of State, County, and Municipal Employees and president of the Coalition of Black Trade Unionists, but in no way did the leadership attempt to integrate the work of this conference into the work of the AFL-CIO. Nor did it make much attempt to trumpet the significance of this conference to the affiliates of the AFL-CIO.[17]

The 2000 elections and the Gore campaign created another strategic quandary for the Sweeney administration in its relations with the Democratic Party. When, the day after the election, no clear winner had yet emerged, the AFL-CIO sent staff to Florida on an ambiguous mission. Staff went into the flash-point voting districts and awaited orders. Arlene Holt-Baker, assistant to the president of the AFL-CIO and one of the best campaign directors within the organization, was sent in to coordinate the operation. However, no instructions were forthcoming about what people were to do. The operation deployed a huge number of staff members, largely to collect affidavits from people alleging voter fraud, problems with machines, and other restrictions on their right to vote. Meanwhile, spontaneous demonstrations were taking place in various parts of Florida against Republican tactics to suppress voters. However, the AFL-CIO staff had instructions not to encourage demonstrations. The staff found itself awaiting a signal that, apparently, would have to come from the Gore campaign. No signal appeared. Thus, while the pro-Bush forces were inciting their supporters to demonstrate (and getting a fair amount of media attention), pro-democracy forces were being held back. The Gore campaign was apparently concerned about its image. Like the Kerry campaign four years later, Gore and his campaign staff wanted to look presidential—even though they had lost the presidency.

The postscript to this event was the inability of the AFL-CIO to respond to the change in national political direction after Bush's selection by the Supreme Court. The organization had no contingency plan for a Bush election. It appeared to have assumed that Gore would win and that no other options were possible. The affiliates received no strategic direction about how to respond to Bush's election. When Bush began courting several affiliates shortly after his inauguration, the AFL-CIO did nothing but complain that it got no respect and was being ignored. The strategic and policy paralysis of the AFL-CIO had become so clear that the ties binding the union movement started to unravel.

BEYOND THE NEW VOICE AGENDA

The unorganized sector of the U.S. working class accounts for 88 percent of the workforce. Union membership has dropped from 15.3 percent to 12 percent during the tenure of the Sweeney administration. Current rhetoric about the failure of the AFL-CIO to increase union density points to the failure of unions to allocate resources or to devise successful strategies for organizing.

The AFL-CIO nationally and locally has never been more than a weak alliance of unions that voluntarily join the federation. Although one can cite outstanding exceptions, the AFL-CIO does not organize workers; national and international unions organize workers.[18] At its best, the federation sets the stage for successful organizing.[19] The AFL-CIO cannot make unions do anything, which is why we must be careful in making comparisons with the role of other national centers, such as the Congress of South African Trade Unions, which may have a greater mandate to institute far-reaching changes. National and international unions are at the core of the question of whether and how workers are organized, and they lack the capacity to be the solution, at least in their current form and with their current visions of the future.

The long-term future of the U.S. union movement depends on action at the local level. Central labor bodies must have the capacity to build local union and labor movements that embrace the true hopes, aspirations, and imagination of working people in communities throughout the United States. The challenge is to link such an effort to local and regional efforts to build working-class power, as well as to link it to the struggle for global justice. We suggest ways to meet this challenge later in the book.

CHAPTER 9

DEVELOPING STRATEGY
IN TIMES OF CHANGE

The Sweeney reform program encountered numerous problems in its efforts to define and carry out strategies that would garner the support of the AFL-CIO membership. These problems, many of which stemmed from changes in the wider economy, were not unique to the AFL-CIO, however; they haunted the entire union movement.

THE PROBLEM OF THE SUNBELT

Labor progressives and reformers have for years discussed the importance of organizing the South and the Southwest, certainly since the failure of Operation Dixie in the early 1950s. Section 14(b) of the National Labor Relations Act, which gives states the ability to adopt so-called right-to-work laws, has always been an obstacle to organizing in those regions, but some unions have persisted.[1] During its first five years in office, the Sweeney administration also put forth rhetoric about organizing the South, but it accomplished little overall.[2]

In early 2000, Sweeney commissioned a new look at organizing the South. The review had two prongs. First, a subcommittee of the AFL-CIO Executive Council was to oversee this work in cooperation with the AFL-CIO's organizing director (Mark Splain, who was chosen at the same council meeting). Second, staff members were to reach out to community-based organizations in the South to enlist their support in this effort.

The entire effort failed and simply disappeared into the wind. For reasons that are unclear, Splain never provided the support necessary for the project to succeed. Moreover, the affiliates that participated, including some that eventually formed the Change to Win Federation, offered only conditional support. One approach advanced by Deputy Organizing Director Nadra Floyd (who was in charge of the project's day-to-day operations) was to select key cities or key sectors around which joint—that is, multiunion—organizing could take place. The affiliates were non-committal about this plan, waiting to see how much money and other resources the AFL-CIO was prepared to put forward.[3] A chicken-and-egg situation unfolded, with the AFL-CIO waiting for affiliates to indicate what resources they were prepared to offer and the affiliates waiting for a signal from the AFL-CIO about its level of commitment. While discussions proceeded within the AFL-CIO and with the affiliates, staff members held meetings with community-based organizations in the South to win their support for (and gain their ideas about) a new southern organizing campaign. Although these organizations were deeply skeptical of organized labor's commitment to organizing the South, most were interested. In Atlanta, at least one meeting with more than a dozen organizations elicited significant interest in a southern organizing project. Despite the promises that AFL-CIO representatives made to community-based organizations in the South, at the Atlanta meeting as well as at other gatherings, that this time the union movement was serious, events showed that it was not serious.

One could easily—and disingenuously—blame the AFL-CIO alone for the failure of this "review" and protocampaign to organize the South. However, any number of international or national unions could have embraced this effort or undertaken the work on their own if they seriously doubted the AFL-CIO's commitment. They did not do so. The few unions already organizing in the South proceeded with their work. Those that were not already active took little or no initiative. Thus, organization of the South and Southwest was not, nor is it today, simply dependent on the actions of the national labor centers. Rather, organizing failures in these regions point to a problem deeply ingrained in the dominant conception of U.S. trade unionism.

CENTRAL LABOR COUNCILS AND STATE FEDERATIONS OF LABOR

As we have seen, central labor councils and state federations of labor were a major focus of the Sweeney administration when it first came into office. The AFL-CIO launched the Union Cities program specifically to revive the central labor councils.[4] CLCs that made a commitment to certain activities spelled out by the AFL-CIO would gain the title of "Union City," which would entitle them to greater resources than they would normally receive. They would also become national models for the rest of the movement.

During discussions about the Union Cities program, AFL-CIO chief of staff Bob Welsh asked, somewhat rhetorically, whether central labor councils needed to rethink themselves and become central workers' councils—that is, widen their focus beyond the role of established unions. This fascinating idea was dropped, though twelve CLC presidents attempted to resurrect it in a paper entitled "Uniting Locally, Growing Nationally" issued shortly before the 2005 AFL-CIO Convention and split. The paper argues, "In order to become the true voice of working people in their community, CLCs should open up their doors to compatible community based organizations outside the Labor movement. Criteria should be developed for membership of community groups, minority unions, and non AFL-CIO unions. Exclusion is a luxury union members can no longer afford."[5]

In the early 2000s, discussions were opened in the Executive Council about including AFL-CIO Constituency Groups (the A. Philip Randolph Institute, Asian Pacific American Labor Alliance, Coalition of Black Trade Unionists, Coalition of Labor Union Women, Labor Council for Latin American Advancement, and Pride At Work) in the central labor councils, and these discussions created quite a stir. The discussions, much like the notion of opening the CLCs to community-based organizations, raised technical questions about who would vote and how, though resting beneath the technical discussion was a political discussion about the appropriate vision for central labor councils. Overall, the leadership placed limits on the extent to which the organization would change the paradigm for central labor councils.

Although certain central labor councils—such as those in Atlanta, Los Angeles, King County (Seattle), North Shore (north, suburban Boston), San Francisco, Milwaukee, Rochester (New York), and Cleveland—attempted to introduce mild-to-significant reforms in their operations, the national AFL-CIO largely scaled down plans to transform the central labor councils.[6] Further, AFL-CIO officials minimized, if not excluded, the CLCs' role in organizing, as mentioned. Though the AFL-CIO relied on the councils at election time, the CLCs' relationship to the larger community did not change very much. The problem most likely lay both in the essential conservatism of the Sweeney approach toward change, which made the national leadership reluctant to push the affiliates, and in the lack of strong advocates of CLCs among the affiliates. The strongest supporters of central labor councils were within the local unions, which makes sense given that the local unions interact regularly with the CLCs. The ambivalence at the national level—as we described in the context of affiliate opposition to geographic CLC-based organizing projects—meant that Sweeney would have to be a strong and outspoken advocate or find an affiliate leader who would step forward. During much of this time—the late 1990s and early 2000s—Machinists president Thomas Buffenbarger was in charge of the Central Labor Council Subcommittee of the AFL-CIO Executive Council. However, he merely went through the motions as subcommittee chair and did not provide strong leadership on the question of central labor councils.

By the late 1990s, a new idea, the New Alliance, emerged that called for reorganizing the state federations and the central labor councils.[7] The proposed process was in many respects quite innovative in that it attempted to fully engage the national affiliates of the AFL-CIO in decisions about the organization and future of the state federations and central labor councils. The process of reorganization proceeded in a few states, including New York,[8] but was derailed by the activities leading up to the 2004 presidential elections as well as by the developing debate over the future of the AFL-CIO itself. The initiative continued, however, in a few states, such as Ohio and Pennsylvania.

Most of the ideas for reforming these bodies—with the exception of Welsh's suggestion, the paper by the twelve CLC leaders, and some earlier propositions by Fernando Gapasin—did not stray far from the existing paradigm of U.S. trade unionism. Reformers should have realized that the national affiliates to the AFL-CIO were largely not won over to the importance of supporting the central labor councils, the state federations, or regional multiunion organizing. They were particularly resistant to CLCs' roles in organizing. The national and international unions saw the central labor councils as interfering in their plans rather than as helping. Some of their resistance understandably stemmed from their desire to conduct strategic organizing by sector. Central labor councils by definition attempt to build the local political and economic power of working people. Their interests are different from, though not necessarily contradictory to, those of the national affiliates. As one international/national organizing director stated in a moment of frankness, "We do not want our local unions lobbying us to organize in locations we do not consider strategic!"

The element that commentators have largely overlooked in the debate between the central labor councils and the national affiliates is the underlying question of power (a question we will pursue in greater detail later in the book). For most national affiliates, the issue of local power is clearly secondary to the notion of sectoral power. Local unions and central labor councils, in contrast, often consider local power in the political and economic realm to be as important as sectoral power. For example, being in a position to influence a local election, a piece of legislation, or a union's contract or bargaining campaign might help build an environment that supports not only organizing but also bargaining.

CHANGES IN TECHNOLOGY
AND THE ORGANIZATION OF WORK

One of the most important books of the mid-1990s to examine the changing terrain of employment, technology, and the process of work was Bennett Harrison's *Lean and Mean: The Changing Landscape of Corporate Power in the Age of Flexibility*.[9] In the book, Harrison demolishes the argument that small businesses are the major source of job creation, a myth long promoted by Republicans and often echoed by Democrats. He examines the changing process of work and specifically the growth of networked production. Major corporations, he notes, are ridding themselves of large core workforces, instead pursuing two approaches. First, they are reducing their core workforce and subcontracting work that they previously conducted in-house. Second, they are using strategic industry alliances to achieve similar goals. Their aim is to increase their flexibility in highly competitive world markets.

The result of these corporate actions, as Harrison points out, is a declining living standard for workers. One example, mentioned earlier in this book, was the devastating impact on largely unionized African American workers of the restructuring of the janitorial industry by office-building owners.

Harrison also points out ways in which the introduction of new technologies has hurt workers. The electronics revolution has not eliminated the working class, nor is the elimination of the working class inevitable as long as the use of technology is regulated by policy or by collective action.[10] But technology has clearly changed the conditions under which the working class works.[11] Moreover, the electronics revolution has eliminated certain types of jobs and reduced the number of people doing other ones. In either case, the reorganization of production along networked lines has shifted the ground under which the union movement has been operating. It has also called into question organizing approaches and forms of organization that have been common in the union movement at least since the 1930s.

The reorganization of capitalism that Harrison discusses, and that is a touchstone for many of the proponents of the "end of work" thesis, has led to the reorganization and recomposition of the working class. The industrial or manufacturing working class has not disappeared, but it has shrunk in the United States as well as dispersed internationally. Examples abound. The steel industry has downsized and shifted. With the introduction of new technologies, minimills have opened, often in rural areas. The choice to move to rural areas of the United States— which is not limited to the steel industry—is reminiscent of the decision by the textile industry to go to the South in the 1920s. The aim? To get away from unions and, in the 1920s, to avoid ethnic groups sympathetic to unions. The choice to locate in the rural *white* South in the 1920s was deliberate, offering a means of driving a wedge between the two major sections of the southern working class: whites and blacks.

Contemporary corporations have similar motives. The rural United States has few unions and, outside the rural South and Southwest, has few people of color. The new minimills (as well as foreign manufacturers' so-called transplants) bring higher wages to these regions than local workers are used to. Thus, corporate managers expect to be able to prevent the establishment of unions in effect by buying people off. This strategy has been unfolding on a large scale in South Carolina along the I-85 corridor.

Manufacturing has been changing in other ways. A steady bifurcation has unfolded, with increases in both high-end manufacturing (for example, aerospace) and low-end manufacturing (for example, light electronics). Los Angeles has become the largest center for manufacturing in the United States, but not by replacing auto, shipbuilding, and aerospace jobs with comparably paid and structured employment. Instead, it welcomes light manufacturing and electronics, along with other forms of small-scale production.

Cities that have traditionally been centers of large-scale manufacturing have seen their economies hollowed out. As Harrison pointed out in a broadsheet, the departure of manufacturers has disproportionately depressed the living standards of workers of color, particularly African American workers. The University of California's Steven C. Pitts makes much the same argument in his important report "Organize . . . to

Improve the Quality of Jobs in the Black Community."[12] In this sense, the proponents of the "end of work" thesis are correct to note the emergence of a stratum of the working class that is structurally unemployed—that is, that has been relegated either to the informal economy or to only periodic employment in the formal economy.[13]

Though some unions have opportunistically embraced outsourcing—one of the features of this reorganization—the long-term impact of this workforce reorganization is mind-boggling. For example, in New York City in 2004, approximately 50 percent of adult Black males were unemployed.[14] What are the implications for a labor movement in the face of such statistics? In fact, this phenomenon and the further hollowing out of communities through disintegration of the industrial working class point to a deadly and intensified stratification of the working class itself.

The "end of work" theorists often ignore the fact that much of manufacturing has shifted overseas. In other words, the global proletariat has expanded.[15] Thus, work that was once the cornerstone of the Global North's economy is no longer centered in the Global North. The Global South is no longer the recipient of archaic technology but is in some cases on the cutting edge. Unions need to factor in this shift when they decide to confront common industries. Several U.S. unions have acknowledged this need over the years but have come up with few truly multilateral strategies to address it.

In a nutshell, the U.S. working class is further stratifying along racial and ethnic lines, as well as in relations to work. The group that some people describe as an underclass or a new proletariat is better described as a redundant or semiredundant section of the working class. Workers in this group are increasingly marginalized, and as we have seen since the Hurricane Katrina disaster on the Gulf Coast, they are subject to a fate that some people would describe as genocide. These populations do not count.

In its early days, the Sweeney administration gave some thought to organizing both the unemployed and the poor. However, this goal essentially dropped off the agenda, to be replaced by periodic financial contributions to groups doing this type of organizing, such as ACORN (Associated Community Organizations for Reform Now). In fact, these groups have not typically viewed the AFL-CIO and the union movement generally as true allies and partners in organizing marginalized segments of the working class; instead they have viewed them as foundations or charities—that is, sources of funds and other resources.[16]

The strategic implications of Harrison's ideas in *Lean and Mean* have not led to a change in the theory and practice of the U.S. union movement, except in a general manner. UNITE, before merging with HERE, began to pay attention to the supply chains in the textile and garment industries and learned that the retail industry in the United States had used Chinese and Taiwanese capital in places like Lesotho to set up sweatshop manufacturing plants. This discovery prompted UNITE to support organizing efforts in that country. This practice was, however, more the exception than the rule. Further, and this practice deserves more attention, the organizing work conducted in these chains was centered or headquartered in the United States and was not a multilateral collaboration.

The Harrison analysis raises interesting questions about the relationship between organizing by industry and organizing by sector. How does one determine which unions should organize the subcontractors or the strategic allies of a core firm? Should one union organize and lead an alliance, or should unions collaborate in some way to organize not only industries but supply chains and strategic alliances?

CHAPTER 10

GLOBALIZATION

The Biggest Strategic Challenge

The ongoing process of globalization has enormous implications for the union movement and the working class. In devising strategies to cope with globalization, unions must contend with three definitions of the term, each of which calls for a different strategy.

- *Version 1*. Globalization is the development of a global economy in which everything is interconnected. Thus, national economies and the nation-state are losing their significance. Globalization is inevitable, and no way exists to stop it.

- *Version 2*. Globalization is a new stage in economic and social relations. Along with the development of a global economy, a transnational capitalist class has emerged that makes the nation-state next to irrelevant. The process by which dominant capitalist powers juggle competing spheres of influence—generally referred to as "imperialism"—is losing its hold because these powers are being subordinated to the objectives of a developing global force, or "Empire."[1]

- *Version 3*. Globalization is the reorganization of global capitalism. This reorganization is part of an effort to address the stagnation of the late 1960s and early 1970s, as well as the effects of the collapse of the Soviet bloc. Globalization is being advanced by national *and* international capitalist forces but is not the inevitable result of anything. Rather it is global capital's response to a particular situation and is therefore the result—fundamentally—of national and international class struggle. *Neoliberal* globalization is one form that capitalist globalization can take, but it is not the only form.[2]

The distinctions between these approaches are not academic. Although the views overlap to some degree, and are strategically consistent in some ways, the most critical distinctions center on two issues: (1) Is globalization equivalent to a global economy? (2) Is globalization inevitable?

Identifying globalization as a global economy is useless as well as incorrect. Capitalism has always been global, as theorist Ellen M. Wood points out in her book *The Origin of Capitalism,* and this is obvious if one remembers the African slave trade and the European invasion of the Western Hemisphere.[3] Without the gold and silver of the Americas or the wealth produced by plantation economies, the system we call capitalism could not have developed. In addition, substantial trade, whether under the nineteenth-century regime of British-dominated "free trade" or during the highly competitive period before 1914, created significant connections between sections of the capitalist world. Thus, capitalism has never been an exclusively national phenomenon.

Even so, the era in which we live departs from these earlier patterns in certain ways. Understanding the concept of *neoliberal* globalization helps us grasp that current events are not simply a continuation of the relationships of past eras. Advances in electronics have enabled people to conduct finance and production in qualitatively different ways and along different lines than in the past. For example, near-instantaneous transfers of capital—taking place in the absence of regulations and restrictions—can undermine currencies and governments. And the introduction of robotics to production is making major sections of the working class both redundant and poor.

Western-style capitalism has been expanding into regions from which it had been restricted, such as the countries of the former Soviet bloc. No matter how we characterize the Soviet system, it was dramatically different from Western capitalism, and it has now become a new horizon for neoliberal capital, as has China. The reversal of socialism in China and the active embrace of capitalism by the leadership of the Communist Party of China have had a dramatic impact on trade and labor relations internationally, giving China a major competitive advantage in labor costs.

International free-trade agreements are also a characteristic of the current era, along with international institutions that enforce such trade regimes. Thus, by defining free trade to its advantage, the Global North has become largely hegemonic in the global marketplace, enabling it to remove all protective barriers the Global South seeks to preserve. "Protection" in the Global North, however, is uneven, supported by governments at certain moments, opposed at others, depending on the dynamics within the ruling circles and in the domestic class struggle.[4]

The accumulation of forces within neoliberal globalization presents, in Bennett Harrison's terms, a "credible threat" to workers in the Global North. In other words, workers and their communities believe that regardless of whether a particular corporation will relocate, it *can* relocate.[5] Neoliberal globalization has come to mean that companies have the ability to move (and certain trade agreements impede efforts to stop them) or the ability to threaten or imply that they will move. Thus, at a moment when the material basis for international working-class solidarity is greater than it ever has been, workers are being forced into a race to the bottom. Workers are increasingly coming to believe either that their survival lies at the expense of other workers, rather than in collaboration with other workers, or that their future necessitates some form of solidarity with other workers. To workers, the forces arrayed against them seem overwhelming, and often mysterious.[6] Recognition of the power of multinational corporations and mobile capital was implicit in the many discussions (which we like to call "the great *un*debate") within organized labor leading to the July 2005 split in the AFL-CIO. As we discuss later, the Change to Win coalition (and later federation) paid little attention to the problems of organizing manufacturing, whereas the manufacturing unions tended to express feelings of despair and fatalism because of their belief that organizing is unlikely, if not impossible, in the current environment.[7]

Workforce competition is, however, not a new problem. Capitalism, by its nature, engenders competition among workers. Though workers competed domestically before the 1950s, competition between workers across borders was less prevalent in that era than it later became, except in relation to issues of migration.[8] Beginning in the 1950s, labor became increasingly aware that competition was not limited to workers within national boundaries and had become truly international. The reorganization of global capital, along with the end of the Cold War and the introduction of the electronics revolution, has since expedited this process.

Yet this development was not inevitable.[9] Advances in technology occur not only because of breakthroughs in science but also in response to larger social forces. Capitalism has required corporations to strive for lower production costs so that they can strengthen their hands against their competitors, domestic or foreign. Thus, competition plays out in the world of technology as well as in the political and economic realms.

Neoliberalism is about more than trade and the production process, however. It focuses on the notion of the public sphere and pays attention to the unbridled use of state violence to achieve the ends of globalization. Fundamental to neoliberalism is the drive to eliminate obstacles to the achievement of profit. In practical terms, this objective requires an emphasis on privatization and the systematic elimination of the public sphere. The United States has been through various rounds of privatization, but beginning in the 1970s, often in conjunction with reactionary tax initiatives, there was an open assault on the public sector by corporate America and the political Right. The tax cuts that followed led to the reduction or elimination of public services and the imposition of fees for remaining services (as a means of offsetting the costs). Increasingly, the tax burden has shifted onto the middle classes and the working class, both in an ideological sense and in a practical one. The ideological side, marked by popularization of the notion of "pay for use," has been just as interesting as and no less devastating than the practical side. The notion is that one should not have to pay for services one does not use. A citizen who does not have children in public schools, according to neoliberal logic, should not be obligated to pay taxes to support the public schools. This notion is one of the most rabid forms of so-called libertarianism, and it strikes at the belief that a public space exists that must be supported by society as a whole. Perhaps this ideology lay behind former British prime minister Margaret Thatcher's famous remark, "There is no such thing as society. There are individual men and women and there are families."[10]

Neoliberal globalization has a military component to reinforce its ideological component. The military component plays out in the context of a post–Cold War world in which the United States as the dominant superpower has no major ideological or military opposition. Though capitalism has always been brutal, and though the United States in particular has had an extremely interventionist foreign policy, the use of military force is no longer constrained by the USSR. It is, however, often veiled ideologically in terms such as "human rights" and "democracy," as in the Iraq invasion.

Yet militarization is not simply about interventions; it is also about the militarization of society. In that area, the capitalist state has evolved into something far more alarming: a new phenomenon we call the *neoliberal authoritarian state*. In a manner reminiscent of comments by Aimé Césaire on the relationship of colonialism to fascism, neoliberal globalization has brought home to the people of the Global North—including to the people of the United States—elements of the horror and authoritarianism that people of the Global South have experienced at the hands of capital.[11] By magnifying the danger of terrorism (by al-Qaeda and similar groups), neoliberal globalization has consolidated a process under way since the early 1980s: the development of a quasi-permanent state of siege or, perhaps more appropriately, a quasi-permanent *siege state*.

This growing authoritarianism, which some describe (inaccurately) as fascism, has become a major feature of neoliberal globalization despite the libertarian rhetoric that often accompanies it.[12] This authoritarianism does not arise in the face of strong resistance to neoliberal globalization (which would be typical of other nonfascist authoritarian responses to a rising mass movement), but rather from the potential for significant mass resistance to the reorganization of global capitalism through neoliberal globalization. This fact does not reduce the importance of the resistance that has unfolded—for example, the activities of the global justice movement in the advanced capitalist countries or the popular resistance movements in the Global South. Rather it recognizes that this resistance has been scattered, particularly in the Global North, while perhaps being a harbinger of things to come.

The phrase *neoliberal authoritarian state* is not a coded reference to the administration of George W. Bush. The evolution of this state has certainly proceeded further and faster (particularly since the terrorist attacks of September 11, 2001) under Bush, but the process is more complicated than the actions of one administration.[13] The neoliberal authoritarian state owes its origins to ruling elites' responses to the social movements of the 1960s and 1970s. Though the state's current focus is apparently to expedite the reorganization of global capitalism and, in the case of the United States, to ensure U.S. domination of this process, strains of militarization and authoritarianism were evident in the repression of social movements in the early 1970s as well as in the conduct of the "wars" on crime and drugs over the decades.

We also see authoritarianism in court decisions about civil liberties and a woman's right to choose. Recent National Labor Relations Board decisions on the right of workers to organize also point in this direction.[14] Despite great democratic victories beginning with the civil rights movement in the 1950s, the field of acceptable discourse, acceptable politics, and, indeed, acceptable criticism of government is now narrowing. All the while, the hold of corporations increases, and governments increasingly see military action as the first, and in some cases only, means of resolving domestic and international controversies.

The neoliberal authoritarian state essentially has a preemptive role, to borrow a formula ironically from President Bush, of undermining actual and potential resistance to the assumption of leadership by pro-neoliberal segments of capital. Implicit in this understanding is that the neoliberal authoritarian state serves as the principal instrument for the reorganization of global capitalism. It does so not as a global state but as a tool for carrying out U.S. imperial aims and ambitions for global domination.

Though we believe that an international infrastructure is being developed to assist in the reorganization of global capitalism—for example, the World Trade Organization—it is not the case, despite the paranoid dreams of the extreme Right, that a global state has come into existence. Although a transnational capitalist class exists, this class does not operate as a cohesive unit outside of the nation-state, at least at this moment in history.[15] Global forces have weakened the nation-state in many respects, particularly in the Global South, but the nation-state has also become stronger in some ways, particularly in its ability to enforce its will on its citizens.

U.S. ruling circles have been divided for decades about the United States' proper relationship to the rest of the world, especially to other capitalist powers. A strong "nationalist" current, for lack of a better term, has alternated between isolationism and xenophobic jingoism (and exhibited a strongly racist orientation). Though this view has existed largely in the Republican Party during the twentieth century, it has never been the exclusive current in the party. Coexisting there, as well as in the Democratic Party, has been a multilateralist current. These currents have tended to find support in different segments of capital, with domestic capital tending to favor isolationism, finance and multinational capital tending to favor multilateralism.

In the 1990s, the distinctions between these worldviews within ruling circles sharpened, as did their similarities. The two groups agreed about the need for a neoliberal approach to globalization (reorganization of global capitalism)—as one could see in political party platforms as well as legislative activity. Bill Clinton's campaign for the North American Free Trade Agreement in 1993, while surprising many of his labor backers, was in effect the formal repudiation, by a Democrat, of the post–World War II social contract. Both segments of the ruling elite have taken steps to build the neoliberal authoritarian state, though at different rates and under different conditions.

Yet the biggest disagreement is about the nature of U.S. global domination—specifically, what form U.S. hegemony should take. Neither segment of capital is willing to concede a leading role on the world stage to another capitalist power. The multilateralists have concluded that U.S. domination must involve cooperation with other capitalist powers. We call this strategy "first among equals," in that the vision is for U.S. domination but not exclusivity. In this view, the Group of 8 (G-8) is the circle within which key decisions about control over the rest of the world can take place, as long as the United States is the leading force there.[16] The multilateralists apparently have made an economic and military assessment that the United States cannot succeed alone. This notion does not, however, mean that the multilateralists—whether of the Bill Clinton type or the Colin Powell type—believe that the United States is unable to act alone if it needs to do so. They are quite prepared to act unilaterally if necessary, regardless of whether such U.S. actions are in accordance with previous agreements or international law. This segment of the ruling circles is intent on constructing the global infrastructure necessary for total domination of the world by global capitalism under the leadership of the United States. This emphasis is not completely cynical in the way of the George W. Bush administration (which tends to ignore international institutions whenever they become inconvenient).[17]

The other segment of the ruling elite has moved away from isolationism to a form of unilateralism. Two documents are relevant to understanding the unilateralists' view of the U.S. role within global capitalism. Some key players in the current Bush administration either came from or have been influenced by the Project for a New American Century (PNAC), a major right-wing think tank. The organization's statement of principles is fairly straightforward, asserting the need to reshape the new post–Cold War global order in line with the interests of the United States.[18] This objective is logically consistent with the Bush administration's September 2002 National Security Strategy Doctrine (NSSD).[19] In the sense that the United States, since its founding, has sought to be a significant international player, we see nothing new here. Yet four key elements of the NSSD suggest a different approach to international affairs that reflects both the post–Cold War environment and the drive to build a neoliberal authoritarian state. These elements include the following:

- The world will be capitalist. No other economic system will be tolerated.

- The United States will determine the form of capitalism that the world adopts. In other words, sovereignty has its limits within the reconstruction of global capitalism.

- The United States will never again have a strong military competitor. This principle clearly looks back at the Cold War.

- If any nation or group disagrees with any of the first three points, the United States reserves the right to unilaterally declare that nation or group to be a terrorist operation and to take any actions necessary to eliminate it as a potential threat.

Interestingly, the United States, in this scenario, does not reserve these rights only for its operations in the Western Hemisphere (the traditional sphere of influence asserted by the United States since the Monroe Doctrine of 1822, and generally recognized by the other major capitalist powers). Instead, it affirms its right to apply each of these points globally.

Which segment of the U.S. ruling circles will successfully operationalize its vision of the foreign-policy role of the United States is far from clear. The neoliberal authoritarian state, however, is likely to persist under either scenario, with implications for the world's peoples and for resistance movements to neoliberal globalization. In the unilateralists' scenario, other capitalist powers will clearly be subordinate to the United States, and international institutions will be of use only as long as they do not get in the way of U.S. global ambitions. This view explains the approach of the George W. Bush administration toward other capitalist powers that disagreed with the U.S. decision to invade Iraq. The unilateralists are looking for subordinates within the U.S.-led global empire. They are not looking to allow other nations the semiprotectorate status that existed in the aftermath of World War II. (In that postwar period, Western Europe and Japan could essentially manage their own affairs—including electing social democrats with welfare-state agendas—so long as they subordinated their foreign policy to that of the United States.) Instead, as President Bush said in September 2001, they see nations as either with the United States or with the terrorists.

For the multilateralists, the neoliberal authoritarian state must advance global reorganization, but in partnership with the other members of the G-8. This view appears to favor a corporatist model of internal governance, a view that holds great appeal for much of the leadership of organized labor, not only in the United States but also in other parts of the Global North. The multilateralists do not turn away from the prospect of a global empire, but they believe it will emerge in a radically different manner than the unilateralists envision. The multilateralists fear that the course pursued by the unilateralists will overextend U.S. power and run the ship of capitalism onto the rocks.

CHAPTER 11

COULD'A, WOULD'A, SHOULD'A

Central Labor Councils
and Missed Opportunities

Before the victory of the New Voice slate in October 1995, many union-ists and scholars believed that central labor councils were moribund remnants of labor history. This view prevailed because of the dominance of national and international unions in the U.S. union movement and George Meany's complete neglect of these local adjuncts to the AFL-CIO. In addition, because local unions were not required to affiliate with the councils, most CLCs lacked the resources to function effectively. National unions replaced central labor bodies as the primary institutions in the union movement at the AFL convention in 1891. That convention established the current per capita structure in which unions pay accord-ing to the number of members they have. Unions voted according to their membership size, and central labor bodies got one vote regardless of how many members they had. Since then, local unions have become subsidiaries of national unions, and national and international unions have dominated the federation on both a national and a local level.

Each national union has a unique history and culture. Thus, the AFL-CIO is a conglomeration of traditions and organizational cultures. For instance, terms have different meanings and significance for different unions. In some unions, a *grievance* is the central mechanism for dealing with employer issues; in others, a grievance may have little impact on the members. *Seniority,* which most manufacturing unions take for granted, has virtually no importance for most building trades unions. *Internal organizing* for most public-sector unions means organizing members of the bargaining unit who are not union members, but for some other unions, it means reorganizing the already organized, and for others still, it describes a dissident group's effort to overthrow the incumbent leadership. *Organizing the unorganized* may be the central work of some unions and be merely an extra activity that is done when the opportunity arises in other unions. And *organizing* itself can refer to organizing people or to organizing "jobs" or employers. Even with these differences, however, the hegemonic culture of narrow, bureaucratic, business unionism engulfs most national and international unions.

When local central labor bodies were the locus of union activity, each union's culture blended the traditions of the trade or occupation it represented with regional traditions, practices, and values. Local unions and central labor bodies were able to affect regional cultures because they were part of the social fabric of communities. When national unions became central to the union movement, however, the traditions, practices, and values extended from national centers to local regions, primarily through guidelines for behavior memorialized in constitutions and bylaws.

Despite lethargy in many central labor councils, research by Fernando Gapasin for the AFL-CIO reveals that many CLCs have continued to function, and some have transformed local union and labor movements in their communities.[1] This research on transformative labor councils, based on interviews with nearly 400 of the 602 CLCs, led to the development of the AFL-CIO's Union Cities program.[2]

The Union Cities program encouraged labor councils to organize new members and support the right to organize, mobilize against employer opposition, build a prolabor political program and hold local politicians accountable to it, promote economic growth, provide economic education to union members, and develop union leadership that reflected the diversity of the working community.[3] In the early days of the New Voice administration, culture change was on the agenda. As Linda Chavez-Thompson, executive vice-president of the AFL-CIO, said in July 1996, "We're aiming to create a culture of organizing throughout the union movement . . . and central labor councils can and will be the center of that culture."[4] In 1996, the original labor council research identified fewer than a dozen transformative CLCs. Since then, the number of transformative CLCs has multiplied. One key to their success is their inclusion and integration of other working-class community forces in strategic planning. And no more dramatic change took place in a local union movement than that in Los Angeles.

THE LOS ANGELES COUNTY FEDERATION OF LABOR:
TOWARD A UNION CITY

The Los Angeles County Federation of Labor (LACFL) formed in 1959 with the merger of one CIO labor council and six AFL labor councils.[5] At the time of the merger, it represented roughly 320 local unions and seven hundred thousand union members. The LACFL's first three principal officers, Sigmund Arywitz, Bill Robertson, and Jim Wood, were straight from the traditionalist mold of union leaders. Thus, George Meany was confident in making his pro–Vietnam War stand in Los Angeles, where, despite strong opposition by the Left, he and LACFL secretary-treasurer Arywitz made sure that the LACFL supported the U.S. adventure in Vietnam.[6] Although dissident left-wing forces had long existed in the LACFL, the federation continued to function as a traditional CLC until the national Union Cities program was launched and Miguel Contreras was elected executive secretary-treasurer in 1996. The LACFL is of interest here because it illustrates how labor movement transformation can start and how the union movement can begin to restore hope to working-class communities.[7]

The transformation of the LACFL has brought enormous changes. The LACFL has directly influenced the selection of the Speaker of the California State Assembly since 1998, and, as of this writing, the former political director of the LACFL, Fabian Nuñez, is Speaker. The federation has also elected numerous prounion people to the Los Angeles City Council. Martin Ludlow, who succeeded Contreras as the executive secretary-treasurer, was a former member of the City Council of Los Angeles.[8] The LACFL was the primary engine for the shift of the national AFL-CIO immigration policy. It was largely responsible for the defeat by a two-to-one margin of Republican-sponsored Proposition 226, which sought to strip political financial resources from unions. The LACFL mobilized broad and consistent support from the entire union movement and the communities of Los Angeles for the Southern California strike of supermarkets by the United Food and Commercial Workers (UFCW), and it built an ongoing fund of over a million dollars to support future union struggles. It fostered a new spirit of organizing, increasing union density in Los Angeles County to almost 20 percent, almost 5 percent more than the state union density. The LACFL has independently drafted and promoted a local initiative for a local tax on utilities to provide tuition money for community college students, thus creating broad support for unions among working-class youth in the Los

Angeles area. It has thus earned a reputation as the most politically influential community organization in Los Angeles County. Though the organization may have missed an important opportunity to unite union and community when the Los Angeles Manufacturing Action Project (LAMAP), which we describe later in this chapter, failed, SEIU's Justice for Janitors, home health-care campaigns, and UFCW's multiethnic campaign at Jimmy Dean's still provided much-needed organizing energy and visibility. More importantly, the interaction between social movement projects and the LACFL helped change the culture of the Los Angeles union and labor movement.

Two social movements changed the LACFL: first, the immigrant rights movement in Los Angeles and, second, the Living Wage Campaign. Leftists played important roles in both these movements. Because the union movement had been slow to organize immigrant workers, numerous immigrant rights organizations had formed to fill the vacuum, such as Hermandad, the Korean Immigrant Workers Association, the Pilipino Workers Center, the Association of Latin American Gardeners of Los Angeles, the Garment Workers Center, and the Coalition for Humane Immigrant Rights of Los Angeles (CHIRLA). As Victor Narro of CHIRLA summed up these efforts, "Immigrant workers are creating their own movement and creating their own union."[9] This movement coincided with the realization that many of the immigrants would become new voters; estimates indicated that in Los Angeles alone, over a million new voters could be registered and mobilized. Contreras, using his own immigrant roots and his long tenure with the United Farm Workers as well as his long affiliation with Latino activists in the Democratic Party, helped form a coalition with the immigrant rights organizations in the Los Angeles area, supported by unions such as HERE, SEIU, and UFW and by scholar-activists of the Center for Labor Research and Education at the University of California, Los Angeles. The LACFL was instrumental in creating a union-based electoral machine that increased Latino voter turnout by over 26 percent. This mobilization was key to the defeat of Proposition 226 and the continued election of prounion candidates in Los Angeles County. By joining forces with immigrant rights activists, the LACFL made clear that it stood for racial justice, and its campaigns helped change national AFL-CIO policy on immigration.[10]

The LACFL further enhanced its standing in the community by building a bridge between two contending communities. Contreras was early to recognize that the traditional liberal coalition between white liberal Democrats (many from the entertainment industry) and the

Black community was rapidly giving way to a new alliance between liberal whites and Latinos. He foresaw that this political shift could exacerbate existing tensions between the Black and Latino communities—which had been evident in the 2000 mayoral race that pitted Mexican American Antonio Villaraigosa against African American–supported James Hahn. Contreras saw an opportunity for the LACFL to contribute to a new alliance between these two oppressed communities, and he hired the staff and developed the political strategy necessary to build this bridge. In implementing his strategy, the LACFL also succeeded in getting another member of Contreras's staff, Martin Ludlow, elected to the Los Angeles City Council.

Championing the Living Wage Campaign in Los Angeles and later Santa Monica placed the Los Angeles union movement at the forefront of the push for economic justice. Local 11 of HERE created an independent nonprofit called the Tourist Industry Development Council, later renamed the Los Angeles Alliance for a New Economy (LAANE). LAANE provided the research and strategic thinking to create two prounion living-wage ordinances in Los Angeles County and the 2004 defeat of Wal-Mart when it attempted to override the veto of the Inglewood City Council. The union and labor movement provided the mass base that gave these movements political leverage.

Leftists also played an important role in building the influence of the LACFL. Within the LACFL were old leftists who had been there from before the merger of the AFL and CIO. Although they would strongly deny any affiliation—probably a throwback to the McCarthy era—most had been affiliated with the Communist Party, and their backgrounds were in basic industries like steel and auto or in communications. The assorted groups of the New Left had roots in the Los Angeles union movement of the 1960s and 1970s. They were in the hotel and tourist industry, the public sector, service industries, the auto industry, manufacturing, nonprofits (especially those promoting the rights of poor people and immigrants), and education (from kindergarten through university level). These New Leftists had received their political training in a variety of left-wing organizations and included nonaligned socialists out of the Chicano Movement as well as Maoist and new Trotskyist groups. These radical organizations not only trained young activists to organize in communities and the workplace but also provided an ideological orientation promoting a vision of social and economic equality and justice. They played roles in strategic thinking, labor education, and consensus building. Some of them organized broad-based discussion groups that contributed strategic and collective thinking for the future of the labor and union movement in Los Angeles. Thus, dozens of ideologically oriented people remained entrenched in the union and labor movements of Los Angeles, and they continue to play a role today in the growth of the social justice movements in the area.

LAMAP: A MISSED OPPORTUNITY FOR RENEWAL

Union activity in Los Angeles provides an excellent example of how the strategic interaction between the union movement and other social movements can revitalize the labor movement.[11] Yet the Los Angeles union movement missed a strategic opportunity to "think globally and act locally" when it failed to act as a strong advocate for the Los Angeles Manufacturing Action Project.

LAMAP raised the question of whether the movement should pay special attention to organizing manufacturing workers. The growth of the Service Employees International Union and UNITE HERE! attests to the shift in the focus of the U.S. economy from manufacturing to services. Organizing in the manufacturing sector is patently difficult when companies can shut down and move plants if unions make progress. And for unions whose primary interest is their own survival, organizing in manufacturing may seem to be a bad investment.

In Marxist economics, the surplus value of capitalism is generated from the exploitation of workers in production. Production includes agriculture, manufacturing, construction, and transportation. Service-sector workers are also exploited in that they are not paid in line with the value they produce; they are part of the distribution system and are paid out of the surplus value generated in production.[12]

Today, U.S. corporations exploit production workers around the world. They have shifted much of their production offshore and import both the products and the surplus value that is generated. The dependence on global production is evident in the number of ships laden with containers docking at Los Angeles and Long Beach harbors. Much of the area's service economy is linked to global production: financiers, lawyers, advertisers, accountants, retailers, communications specialists, and many other managers and professionals are busy coordinating the global economy, and taking gigantic profits from it.[13] Many low-wage service workers, those employed in hotels, restaurants, child care, housecleaning, and the like, provide personal services for these managers and professionals of the global economy. In other words, Los

Angeles sits on top of a system of global exploitation, and its wealth depends on the extraction of wealth from poorer nations. When public- and service-sector unions pressure corporations to pay their workers more, they are, in part, asking for a bigger share of the wealth stolen by capital. That they should be paid a living wage is consistent with basic human rights and decency. Nevertheless, from an economic point of view, raises in their wages do not threaten the regime of capital accumulation in the same way that raises in agriculture or manufacturing do.

Manufacturing in the United States has evolved in two directions: high-end (high-tech) production and low-end production. Much semiskilled work has gone away, because of both technological changes and companies' decisions to move production offshore to maquiladoras in Mexico or to China or other Asian countries. High-end production, for example, takes place in the computer industry (as does low-end production, interestingly) and aerospace, whereas low-end production includes sectors such as light electronics, garments, and parts. Manufacturing workers in Los Angeles are in a peculiar position. They are generally the leftovers of a system of production that has partially moved abroad. They work in the sectors of production that their employers either cannot move or have not moved yet. The fact that the manufacturing sector has a higher proportion of immigrant workers than any other sector, and typically some of the lowest-paid workers, is no accident. The very presence of immigrant workers reflects, in part, the pressures to migrate inherent in global capitalism. Moreover, immigrants are in demand by the remaining domestic production industries because employers in these industries can take advantage of the political disabilities, including the denial of full citizenship rights, of these workers.

Unions need to organize manufacturing workers in Los Angeles for a number of reasons: the workers are crucial to capital accumulation and therefore represent an important front in the class struggle; they are among the most oppressed and exploited of workers and need the protection of unions to defend themselves; and they are linked to exploited and impoverished production workers in the same industries around the world.

Many people on the left recognize the need for international solidarity in the class struggle. Workers of the world need to unite, and the possibility of coordinating workers' actions grows as capitalism becomes an increasingly integrated global system. The ideal way to build international linkages is for each country to develop its own union movement, which can then join with others in confederation. Too often, the U.S. union movement dismisses unions in other countries, especially in the Global South, as weak, nonexistent, or corrupt. The U.S. union movement needs to hold up its part of the tent. If manufacturing workers in the United States do not organize, growing unions in the Global South will lack the key U.S. allies they need to forge solidarity in the larger fight against global capital as well as the fight against specific sectors of manufacturing capital.

U.S. unions have a responsibility to educate workers to think and act locally and globally, because their future depends on doing so. Los Angeles provides a perfect example of this strategic perspective. Certainly, protecting the ability of workers internationally to unionize and improve their standard of living helps raise the standard of living for workers around the world. Workers in the United States can reverse the international race to the bottom by forcing transnational corporations like Wal-Mart to relinquish the superprofits they make by not paying workers a living wage and by not providing adequate health care, relying instead on the government to provide their workers with health care. Transnationals like Wal-Mart are subsidized by other companies as well. Because of Wal-Mart's dominant position in retail, it can require shipping companies, transportation firms, railroads, trucking companies, storage firms, and suppliers to provide preferential pricing. Indeed, it can now shape the retail policy of suppliers. Because transnationals can control the supply chain, exerting pressure on suppliers anywhere in the world as well as at the local market, they have tremendous control over both the local and the global economies.[14]

About 13 percent of the goods produced on the Pacific Rim arrive at the Port of Los Angeles and are transported, stored, and manufactured in the Alameda Corridor. This 120-square-mile corridor stretches from downtown Los Angeles to the Port of Los Angeles and contains almost two-thirds of the approximately 465,000 manufacturing jobs in the city (down from approximately 700,000 around 2000). The Alameda Corridor is the primary access point for Pacific Rim goods in the United States. Organizing the workforce of mostly immigrants and workers of color in the Alameda Corridor would not only be a step toward democracy for all working people but also an opportunity to think and act locally and globally.

Given the great variety of small manufacturing shops in Los Angeles and the fact that workers do not have stable employment, the idea of multiunion geographic organizing is attractive. Of course, this idea is not new; indeed, it played a role in LAMAP. Still, the potential for strategic gains is huge if unions were to give up their jurisdictional squabbles and reach for the greater good they could gain by working together. The Alameda Corridor appears to offer rich possibilities for strategic collaboration. Not only is it populated with a large number of manufacturing plants, it also contains a number of residential communities housing the workers who are employed in those plants. Thus, unions have an opportunity to couple industrial and community organizing. Furthermore, the ports of Los Angeles and Long Beach lie at the end of the corridor, and the unloaded goods are shipped up the corridor to feed local industries and retail establishments, as well as to be prepared for shipment to the rest of the country. Both the International Longshore and Warehouse Union and the Teamsters are in a position to disrupt these flows, if the manufacturing unions of this city were willing to engage in a serious, broad-scale, multiunion organizing drive. Unfortunately, as LAMAP showed, petty power games and arguments about dividing the spoils made it impossible for the various unions to work closely enough to pull off this ambitious project.

The Los Angeles County Federation of Labor seems a likely place to start thinking outside the standard limitations of the union movement. Despite great praise for the LACFL's accomplishments, the federation has seemed trapped in some old-style thinking. Its leadership has been unwilling to provide a vision for its member unions, instead simply following and supporting the actions the member unions are willing to take. If no manufacturing unions have been willing to take on the difficult task of organizing Los Angeles manufacturing workers, then the LACFL has not been willing to do so either. An alternative, perhaps, might have been to pursue a course similar to the Stamford, Connecticut, geographic organizing project, which brought together assistance from the national AFL-CIO, the central labor council, and the local unions, along with some national and international union assistance, to develop a regional approach. The LACFL has been (and still is) in a good position to advance this strategy, particularly in the aftermath of the split in the AFL-CIO and with labor's desperate need for large-scale organizing projects.

One weakness in the current "strategic organizing" concept of the AFL-CIO, and, after the split, the Change to Win Federation, is the focus on industries that cannot run away to avoid unionization, such as public-sector or service industries. The ability of some manufacturing enterprises, like garment factories, to export jobs to nonunion or offshore locations paralyzes many unions. Into this gap have stepped a number of independent and union-supported projects, such as LAMAP, though these projects too, as noted, have run into challenges.

LAMAP was founded in 1992 by leftists and other veteran organizers in conjunction with, but independent of, unions. The founders envisioned the project as a community development program that could bridge ethnic communities, incorporate the expertise and prestige of universities, and harness the organizing power of multiple unions. LAMAP chose the Alameda Corridor as its organizing target and pioneered large-scale, multiunion labor-organizing drives that targeted whole industries rather than individual shops. It also designed a large-scale community component that included classes in English as a second language and citizenship (empowerment programs) and mobilized college students to volunteer in the campaign.

However, LAMAP, much like other creative programs (such as the California Immigrant Workers Association), died for lack of union support. Despite high praise from several international unions and acknowledgment from John Sweeney that LAMAP was a model for organizing, the national and international unions—with the exception of the Teamsters, then led by Carey—would not support an "outside" entity like LAMAP, and the project had to shut down in January 1998.[15]

One of the consistent messages in the demise of LAMAP was that, despite the LAMAP founders' ties with unions, many unions considered LAMAP to be an outside organization. The common refrain from these unions was, "Why ask them to do what we should do ourselves?" This statement makes no sense within the self-contained post–World War II context of the U.S. union movement. To do what LAMAP wanted to do, a local union would have to decide to organize workers throughout an industry, across industries, and in its community. It would have to be able to draw upon resources large enough to field the necessary numbers of staff and rank-and-file organizers. It would have to have the desire, knowledge, resources, and structure to incorporate community issues and strategies into its organization and to help accomplish community as well as union goals. The local union would also need to have clear jurisdiction with unions representing workers in other sectors. Clearly, few unions working by themselves could do what LAMAP was designed to do.[16] LAMAP attempted to be the vehicle by which unions could learn how to organize in a flexible-manufacturing environment, but it also offered a way for unions to combine resources to organize a whole geographic area rather than pursue the traditional incremental organizing of "hot shops."

For some leftist trade unionists in the Los Angeles area and around the country, LAMAP was a beacon of creativity pointing the way to success in organizing then and in the future. As we have noted, the AFL-CIO's central labor councils are logical institutions for spearheading such a broad restructuring of the union movement. They could coordinate resources to enable "regional unionism." Other commentators, such as Joel Rogers, have also suggested regional unionism in one form or another. We envision cross-sector, whole-industry, or geographic organizing, along with the development of worker centers, community issue-based organizing, or more orthodox collective-bargaining strategies.[17] Multiple labor councils could forge organizational links, even between states, to facilitate organizing over larger geographic areas. To do so, they would need to develop regional organizing strategies that effectively combat the regional strategies of the transnational corporations. At the risk of advocating "one big union," we could even see an effort to extend regional unionism to all of Southern California and, in a much different form (respecting national differences), to Mexico. We see only one problem: to paraphrase a statement by Samuel Gompers, the AFL-CIO is a federation held together with a rope made out of sand. Because national and international unions are autonomous, the AFL-CIO can only attempt to persuade unions to coordinate their efforts. It cannot compel them to do so.[18]

THE CHARLESTON 5: A PATH NOT TAKEN

Every movement has missed opportunities. The Detroit newspaper strike and the A. E. Staley lockout, which overlapped Sweeney's assumption of office, were mass struggles that seemed certain to be points of concentration for the Sweeney administration in mobilizing the union movement. In both cases, however, politics with the affiliates apparently got in the way of leadership. Thus, though the strikers and their supporters expected the New Voice team to champion their cause, they were to be disappointed. No significant support came from the national AFL-CIO, despite promises, implied or explicit. Both struggles ended in defeat, at which time people pointed fingers in various directions in recrimination. The complicated story of the Charleston 5 is one example of the start-stop approach that caused the national AFL-CIO to miss an opportunity to ignite a fire throughout the labor movement.

In early 2000, dockworkers in Charleston, South Carolina, members of Locals 1422, 1422A, and 1771 of the International Longshoremen's

Association, were conducting protests against the use of a nonunion stevedore company to unload shipping. The ILA in the South is largely African American, and Local 1422 was led by Kenneth Riley, a young African American who was, by coincidence, the chair of an opposition group within the ILA known as the Longshore Workers Coalition. The ILA has a long history of documented corruption, mob involvement, and lack of democracy. Riley and others had mounted a campaign to fundamentally reform the union.

The attorney general of South Carolina, Charles Condon, apparently made a decision to move against Local 1422, one of the strongest union and African American institutions in the state, through use of provocation. His motives have never become clear, though we can infer that he aimed to weaken worker organization at a time when South Carolina's political and economic elites had opened the state to global capital. Foreign transplants from Europe along the state's I-85 corridor had been moving elsewhere in search of even cheaper labor. Condon may also have wanted to send a signal to South Carolina's substantial African American population that it could take its demands for economic justice only so far. In either case, with the mobilization of well-armed and very threatening state police, Condon's forces were able to inflame a tense situation and foment an altercation between the police and protesting dockworkers. Five dockworkers were ultimately charged with inciting to riot and rioting.

Local 1422 received additional support from the maverick South Carolina AFL-CIO. Led by the innovative and progressive Donna Dewitt, the South Carolina AFL-CIO immediately recognized the importance of this burgeoning struggle and joined hands with the Local 1422 leadership to construct a national outreach program. The organizers simultaneously turned to the national AFL-CIO and to the Black Radical Congress, a network of Black leftists that had formed in Chicago in June 1998.[19]

ILA Local 1422 received little support except from the West Coast dockworkers union, the International Longshore and Warehouse Union. Providing more assistance than the ILA, the ILWU helped support a national defense campaign by contributing financial and in-kind support to help develop a legal defense and by publicizing the case (which it did through its union newspaper). The importance of the ILWU's support cannot be overstated, because the union's participation legitimized the struggle in the union movement as a whole.

The story of the subsequent campaign could fill a book.[20] A committee formed in South Carolina, with the assistance of the national AFL-CIO, to plan a national defense campaign for the five dockworkers. To John Sweeney's credit, he became an enthusiastic and outspoken supporter of the campaign when he learned of it. Sweeney's enthusiasm was greater than the initial enthusiasm of many of his top staff, who at first did not see anything in the case to justify national AFL-CIO attention. Sweeney authorized AFL-CIO staff involvement in the campaign and called upon affiliates to become involved. The leadership of the ILA seemed to have no interest in a successful campaign, yet had no way to articulate such a message. Sweeney regularly asked John Bowers, president of the ILA, for updates on the Charleston 5.

The Charleston 5 campaign, coordinated through national AFL-CIO staff but under the political leadership of dockworkers, took off like wildfire. Local defense committees formed around the country to support the Charleston 5. The campaign united issues of race and workers' rights like few campaigns had in the recent past. Other organizations became involved in the case, most importantly the Black Radical Congress, which helped develop certain defense committees as well as build support for the historic June 2001 Charleston 5 demonstration in Columbia, South Carolina.

Affiliate support for the Charleston 5 campaign was mixed. To be fair, organized labor in the United States was not used to such a campaign. Some affiliates contributed resources, but no affiliate took up the campaign with the enthusiasm that the ILWU did. For the ILWU, the Charleston 5 campaign became a major way to demonstrate the power of solidarity. Unfortunately, most other unions did not share this commitment, regardless of the level of rank-and-file interest.

One of the most unusual aspects of the Charleston 5 campaign was its success! By building the visibility of this case and systematically isolating Condon (for example, by driving a wedge between him and other political figures in South Carolina), the unions caused the state's case to collapse, which led the court to reduce the charges and issue only minor fines. Condon had been so desperate to keep his case alive that shortly after the 9/11 terrorist attacks, he attempted to compare the Charleston 5 to terrorists! This ploy did not work, and everything unraveled for Condon thereafter.

Despite the success of the campaign, the AFL-CIO never capitalized on its victory. In fact, in the immediate aftermath of the 9/11 terrorist attacks, some people in the AFL-CIO wanted the national defense campaign coordinating committee to call off plans for a demonstration on

the first day of the trial (the trial never took place). The national committee correctly resisted this suggestion and went forward with its plans.

Yet, despite the success of the campaign, nothing changed. Riley and
the defendants went on a national tour, albeit one that was not organized
by the AFL-CIO. No large-scale publicity about the victory materialized,
and no celebration took place. At a time when the labor movement,
under severe attack, sorely needed a victory, it had achieved one. Yet
movement leaders did little but yawn, turn over, and go to sleep. The
critical lessons of this campaign were all but forgotten.

One must ask why the AFL-CIO failed to take advantage of this
opportunity. No one seems to know why or to want to explain this
failing. Were the lessons of the campaign, such as the following, too
unorthodox?

- Build a national defense coordinating committee with a real com-
  mitment of resources.
- Ensure that the political leadership for the campaign comes not
  from Washington but from the forces on the ground.
- Gain the active support of the state federation of labor.
- Promote a broad united front with basic principles of unity that
  encourage many forces to join.
- Establish high visibility for the campaign; seize the moral high
  ground.
- Invite nontraditional activist forces to participate.
- Coordinate internationally with other unions.
- Prepare for militant action.[21]

Perhaps some leaders of organized labor thought that the campaign was
not significant because of the small number of workers involved in
Charleston. Nevertheless, the Charleston 5 campaign charted a path
that was largely alien to organized labor and that was largely avoided
even during the Sweeney era.

CHAPTER 12

INTERNATIONAL AFFAIRS, GLOBALIZATION, AND 9/11

In international affairs, the high point of the Sweeney administration was John Sweeney's appearance before a plenary of the World Congress of the International Confederation of Free Trade Unions (ICFTU) during April 2000 in Durban, South Africa. By then, the AFL-CIO had taken major steps away from Cold War trade unionism by appointing a progressive international affairs director, consolidating AFL-CIO–sponsored international labor institutes into the American Center for International Labor Solidarity, and opening or strengthening relations with certain key Left-led national labor centers. Thus, the organization was not only changing its image but was actually gaining some favor with many trade unionists around the world.

However, the transformation was uneven. In Latin America (with the major exception of relations with Cuba and later in Venezuela) and Africa, the AFL-CIO showed new openness to relations with many, though not all, Left-led labor unions and centers. In Asia, the AFL-CIO's relationships were still haunted by the Cold War, and the organization was more wary. Though it developed relations with the more left-leaning Korean Confederation of Trade Unions (KCTU), the AFL-CIO refused to entertain serious relations with the Philippine labor federation known as the Kilusang Mayo Uno, a left-leaning federation that is part of Bagong Alyansang Makabayan (the New Patriotic Alliance). Europe was even more complicated, and a struggle took place within the Sweeney administration about whether the AFL-CIO should have *any* operation in Europe (particularly in Eastern Europe) given that the European Trade Union Congress was quite functional and was the logical organization to work with the newly emerging trade union federations in Eastern Europe.

In any case, Sweeney's appearance in Durban was highly significant. He set to work meeting with leaders of large and small labor centers and took two stands that are worth noting. First, he advanced, along with other allies, the need for a Millennium Review Commission that would think through the role of the ICFTU in the post–Cold War world. This step was critically important because the ICFTU was primarily a vestige of the Cold War, and some people were questioning its reason for existence in the years after the end of that conflict.[1] Additional and no less important matters had emerged, especially the role of national labor centers from the Global South. The ICFTU had always been dominated by national labor centers from the Global North, such as the British Trade Union Congress and the AFL-CIO, yet the international trade union movement was more vibrant in the South than in the North. What role could these centers play in leading the twenty-first-century ICFTU?

Sweeney took his second stand on globalization. In his plenary speech, Sweeney blasted globalization and its impact on the global working class.

> At the AFL-CIO, we are clear about what is at stake. We are in a conflict between two visions, two worlds. On the one side is a world defined by global capital and corporations, enlisting state power to free themselves from civilizing rules. They span the globe with the power to destabilize governments, to reverse generations of progress in a matter of weeks. They have created an economy in which the assets of the three richest billionaires exceed the gross national product of 48 countries and their 600 million citizens.
>
> This global order is neither a force of nature, nor the inevitable product of technology. It has been forged by governments, envisioned by conservative ideologues and enforced by corporate muscle. It is the construct of the conservative movement led in the West by Thatcher, Kohl and Reagan when they took control of the commanding heights a quarter century ago. Deregulation, privatization, globalization and austerity became the order of the day. The price of everything was deemed more important than the value of anything.
>
> Workers across the world were targets of their offensive. In Europe and the U.S., unions and the civilizing rules so vital to markets are still under attack. In the developing world, the so called "Washington consensus" on deregulation, privatization, and free trade was enforced by private investors and public institutions.

We've seen the result. The spread of sweatshops. The resurgence of child labor, prison and forced labor. Three hundred million more in extreme poverty than 10 years ago. Countries that have lost ground. A boom in busts in which a generation of progress is erased in a month of speculation. Workers everywhere trapped in a competitive race to the bottom.

As Seattle showed, working families do not accept the notion that there is no alternative. There is another vision, another world. Citizens of conscience across the world are beginning to object. Students are organizing against sweatshops. Women are marching against violence. Children rise to reclaim their childhood. Sensible economists are dissenting from the conservative catechism.

At these meetings, in this moment, at this place, it is vital that we lay specific plans to raise the heat. That we share ideas to insure that no one shall divide us, North against South, rich nation against poor nation.

The global economy that the corporations have forged can only be tamed by the international solidarity of working families everywhere. For the AFL-CIO, Seattle marked a turning. We heard the stirring calls of our brothers and sisters from across the world. We deepened our appreciation of a truly international global agenda that works for working people.[2]

Delegates were impressed by these remarks, which seemed to pull very few punches and would have been inconceivable coming from any previous AFL-CIO president.

Yet, in slightly more than one year, many of these relationships were, if not shattered, called into question by the response of the AFL-CIO to the terrorist attacks on September 11, 2001. In some respects, the AFL-CIO's response to September 11 had its roots in the organization's understanding of globalization.

As we have seen, globalization is not solely about corporations' actions. Nor is it solely about new technology or about the attitude of capital toward labor. Globalization is about the reorganization of global capitalism, and within that process, the role of nation-states is critical. Yet most of the U.S. trade union movement perceives globalization either as the inevitable process of capitalism or as the product of the activities of multinational corporations. Union leaders almost never connect globalization (particularly the military side of globalization) to U.S. foreign policy, except when it relates to U.S. trade policy.

As progressive as Sweeney's Durban presentation was, it contained no significant critique of U.S. foreign policy. For the leaders of organized labor in the United States, globalization was about free trade and the movement of capital, and therefore the failure of the federal government to take a firm stand in defense of working people. But they did not discuss the relationship between globalization and underdevelopment—that is, the manner in which globalization furthers the underdevelopment of the Global South. And they did not consider the relationship between globalization and the U.S. predilection to prop up regimes that serve its interests and have accepted the dictates of the so-called Washington Consensus.[3] In that regard, globalization was almost a safe topic.

Even with this incomplete understanding of globalization, the AFL-CIO and several of its affiliates recognized that the rank-and-file members of the union movement had at best a superficial understanding of globalization and global injustice. Thus, the AFL-CIO commissioned the Global Fairness educational program. Modeling the program generally on the Common Sense Economics education program, AFL-CIO leaders hoped to use the Global Fairness program very broadly to raise members' awareness of trade and global policy. The program, which unfortunately gained little traction, suffered from some of the same problems that the larger analysis did. It failed to link globalization to the position of the U.S. state in the world and the strategies of its ruling elites for maintaining that position.

The AFL-CIO's limited view of these issues was reflected in its reaction to the 9/11 terrorist attacks. As in many other places, the attacks created panic within the union movement generally. Almost immediately, the Sweeney leadership tried to convey to President Bush that the time had come for a truce between labor and capital. The reasons for this message became clear from the actions of business after the attacks. The airline industry, for example, began restructuring and laying off workers, carrying out cuts that would have helped the industry in any case. Workers were reeling from the layoffs, yet many felt that they could not speak up during that dark hour.

The AFL-CIO chose this moment to take out two-page spreads in some of the most prestigious U.S. newspapers. At the reported cost of approximately $750,000, these ads announced that the AFL-CIO, on behalf of the U.S. worker, supported President Bush's war against terrorism. The ads asked only that the president not forget the U.S. worker.

One cannot easily ascertain the strategic objective of this ad. The fact that the AFL-CIO opted to run an ad in this situation, whereas it had issued nothing other than press statements in response to the everyday attacks on U.S. workers before September 11, is itself noteworthy. Clearly the Sweeney administration assumed that in the face of the al-Qaeda attack, Bush would seek allies in U.S. labor. But nothing could have been further from the president's plans. The Bush administration had decided to carry out a war on two fronts: a foreign war against al-Qaeda (and Saddam Hussein's Iraq) and a domestic war against the U.S. worker.[4] In fact, when the AFL-CIO and—separately—its affiliate the American Federation of Government Employees offered the Bush administration assistance in this time of crisis, they were both rebuffed.

In the background, another drama was playing out. Following the terrorist attacks, several national labor centers from the Global South, including the Korean Confederation of Trade Unions, the Brazilian Central Unica dos Trabalhadores (CUT), and the Congress of South African Trade Unions (COSATU), issued statements calling upon the United States to respond to the terrorist attacks carefully and not unleash a war. These movements expressed their sorrow about the attacks and opposed the attackers, but they did not support a U.S. military response.

The AFL-CIO's response was to draft a letter to each of these federations telling them that they had no right to comment on the 9/11 attacks without clearing their statements with the AFL-CIO. The letter then defended Bush's war against terrorism—in this case, the bombing and invasion of Afghanistan. The first draft of this letter was unacceptably condescending. Fortunately, cooler heads prevailed, but the final version still took leaders of these national labor centers by surprise. They did not know how to respond to the letter's chauvinistic tone and approach. Ultimately, they took an interesting tactical approach: they ignored the AFL-CIO letter altogether.

This incident is worth noting for several reasons. The most important is that the AFL-CIO leadership, including most of its top staff, fell prey to one of two problems: either individuals had no frame of reference enabling them to understand the concerns of these national labor centers, or, as a result of the September 11 trauma, they erected a solid wall of denial preventing them from recognizing that the attacks and any potential U.S. response would certainly raise concerns in the Global South. None of the national labor centers (KCTU, CUT, and COSATU) supported the 9/11 attacks, even implicitly, but they did hope that the AFL-CIO and other forces of goodwill would appreciate the view of U.S. foreign policy among people outside the United States: that it is perceived as imperious, militaristic, self-serving, and offensive. None of these concerns resonated within the leadership ranks of organized labor in the United States, nor did the leaders show interest in discussing these issues. Perhaps the situation was too raw, yet very little has happened since then to suggest an interest in examining these questions. One might argue that the July 2005 AFL-CIO Convention resolution opposing the invasion of Iraq contradicts this point.[5] However, the resolution would not have succeeded without the work of the progressive U.S. Labor Against the War (USLAW).[6] Even in light of that group's work, the leadership has not conducted a full review of U.S. foreign policy as a matter of central importance to the vision and strategy of organized labor in the United States. The leadership of organized labor (both within the AFL-CIO and within Change to Win) has been profoundly resistant to considering the Global South's view of the United States. Clearly such a review would be a source of discomfort, but it could help U.S. labor leaders understand why many in the Global South are skeptical of the sincerity of U.S. intentions, including those of the U.S. union movement, on the world stage.[7]

The AFL-CIO's response to the buildup to the invasion and occupation of Iraq further reveals the confusion within the leadership about how to deal with U.S. foreign policy. Despite the overwhelming evidence that the Bush plan to attack Iraq was grounded on ambitions other than the desire to take out Iraq's much-touted (but nonexistent) weapons of mass destruction and (equally nonexistent) links to al-Qaeda, the leadership of most U.S. unions refused to speak out on Iraq. The fear of being perceived as unpatriotic and the hardwiring to support most U.S. foreign-policy initiatives that involve troops led to dead silence in the face of the buildup, at least until the eve of the invasion.

In advance of the invasion, the AFL-CIO finally issued a statement that opposed the use of military force. Yet once the invasion commenced, the AFL-CIO issued two contradictory documents. The formal statement noted that because the war had begun, everyone needed to get behind the troops and support them. The cover letter, however, conveyed a different message. It noted that the United States would not have had to face the prospect of lost lives had it followed a diplomatic path. The double message of the documents effectively neutralized any antiwar response by the leaders of organized labor, at least until later in 2003, when a grassroots initiative took over.

U.S. Labor Against the War emerged in late 2003 as an ad hoc organization seeking to articulate a different labor message on the Iraq war and to challenge the U.S. union movement's stand on the war. USLAW soon became a major force in galvanizing antiwar sentiment within the union movement, ultimately triumphing, as we noted above, at the July 2005 AFL-CIO Convention by winning the passage of a resolution calling for withdrawal of U.S. troops from Iraq.

Taken as a whole, the Sweeney administration either would not or could not lead a challenge to U.S. foreign policy. It made a small break with previous AFL-CIO administrations in recognizing the danger globalization holds for the world's workers, but it has nonetheless been willing to accept the notion that globalization can be reformed, particularly if workers and unions have input in the international infrastructures supporting global capital.[8] It has refused, however, to draw a link between corporate globalization and the military globalization taking shape in U.S. foreign policy. The AFL-CIO and CTW leaderships appear to equate patriotism with support for U.S. foreign policy and are clearly reluctant to entertain broad-based discussion of U.S. foreign policy within the ranks of the union membership. This view is entirely consistent with that of Gompers, who, following the Spanish-American War, saw the future of U.S. organized labor bound up with the foreign policies of the U.S. government.

PART FOUR

WHEN SILENCE ISN'T GOLDEN

It is we who plowed the prairies; built the cities
where they trade;
Dug the mines and built the workshops;
endless miles of railroad laid.
Now we stand outcast and starving,
'midst the wonders we have made;
But the union makes us strong.

Ralph Chaplin,
"Solidarity Forever,"
1915

CHAPTER 13

RESTLESSNESS IN THE RANKS

Perhaps one of the greatest ironies of the circumstances leading up to the split in the AFL-CIO, a split led by the Service Employees International Union, was that during most of John Sweeney's tenure as AFL-CIO president, many of the affiliates viewed the AFL-CIO as the "AFL-SEIU." This characterization was the result of several factors. Obviously, Sweeney, having come from SEIU, was a source of suspicion among the pro-Donahue forces, and any action he took was the subject of caricature. Nonetheless, real issues were at stake, though interpretations of them differed.

Sweeney brought with him to the AFL-CIO three key individuals: Bob Welsh, his chief of staff at SEIU, who became the AFL-CIO's chief of staff; Denise Mitchell, who continued in her role as assistant to the president for public affairs (media); and Jon Hiatt, who continued his role as general counsel, but now for the AFL-CIO. These staff members joined Gerry Shea, a longtime Sweeney ally who had earlier gone to the AFL-CIO to work with Donahue. Shea became assistant to the president for governmental affairs.[1] Thus, key positions were in the hands of people with direct or indirect ties to SEIU. Nothing should have been surprising about this move, given that a new president typically likes to surround himself or herself with people who are known quantities.

What transpired next, however, was far more complicated. Contrary to the mythology that Sweeney and Welsh went out of their way to recruit SEIU personnel to fill positions at the AFL-CIO, the new leaders actually made a sincere attempt to bring in first-class staff from other affiliates. This effort encountered resistance from the affiliates themselves, with the affiliate presidents often blocking recruitment attempts.[2] Sweeney increasingly drew on SEIU staff people as a result.

Sweeney became the target of some unfair attacks, sometimes by the same unions that had refused to let him recruit their staff, for increasing the SEIU presence in the AFL-CIO. For those who did not know what was actually going on, this hiring trend led to increased suspicion.

As the years proceeded, the affiliates measured virtually every one of Sweeney's decisions by whether his actions benefited SEIU. The 2000 debate about the AFL-CIO's core jurisdiction is a case in point.[3] The real question at stake in this debate was whether the union movement would conduct strategic organizing; however, opponents of Sweeney's proposals for core jurisdiction—including some unions currently in the Change to Win Federation—described the proposals as a naked attempt by Sweeney to ensure hegemony for SEIU, particularly in health care. Some of these attacks, when affiliates were being more generous, emphasized Sweeney's alleged bias favoring service-sector unions. This latter concern was in evidence in debates about trade from 1999 on, including in allegations that Sweeney was not as forceful about trade issues as he should be because of his origins in and bias toward the service-sector unions (which are theoretically not as affected by international trade as the manufacturing sector is).

Much of these innuendos, half-truths, and caricatures substituted for genuine debate about the purpose and operation of the AFL-CIO. Thus, instead of conducting an honest and open debate about international trade, affiliates viewed Sweeney's actions through a lens placing the service sector in conflict with the manufacturing sector. As a result, they missed opportunities to debate other important matters, such as how to understand globalization or how to conduct relations with the Clinton administration.

The tensions that eventually led to the polarizing split stemmed from the very beginning of the Sweeney administration. Sweeney's consensus-based leadership style led to a series of advances and retreats on various initiatives, thereby frustrating key allies, such as SEIU's Andy Stern, and only temporarily placating opponents. The lack of a truly open forum for debate, and the toxic culture within the overall union movement that denies the importance of debate, conspired to prevent the development of an atmosphere of trust and to convince affiliates that their concerns were being heard.

This problem had many faces. The 1999 early endorsement of Al Gore for president was extremely controversial, for instance. Sweeney was convinced that if the union movement did not influence the Gore campaign quickly, Gore would lose and Senator Bill Bradley would win the nomination only to lose the general election. Several affiliates pushed back on hearing of the move toward early endorsement, but the only glimmer of debate came at the August 1999 AFL-CIO Executive Council, where the late UAW president Steve Yokich made an unusually candid and impassioned argument against an early nomination, citing the failure of the union movement to gain sufficient guarantees from the Gore campaign of his support on key worker issues. Yokich wanted the AFL-CIO to hold out longer and press the Gore campaign harder. He received a polite hearing, but his audience ignored his argument, and the early endorsement was advanced at the October 1999 Convention.

The affiliates also became increasingly suspicious of AFL-CIO staff of all backgrounds. Whereas Sweeney, as an individual, was held in great respect by most of the affiliate leaders, choruses criticizing the staff increased in volume. For instance, affiliates criticized the Field Mobilization Department—which Sweeney had reconstructed and renamed as the staff arm to work with central labor councils and state federations and in various campaigns—for being bloated, unfocused, and often useless. More unsettling, however, was the sense among affiliates that the AFL-CIO staff, including but not limited to people in Field Mobilization, was telling the affiliates what to do and was treating the affiliates as local unions rather than as fully independent union organizations.[4]

In the debate leading to the AFL-CIO split, SEIU president Andy Stern said that he had attempted to offer suggestions and criticisms for years but had not been heard. He was undoubtedly correct, though this fact in no way justifies the circumstances under which the split took place. Tensions and frustrations were evident as early as the October 1999 AFL-CIO Convention. They intensified throughout 2000 with the core jurisdiction debate and preparation for the 2000 presidential election and finally led to the paralysis we discussed earlier in the immediate aftermath of the November/December 2000 selection of George Bush.

A SPLIT THAT BEGAN IN SILENCE

The signs that the AFL-CIO was fragmenting appeared immediately after George W. Bush was sworn in as president. Bush made an interestingly calculated outreach to certain unions, including the Teamsters and

Carpenters, to begin discussions about his policies. But he ignored the AFL-CIO. Though some affiliates immediately denounced the Bush administration's tactics, other unions quietly met with the new administration. The Sweeney leadership seemed to have lost the authority to hold these unions in check. In particular, many people saw the Teamsters' response to Bush as an act of revenge for the AFL-CIO's perceived interference in Teamster internal affairs.[5]

Discussions that led eventually to the New Unity Partnership, and in due course the split in the AFL-CIO, seem to have begun very quietly and informally some time in 2001.[6] As of this writing, no details are available about the discussions or the participants, but at some point in 2001, the tensions and frustrations that had been mounting led some affiliates to consider taking new actions to protect the future of organized labor. The sources of frustration ran the gamut from disagreements with Sweeney's leadership style to questions about the usefulness of AFL-CIO staff and the slow pace of organizing among the affiliates.

The catalyst for the split was clearly the decision by the Carpenters Union to withdraw from the AFL-CIO. Tensions with the Carpenters had been rising since Sweeney took over the AFL-CIO. Douglas McCarron, president of the Carpenters Union, had risen to power shortly before the 1995 contest for the AFL-CIO presidency. Reversing the position of his union, McCarron threw his support to Donahue. He then began reconstructing the Carpenters Union in fundamental ways.

Never ashamed of being compared with the infamous Al "Chainsaw" Dunlop from Sunbeam (known for rebuilding organizations by virtually destroying them), McCarron transformed the Carpenters Union into a highly corporate organizing machine guided by a particularly blatant form of right-wing trade unionism. McCarron denuded the Education Department of the union, for instance—a department that had an impressive reputation with the building trades and, for that matter, within the union movement generally. He cut other functions that he considered irrelevant to organizing and then turned his attention to restructuring the field and especially to altering the power of the local unions so that the individuals he appointed held control. Union consolidation took place, and McCarron eliminated any notion of local union autonomy, all in the name of supporting organizing.

McCarron raised many eyebrows as he relentlessly transformed the Carpenters Union. First, he envisioned the union as a limited structure with a narrowly defined purpose: collective bargaining. In his view (as demonstrated by his priorities), other functions, such as education and civil rights, were clearly subordinate to this purpose, if not distractions to be dropped altogether. Second, McCarron argued for reorganizing the building trades to do away with separate craft unions and form one union. The idea of applying industrial unionism to the building trades was not new, but the rationale was: to make life easier for employers. McCarron's union was to provide a mechanism for "one-stop shopping" by employers. This peculiar pro-employer orientation continued to emerge as the sparring within the AFL-CIO leadership continued over the next several years. Third, McCarron's views of politics placed him squarely within the camp of George W. Bush. He largely ignored every action that the Bush administration took against workers and unions (and he certainly ignored Bush's international agenda), looking upon Bush as a friend and inviting him to Carpenters Union conventions.

McCarron took the position that the AFL-CIO had the wrong priorities and was not spending its resources appropriately. Interestingly, just as with some of his future allies in the New Unity Partnership and the Change to Win coalition, McCarron did not express his views openly at AFL-CIO Executive Council meetings. In fact, he avoided Executive Council meetings like sailors avoid a plague ship. When he did attend, he put in only brief appearances and said not a word. Although McCarron had plenty of opportunities to publicly raise differences with Sweeney and other leaders about the direction of the AFL-CIO, he seized none of them. Instead, he folded his tent neatly and quietly and disappeared. Outside of Executive Council meetings, however, McCarron rarely muted his voice.

The response to McCarron in the union movement was both complicated and contradictory. He alienated many in the building trades with his notion of one-stop shopping for contractors; they considered his position to represent either quintessential class collaborationism or advocacy of a turf war with other building trades unions.[7]

Progressives' response, however, was even more interesting. Former AFL-CIO organizing director Richard Bensinger, a strong and committed progressive trade unionist, cultivated a fairly close relationship with McCarron, citing McCarron's strong dedication to organizing. This view began to take hold in various circles, ultimately finding voice among leaders of the SEIU and other unions. It is therefore worth examination.

For many labor progressives, the element at stake in McCarron's restructuring of the Carpenters Union was not the number of workers he had organized or the character of the union he was building. Rather, McCarron's maverick and audacious approach was attractive to many a trade unionist who was disappointed by the slow pace of change in most of organized labor.

Thus, segments of the left wing of labor decided to ally themselves with pragmatists (and, indeed, with the traditionalists at times) under the practical *and* ideological domination of the pragmatists. We call this move the "ideologizing of organizing," which holds that organizing workers into unions is, in and of itself, a progressive, if not revolutionary, action. When one ideologizes organizing, one chooses to ignore the character of the union or unionism and proceeds with the conviction that things will work out in the end. Thus, progressives decided that McCarron's politics and restructuring of his union were, at best, of secondary importance to his commitment to organizing.

Though workers are generally better off being in unions than not, we must ask serious questions about the ideologizing of organizing. For example, in the extreme situation in prewar Germany or Italy, where workers were organized into fascist unions, should we withhold judgment about the unions' political and ideological context? Hardly. The United States has a history of mobbed-up unions' undertaking organizing for reasons that have nothing to do with the conditions of the workers. Are we incorrect to analyze the nature of such unions and raise doubts about the prudence of encouraging workers to join these organizations?

Organizing does not take place in the abstract, yet the proponents of the ideologizing of organizing (a term they would not accept) have defined the satisfactory outcome of organizing in a highly pragmatic way: as the incorporation of workers into a union with a collective-bargaining agreement. McCarron's corporate model is not simply hierarchical; it is also effectively patriarchal, because it removes the organization from the hands of workers and empowers the union leadership to make virtually every decision for the workers.

This approach also holds, whether explicitly or implicitly, that issues outside of collective bargaining are irrelevant. Thus, whether McCarron supports the illegal war in and occupation of Iraq or whether he is close to Bush is unimportant as long as he is committed to organizing. The implications of this view are scary to many in the union movement.

The ideologizing of organizing in the trade union movement is a response to the collapse or absence (depending on one's point of view) of a *Left project*.[8] The crisis of socialism—uncertainty about the best path toward creating a progressive, postcapitalist society—has been significant not just to the Marxist-Leninist or communist Left but also to social democrats and other people with leftist tendencies. For those on the left who saw in trade union work one of the fronts (if not the principal front) for building class consciousness toward a project for socialism or postcapitalism, a void opened up beginning in the late 1970s, when significant questions were raised, practically and theoretically, about a postcapitalist vision. Instead of launching a Left project to transform unions into vehicles that could contribute to the struggle against capitalism and for social justice, the crisis of socialism opened up the question of whether anything is capable of replacing capitalism.

For those who either did not wish to face this question or succumbed to feelings of defeat, the next question was what course of action was possible for people committed to improving the conditions of the working class. In giving up on the possibility of a progressive, postcapitalist project, segments of the left wing of labor tended to treat the organization of workers into unions as the central project. Indeed, although the attack on workers by capital made the building of working-class organizations, including but not limited to trade unions, a critical task, the urgency of this work obscured people's recognition of the larger challenge of social justice. Those who would ideologize union organizing seemed, at least at first glance, to be at the cutting edge of trade union politics. Yet in abdicating a Left project to focus on the purity of organizing, those who ideologized organizing began moving down a slippery slope. They seemed to have put on blinders that forced them to look at the world from a very narrow perspective.

McCarron's break provided an unexpected opening for other affiliates to articulate broader concerns about the direction of the AFL-CIO (the opportunity was "unexpected" in that McCarron had few public allies on the Executive Council). His split apparently catalyzed informal discussions within SEIU that led building services director Steven Lerner to leak a paper discussing what the union movement needed to do to experience a revival. An official version of this paper, "United We Win," ignited a badly needed discussion about the future of organized labor. Unfortunately, though Lerner's paper ignited a discussion, the debate failed to unfold in a comprehensive and broad-scale manner, giving rise to our use of the term *undebate* to describe the two years before the AFL-CIO split.

SEIU was the first to raise the core arguments, later echoed by its allies in the New Unity Partnership and still later, by the Change to Win Federation.[9] After acknowledging the crisis facing the union movement and the continued decline in the percentage of workers represented by unions, the groups advanced the following "solutions":

- *Consolidation.* The starting point for the SEIU, one related to its position on core jurisdiction, was that a surplus of unions was creating overlap and inefficiency in organizing and representing workers. The labor movement therefore needed to consolidate.

- *Core jurisdiction.* Beginning around 2000, Sweeney attempted to advance a discussion of core jurisdiction in the AFL-CIO. SEIU took this move as an endorsement of its vision of a new unionism. A definition of the core jurisdiction would determine how many unions were permitted in the federation. Thus, SEIU proposed reducing the number of unions according to a common jurisdiction.

- *Pragmatic international solidarity.* Although SEIU acted as if it had invented the idea of forging international solidarity with unions in the same or similar jurisdictions, it was far from the first to make this case.[10] However, SEIU initiated more high-profile contacts with other unions overseas than most other U.S.-based unions had and frequently made a point of ignoring the so-called global union federations covering or responsible for that sector. In fact, people within SEIU privately suggested that their organization was doing, internationally, what the global union federations *should* be doing (and in some cases SEIU was clearly right). SEIU was, in effect, prepared to put its money where its mouth was. It saw the need for a global union to address a global industry.

- *Domestic political flexibility by organized labor.* The notion that organized labor cannot afford to ally itself with only one political party or position on the political spectrum has been the source of much controversy. The idea that organized labor has no permanent friends or permanent enemies, only permanent interests, is straight from Gompers (as are most of the points above). In this case, SEIU said that the Democratic Party had been given a pass by organized labor and that the Democrats needed to be challenged to be accountable to the demands of labor.

Though the arguments advanced by SEIU and others could have represented the beginning of a promising debate, they failed to do so. The analysis that was so desperately needed to chart a new course was not forthcoming, except at a superficial level. Thus, the storm clouds brought in much wind but little rain.

CHAPTER 14

CHANGE TO WIN

A Return to Gompers?

We get a sense of back to the future when we read some of the notions that passed for new ideas in the AFL-CIO's debate. Indeed, beneath the surface, we see the ideas of both Samuel Gompers and Walter Reuther.

When we look at the four solutions proposed by SEIU, and later by the New Unity Partnership and Change to Win, several points come to mind. First, no fundamental differences—at least no split-worthy differences—exist in the union movement about the issues in question: consolidation, core jurisdiction, pragmatic international solidarity, and political flexibility. Second, the people presenting these concepts have generally done so with no historic context, a point that is especially relevant to the issue of union consolidation. Third, one reason that no strong differences have emerged is that the two sides of the divide in organized labor share a common ideological assumption that goes back to Gompers.

Perhaps the most striking feature of the debate, including the four proposals and their opponents' rejoinders, is the lack of context—that is, the lack of analysis of the current global and domestic situation. On occasion, rhetoric tried to pass for analysis. For example, at the fall 2004 Cornell University Global Unionism conference in New York City, two leaders of the CTW coalition offered exciting and moving speeches about the state of workers in the United States and about the state of the union movement. Yet these presentations paled next to the true analysis by General Secretary Zwelinzima Vavi of the Congress of South African Trade Unions, who took on the questions of globalization and economic development and linked them to the union movement.[1]

The debate tended to focus on a few themes: the wrongs faced by the U.S. working class, the impact of globalization, acknowledgment that the U.S. movement has not been proactive in organizing, and recognition that something needs to change. The absence of concrete analysis impeded the ability to come up with substantive solutions, particularly given that union members' declining share of the workforce opens the door to myriad possible conclusions about the future direction the union movement should take. Absent from the discussion was any significant attention to the political and economic factors in which the working class struggles against capital. For example, the question of technology (both as a response to class struggle and as a response to competition among capitalists) was not a high-priority topic. The introduction of new forms of technology, particularly computerization and robotics, raises significant questions about the shape of the workforce generally and the working class in particular. Skilling and deskilling of work, not to mention questions of distance work and the changing size of workplaces, have a major impact on any organizing strategy. Yet the discussion we call the "undebate" never tackled these questions; no one even put them on the table for future discussion.

The proponents of change—and eventually of the split—appeared to steer clear of such an analysis. As became clear over time, however, the debate carried an implicit analysis. The following sections look at each proposal in turn and explore how each stacked up against the orientation of the Sweeney team.

CONSOLIDATION

For many U.S. trade unionists, proposals suggesting union consolidation both made immediate sense and were unthinkable. Despite the formal number of unions in the AFL-CIO (approximately sixty-three prior to the split), the majority of union members are represented by only ten to fifteen unions. The call for consolidation was at least an attempt to deal rationally with the problem of inadequate resources. Some unions are so small that they are unlikely in today's world to gain the resource capacity they need to grow. Thus, from one perspective, consolidation into a smaller number of unions with greater levels of resources would increase the possibility of movement growth. To support this argument, at least in the late 1990s and early 2000s, some in the U.S. trade union movement cited the example of Australia as a potentially hopeful direction to follow.

Declining union membership in Australia brought with it, much as in the United States, a series of discussions, some of which concluded that mergers would be the best way to halt the deterioration. From the early 1990s, when the Australian movement had 295 unions, consolidation has evolved to the point that 20 unions, constituting a mix of multijurisdictional and industrial unions, now represent 80 percent of all union members. Not only did this consolidation fail to halt the membership decline, but also the Australian working class came under assault by political conservatives in the government, a situation that the union movement seemed unable to stop.[2]

Neither the proponents of consolidation nor the Sweeney camp brought up the real-world outcome in Australia when discussing the issue of consolidation. At best, and in more informal settings, some proponents of consolidation implied that the U.S. movement might have something to learn from Australia, but they then backtracked on the theory that the Australians did not put sufficient resources into organizing at the same time that they were consolidating. The call for consolidation further ignored a critical fact: some unions, despite their size, have power because of the important space they occupy in the economy. Thus, the International Longshore and Warehouse Union (ILWU), representing dockworkers and warehouse workers on the West Coast and in Hawaii, has substantial power in the longshore industry (and in the state of Hawaii given the nature of the state's economy). A merger with another transportation union would not necessarily enhance the power of these workers, though building links with other such unions would certainly be beneficial. In contrast, the United Food and Commercial Workers union, although it is very large, is not necessarily a powerhouse in its key sectors.[3] Elevating consolidation to a principle, or identifying it as the key link to building power, ignores the importance of analyzing the balance of power in each industry and identifying the pressure points through which a given union can exert or influence power.[4]

CORE JURISDICTION

Trade unionists familiar with the often-senseless competition among unions for workers, regardless of the historical origins of the unions involved, saw in the call for core jurisdiction an attempt to rationalize the approach taken by unions to organizing unorganized workers. Essentially following from the notion of one industry/one union, the proposals for core jurisdiction were straightforward. Unions should focus on the type(s) of workers who are the core of their identity and work. The most obvious examples are in manufacturing; for example, the assumption would be that the United Auto Workers would focus on auto-related workers as well as on aerospace workers. An expanded notion of core jurisdiction is also possible: for example, the UAW could take on the mantle of organizing other metalworkers (which was the plan when the UAW, United Steelworkers of America, and International Association of Machinists discussed merging in 1995). In the service sector, the American Federation of Teachers has a core jurisdiction in education and health care (specifically nurses). Thus, its organizing would focus on workers in those arenas rather than, say, those in fast food.

The core jurisdiction concept met major resistance, including from some unions currently in the Change to Win Federation. Ironically, some of the same unions that have recently joined hands with SEIU accused the Sweeney-led AFL-CIO of pushing the concept of core jurisdiction in order to benefit SEIU! In fact, during the heated discussions in the weeks before the AFL-CIO Convention, when unions were, theoretically at least, attempting to clarify their positions (and Change to Win was attempting to assert and clarify its alleged principled differences with the Sweeney leadership), the CTW forces stumbled over this concept. In a fascinating interview with key union leaders, activist-scholar Janice Fine posed the question of core jurisdiction to CTW stalwart and Teamster president James Hoffa:

> Q: James Hoffa, the Teamsters are the most general union of all. Why
> are you on a team that is so clearly emphasizing uniting workers
> by core industries? You organize in every industry. Are you going
> to stop doing this?
>
> Hoffa: Absolutely not. We would not give up members. But we feel that if
> a union is going to get the organizing rebate money from the AFL-
> CIO, it should be for organizing in their core industries, not just
> for going out and organizing zookeepers or something like that—
> what we have at the San Diego Zoo. We have from A to Z in our
> union, airline pilots to zookeepers, but we felt that the money that
> comes from the rebate program should go to each union for orga-
> nizing their core industries. We will never just be a trucking or
> transportation union. We will always be a general union, and we
> are not giving up our right.[5]

Some would see this response as a case of "do what I say, not what I do."

Core jurisdiction proponents ignored some significant implications of the notion. Larry Cohen, president of the Communications Workers of America (CWA), suggested some of these implications before the split. In a speech at a December 2005 conference in New York City sponsored by the journal *New Labor Forum,* Cohen, then CWA executive vice-president, asked, "What is the relationship between industry and enterprise?" We would deepen this question and ask, what is the relationship between ownership and product? If General Electric owns NBC, for instance, what should be the relationship between unions representing workers in both "industries"? Indeed, what is an "industry" in this era of networked production and diverse ownership?

The discussion seemed to have overlooked other concerns. In some sectors, new and old, workers tend to identify on the basis of trade or craft. Ironworkers, for instance, although part of the larger building trades industry, do not identify with construction workers in general and certainly do not identify with employers. Though some form of industrial organization for building trades workers has long been under discussion, such a method may well not be ideal and is unlikely ever to become the exclusive form of organization of workers in the building trades. In fact, given the changes under way in the nonunion sector of the building trades, we might see the emergence of different forms of organizing. An analogy is the organization of shipyards, which have both industrial forms of organizing (represented by the former Industrial Union of Marine and Shipbuilding Workers of America—which in the 1980s merged into the Machinists) and the Metal Trades Councils, which organizes skilled craft unions by craft.[6]

In the computer industry, this question has already emerged. One could make an argument for organizing all workers—wall-to-wall—within the computer industry. However, identification by skill or trade—for example, for computer programmers—may become the point of reference for organizing. What would this form of organization mean for core jurisdiction?

Core jurisdiction has an interesting geographical dimension. Labor history offers examples of workers in specific areas, such as cities or counties, who have rallied to a union outside of their industry because of the union's strength and reputation in their area. The United Mine Workers of America, United Auto Workers, International Longshore and Warehouse Union, and United Electrical Workers, among others, have had such experiences. The UMWA might organize workers outside of the mining industry because of its relative strength in a particular community. The ILWU has become the most significant union in Hawaii, organizing far beyond its official jurisdiction. In Boston during the 1980s, workers from various sectors were often attracted to HERE Local 26 because of its creativity, militancy, and influence within the city. Such activities do not fall so easily into the practice of organizing any workers that happen to be available.

In the United States of the twenty-first century, a new geographic issue calls into question a narrow interpretation of core jurisdiction. Today entire states, such as Mississippi, have minimal unionization. A union with enough resources might choose to organize workers in the state of Mississippi beyond its jurisdiction. Such a decision need not be frivolous if such a union makes a commitment to the state. In fact, such an approach might be necessary to organize workers in the U.S. Sun Belt.

Thus, the elevation of core jurisdiction to a principle missed a larger and more critical point. Are unions prepared to make a long-term commitment to organizing workers on a rational basis? To what extent are union leaders making decisions according to a strategic plan for an industry, occupation, geography, or other factor as opposed to capitalizing on the opportunity of the moment? By posing the problem narrowly, CTW locked itself into an internally inconsistent approach and risked strategic shortsightedness.

PRAGMATIC INTERNATIONAL SOLIDARITY

True international labor solidarity has both haunted and eluded the U.S. trade union movement for most of its existence. Forces within the Left of the union movement have, over time, attempted to promote a dual notion of solidarity that combines *sectoral solidarity* and *social justice solidarity,* for lack of better terms. The official trade union movement practiced an additional form of "solidarity"—using that term very broadly—in taking a position against communism during the Cold War: "solidarity" with anticommunist and anti-left-wing forces.

Leaving aside Cold War unionism (an oxymoron), sectoral and social justice solidarity have both been features of U.S. trade unionism, but neither has held sway in the U.S. labor movement. Sectoral solidarity is the unity of workers in the same industry or sector of the economy. The longshore industry is a case in point: international solidarity among dockworkers has been a feature of the union's life and thinking for decades. Many other unions have adopted such sectoral, or *pragmatic,* solidarity on a more tactical basis—that is, when they considered it beneficial to the U.S.-based union.

Social justice solidarity is a broader concept of international working-class unity. Whether in the relatively recent past, such as U.S. workers' unity with workers and peasants in Latin America struggling against U.S.-backed repressive regimes in the 1980s, or U.S. workers' support of the antiapartheid movement in South Africa, such expressions of solidarity have gone far beyond the pursuit of sector-based or self-interested unity.

Change to Win advocated a form of sectoral or pragmatic solidarity. The activities of SEIU and UNITE HERE! have elements of this approach. First, the unions advocate unity based on sector and on common interests. Second, and in practice, the initiative comes from the U.S. side and does not generally grow out of a reciprocal relationship. Third, despite the existence of global union federations, the unions tend to downplay the importance of reconstructing these institutions to suit the needs of the twenty-first century.[7] Fourth, and quite ominously, the advocates of pragmatic solidarity began espousing the need for one global union in each sector (or industry) without careful attention to the implications of this notion.

In general, nothing is wrong with pragmatic solidarity. Building ties along sector or industry lines can broaden an organization's concept of self-interest, and in some cases, the notion of class interests. Yet the pragmatic solidarity advanced by CTW, as with its other positions, lacks the support of a comprehensive political and economic analysis. In some cases, it also seems to lack historical analysis.

In view of U.S. history, the first and most obvious question is whether the solidarity proposed by CTW will be reciprocal. Usually justifying their positions by citing various statutes, U.S. unions notoriously—with few exceptions—find reasons *not* to express practical forms of solidarity with unions overseas. For example, whereas in the 1980s, South African trade unions conducted a sympathy strike with U.S. workers in Freehold, New Jersey, one cannot easily find examples in the recent past of similar actions by U.S.-based unions, with the notable exception of the ILWU. Thus, one might ask whether the international pacts under consideration would be strategic alliances or alliances of convenience.

This question came to the fore in 2002–03 when UNITE (before its merger with HERE) sought to build a global coalition of garment workers unions. The formation of this coalition signaled criticism of the global union federation for the sector (the International Textile, Garment, and Leather Workers Federation). The coalition, however, both in the manner in which it was formed and in the way it was led, reflected the needs of UNITE more than it reflected the needs of the coalition partners. Though the coalition was not itself a bad initiative, it appeared to be more of a support group for UNITE than a multilateral alliance of partners taking on a set of common opponents.

In turn, little evidence exists that CTW analyzed the strengths and weaknesses of the global union federations to help formulate an approach to these institutions. Some people delivered speeches about the archaic nature of various labor bodies but offered no leadership in determining which labor bodies are archaic and why they are so. Without analysis of these institutions, no one can determine whether their dysfunction stems from poor leadership or from a systemic problem. Further, no one has attempted to define conditions and requirements for reforming them. One troubling feature of the current discussion of pragmatic solidarity has been support for establishing one global union (rather than a global union federation) for each industry. At first glance, this proposal appears to be a rendition of the old Wobbly notion of one big union, but upon further inspection, it is not quite that.[8] Beginning in the late nineteenth century, the notion of *international trade unions* took hold among U.S. trade unionists. This concept was a U.S.-based (and U.S.-centric) view of unions that emerged and coincided with the birth of U.S. imperialism. Many U.S. trade unionists at the time seemed to view so-called international trade unionism as a form of trade union Manifest Destiny. Paul Buhle noted, for instance:

> The AFL president [Gompers] had meanwhile already quietly laid out plans for a business union internationalism. Endorsing the "ward" status of U.S. rule in Puerto Rico and the Philippines, he insisted upon the right to create AFL-style unions in such places as the U.S. conquered. He rationalized that colonial status would give workers the high wages to buy American products and simultaneously make products manufactured in these places sufficiently expensive that American capitalists would become uninterested in exporting jobs there.[9]

For this reason alone, U.S. unionists must be careful in their use of certain terms.

When CTW leaders refer to *a* global union for each sector, do they really envision only one union per sector? Do they mean that all janitors or truck drivers, whether in Buenos Aires, Berkeley, or Belgrade, will be in the same union? If so, where is the corresponding discussion of nation-state foreign policy, specifically the relationship of the U.S. government to the workers and other peoples of the various countries? Who would run these global unions? What level of autonomy—if any— would national unions have?[10]

Given the lack of any answers to these questions, we must ask if the use of the phrase *global union* is simply a semantic matter—that is, that the proposal does not envision literally *one* global union for each sector but really a revamping of global union federations. Or, in the alternative, is the idea that unions in the same sector would meld into one international union for that sector of the economy?

We see many practical reasons for demanding further exploration and explanation of CTW's and others' concept of global unionism. For example, given that most of the world and certainly most international trade unionists are against the U.S. occupation of Iraq, does the CTW concept of global unionism provide a mechanism through which a global union of food workers, for the sake of argument, could take a position against the U.S. invasion that was binding on U.S. members? Could such a global union demand that the U.S. affiliate work against the invasion? If not, perhaps the CTW is not talking about a global union but about revamped global union federations.

DOMESTIC POLITICAL FLEXIBILITY

In the AFL-CIO debate, a critique that initially sparked interest and support among progressives evolved into an ahistorical and perplexing position on electoral politics. Attempting to distinguish itself from the Sweeney leadership, which has had a nearly uncritical relationship with the Democratic Party, the CTW coalition denounced the organization's partisanship. It argued that organized labor must distance itself from any political party and noted that the AFL-CIO seemed more concerned about cementing its ties with the Democratic Party than about ensuring that workers receive proper representation in the political realm. Thus, the CTW announced that organized labor's political allegiance could no longer be taken for granted.

Had the story ended there, it might have signaled the start of new and creative politics. Instead, as the outlines of the rhetoric have been filled in, we find that "independence," for the CTW Federation, is more of a retreat into a Gompers-like stance. It does not mean the establishment of a political organization or party to represent the interests of the working class; it describes the ability of organized labor to do a dance between the two established political parties.

For all of the CTW camp's criticism of the AFL-CIO for devoting too many resources to politics and not enough to organizing, the CTW affiliates have offered a great deal of financial support to political candidates. SEIU, for instance, devoted millions of dollars to the 2004 presidential elections. In fact, CTW leaders, including former HERE president John Wilhelm (now head of the hospitality division of UNITE HERE!), have touted the importance of the AFL-CIO's role in politics:

> *Wilhelm:* My own view about the AFL-CIO, and I've expressed this view to President Sweeney and the executive council, is that after the November [2004] elections, the AFL-CIO should do two things: I think that it should do politics, and I think it should do Wal-Mart. . . . But there's a diversity of opinion on that, and frankly there is no consensus about the role of the AFL-CIO in organizing at all. I think there's a general consensus about the role of the AFL-CIO in politics, in national politics, but there isn't any consensus on the AFL-CIO's role in organizing.[11]

Wilhelm's remarks offer a more balanced view of the relations between politics and organizing than those that the CTW coalition presented to the AFL-CIO Convention. Indeed, the last sentence in the Wilhelm interview—cited above—is critically important. Wilhelm acknowledges that, at the time of the interview (2004), the AFL-CIO had no consensus on its proper role in organizing but it had forged consensus on politics. If he is right, on what basis can someone criticize the AFL-CIO for being too involved in political action? This revelation by Wilhelm points to the fact that the role of the AFL-CIO in organizing had never been clearly established during the Sweeney years and should have been the subject of a comprehensive struggle rather than an exchange of rhetoric.

The CTW Federation, however, seems to see a need to cultivate stronger relations with the Republican Party as a counterweight to the Democrats. This strategy has a certain logic, given that the Carpenters Union has strong ties with the Bush administration, and the Teamsters Union has a long history of relations with the Republicans. SEIU itself, in 2004, provided the Republican Governors' Association with a contribution of $500,000.

However, the CTW position rests on a problematic premise. The Republican Party had no social forces committed to organized labor. The pro–New Deal members (or those that offered critical support to the New Deal) that existed in the Republican Party at one point, such as Nelson

Rockefeller and Jacob Javits, have vanished or been marginalized.[12] In their place are people who are willing to take union money and manipulate divisions within the ranks of organized labor but who do not advance even the narrowest defense of trade unionism. The Republicans are generally hostile to the interests of organized labor—as an institution—and the working class. Moreover, the party does not offer the formal acceptance of unions that one finds in the Democratic Party, even within its more conservative wing, such as the Democratic Leadership Council.

The real-world politics of the CTW Federation will undoubtedly prevent it from venturing down the path of legitimate independent working-class political action. The components of the CTW Federation are themselves quite divided about unions' proper role in politics. Their initial inability to take a stand on the Iraq war, for instance, is a sign that CTW's internal contradictions were not dissimilar from those within the AFL-CIO, which not until the 2005 convention, as a result of the excellent work of U.S. Labor Against the War, was able to agree to call for a withdrawal of U.S. troops.[13]

In effect, CTW, following the Gompers tradition, accepts politics as based in the two-party system and believes that the role of the trade union movement is to operate as a pressure group on one or the other of the two fundamentally capitalist parties. Although the U.S. electoral system complicates efforts to form minor political parties, the CTW Federation does not appear to be entertaining the thought of forming a legitimate political organization (nonparty) to advance working-class interests.[14] This stance seems to abdicate the notion of class politics and see the union as a pressure group or special interest group for a particular constituency. For the coalition, as for Gompers, the working class is a fishing pond from which the union movement can catch or attract members, rather than a social force that the union movement hopes to organize and mobilize toward a broader progressive project.

All in all, the arguments advanced by the CTW are not particularly profound or revolutionary, but instead are a twenty-first-century version of the vision advanced by Samuel Gompers. They represent a *neo-Gompersian* perspective because of the absence of a transformative project; the absence of a true master narrative to link the economic struggle with other struggles for social justice; and, fundamentally, explicit acceptance of the role of the union movement as a junior partner of capital. Finally, Gompers was the architect of a form of unionism that became known as *job-conscious unionism, pure-and-simple unionism,* or *bread-and-butter unionism.* In this form, the role of the union was not a political one, and, indeed, had no broad social parameters. Not only did job-conscious unionism focus on the problems at the job (or in a more liberal fashion, in work) to the exclusion of other arenas, but it also defined political activity in fairly narrow terms. Thus, not only did Gompers-style unionism abdicate a transformative project, but it abdicated any project outside of guarding the economic gate for those lucky enough to have entered. In this sense, the CTW approach fits well within this mold.

In reviewing the CTW side of the split in the AFL-CIO, we must draw from piecemeal information, because the views of CTW are far from consolidated. Yet the most articulate views on the desired form of trade unionism come from SEIU, specifically from SEIU's president, Andrew (Andy) L. Stern.

Stern, despite years as a progressive (if not leftist) trade unionist and chief architect of SEIU's expansion and influence, has ironically come to represent quintessential neo-Gompersism within the trade union establishment. This evolution has been extremely controversial and has been difficult for many of his supporters and friends to accept.[15] A series of controversial interviews and statements raised many an eyebrow in the weeks leading up to and following the split. They seemed to indicate an approach to trade unionism and an understanding of contemporary capitalism out of touch with the realities of class and power in the United States. The April 2005 issue of *HRO Today* contains an article entitled "Is Outsourcing the New Union Movement?"[16] The article lauds Stern's maverick style and vision, though largely from the standpoint of management.

In addition to distancing himself from any form of Marxism and embracing globalization, Stern has emphasized the role of the union in helping businesses become more competitive. The author notes that Stern endorses the concept of helping companies share the risk of worker dislocation. The author further notes that Stern does not reject outsourcing, particularly given that SEIU represents outsourced workers.

Perhaps the most controversial part of the interview was Stern's critical support of private retirement accounts (an idea that President Bush has advanced). To be fair, such an account would accompany social security and would allow workers to contribute funds. It would also be portable. In other words, it would be an extension and modification of 401(k) plans. Yet in the context of right-wing attacks on social security, what are the implications of flirting with concepts such as private retirement accounts?

These suggestions have an interesting ideological thrust. Stern, following in a tradition that has existed within SEIU (and for that matter within sections of the union movement), treats globalization as accomplished fact, out of the hands of humans, and, in essence, a value-neutral process of economic evolution. Thus, for him, the main issue is to get ahead of the curve and influence the manner in which globalization operates. He sees no point in attempting to resist globalization because it is inevitable.

SEIU had a similar response to health-care industry reorganization in the early to mid-1990s. The SEIU leadership (which then included Sweeney, who was SEIU president) concluded that health-care industry reorganization—particularly the end of public-sector hospitals—is inevitable, managed care is here to stay, and no one can do anything about it. Thus, SEIU saw no point in resisting the privatization of municipal health care. Rather, the union would have to accept the restructuring of health care and develop a strategy for taking maximum advantage of the inevitable changes.

Although SEIU has done some exceptional health-care organizing, its approach to managed care confronted immense problems, not the least of which was the attitude of most other unions in the public health-care sector. More important, though, was the economic determinism that guided its analysis.[17] The leadership made little effort to consider which political forces, including which struggles, might influence the outcome of health-care privatization. Such considerations are critical in municipal settings given the opportunity to mobilize other social movements in response to privatization. Thus, in city X, a privatization effort may not be stoppable, less because of industry trends than because of the balance of forces, yet in city Y, another outcome may be possible.

The deeper problem in SEIU's analysis is the sense that developments such as health-care privatization are independent economic trends over which mere humans have little influence. However, industry developments are driven by a set of factors that include, but are not limited to, class struggle (broadly defined), competitiveness, introductions of new technology (often in response to class struggle), as well as broader ideological forces. Economic trends rarely operate in isolation.

As we have noted, globalization, particularly neoliberal globalization, is not out of the control of human beings. It is, instead, the result of human actions, largely the concerted efforts of governments and multinational capital to influence the global reorganization of capital itself. To treat this campaign as inevitable is to give up on the possibilities of a proactive working-class strategy for power. If one accepts the deterministic view, the actions of the working class become constrained entirely by the decisions of capital. Despite Stern's characterization of creative CTW leadership, CTW finds its creativity limited to reacting to or responding to the developments of capital.

Unfortunately, Stern's neo-Gompersian views do not end with these references. An August 1, 2005, interview on CNBC, combined with remarks Stern offered at the CTW founding convention, confirms that the CTW project, at least from the standpoint of its principal designer, is *not* a project for leftist or transformative trade unionism but is instead a project that is very familiar on the U.S. scene.[18]

In the CNBC interview, conducted by Ron Insana, Stern offered a clear vision:

> *Insana:* Why did you break from the AFL-CIO?
>
> *Stern:* Well, Ron, I don't need to tell you that we are living through the most significant transformative economic revolution in world history, and American workers, although there's growth as you just noted in the economy, it's not distributing. They're not finding their work valued and rewarded, and we need to build a new, dynamic, modern, flexible, innovative labor movement that can be good partners with our employer and we started down that road last week.
>
> *Insana:* Let me ask you to define what that means and how it's different from the movement that is, you know, essentially led by the AFL-CIO.
>
> *Stern:* Well, our labor movement was built around an industrial economy back in the 1930s. It was sort of a class struggle kind of unionism, but workers in today's economy are not looking for unions to cause problems; they're looking for them to solve them, and this means just like Ireland where business and labor and government all began to work together, we need team America to really work together if we're going to reward American workers' work, and to make sure that they still can live the American dream.

In the same interview, and at the CTW convention, Stern outlined his view of unions' key role in the labor-capital partnership. One reporter at the CTW convention noted the following during a press interaction: "However, Andy Stern, who is widely regarded as the driving force behind the break of the seven unions with the AFL-CIO in July, made it clear in a session with reporters that he regards 'class struggle' unionism as outdated. 'We need to partner with business and with government,' he said. This is a time when 'America's economic leadership [in the world] is being tested.'"[19] The odd aspect of this performance, though it is quite consistent with Gompersian unionism, is that at a point when one would expect CTW to be at least feinting to the left, if not shifting to the left, its prime theoretician focused on the relationship of organized labor to capital.

Though some argue that Stern's stance in the pro-business mainstream media is merely a ruse to hide his true class-struggle politics, he has put forth the same line of argument in prolabor media. Moreover, the interview at the CTW convention was with a group of journalists from across the political spectrum, and in most of the interviews he has given since the AFL-CIO split, including his *60 Minutes* interview on May 14, 2006, he has articulated the same basic line of argument.[20] If his stated position in these interviews is a ruse, one might wonder when he will present his real politics and whether that position will be believable after repeated airings of his other arguments.

Stern's analysis has several problems

- The notion that workers do not want unions that cause problems is interesting, if for no other reason than the manner in which Stern formulated the statement. Someone could conclude that Stern sees class struggle as the result of troublemaking by workers or unions rather than as the contention between classes over power. Stern's view also suggests that class struggle can be turned on and off. But most important, his argument is likely the result of poll data that have circulated around the union movement for some time indicating that workers are not looking for trouble at the workplace. How should one interpret these poll results? Who actually looks for problems? Workers want to be left alone and work in peace, and they want acknowledgment of their creativity and intelligence. The problem is that employers get in the way. For a union leader to simply report on the current state of consciousness of many, if not most, workers is to ignore the leader's important role as one who *influences* consciousness.

- The notion of "team America" seems to be a recurring theme for Stern, and it raises questions about his views of the relationship between labor and capital in the United States, as well as in the global picture. First, the Irish example Stern cites—which is regularly cited by advocates of tripartism—is particular to Ireland. The Irish economy and the U.S. economy are not comparable. The Irish economy exists within an unusual setting. It is in the southern part of the Irish nation, split off from the British-controlled north, and these political-strategic factors influence the manner in which the economy and politics of the entire island operate. Specifically, stability in the south of Ireland has been a priority given the historic instability and national liberation struggle in the north of Ireland. The Irish model is also at odds with the neoliberal model that has been spreading across Europe and, as we have discussed, that has become the approach most favored in the "developed" capitalist world. Finally, no significant section of U.S. capital is advocating an Irish model of tripartism. The reality is precisely the opposite.

• The team America idea also raises questions about the relationship of the U.S. worker to workers in other parts of the world. If the U.S. worker should mainly focus on helping U.S. capital become more competitive internationally, how should working classes in other countries relate both to their own corporations and to U.S. workers? For all the international work of SEIU and some other members of the CTW coalition, should workers have to choose between supporting the expansion of U.S. capital and supporting the strengthening of workers in other countries? As with Gompers one hundred years ago, the team America concept does not lend itself to an answer, or at least to a progressive answer.

CHAPTER 15

ANGER, COMPROMISE, AND THE PARALYSIS OF THE SWEENEY COALITION

In the period leading to the split, the Sweeney coalition seemed to be playing a constant game of catch-up with Change to Win. Yet no one in either group attempted to transform the limited framework in which both sides were caught. In considering the Sweeney response to the CTW challenge, one needs to examine the tactical situation as well as the theoretical and programmatic response.[1] Tactically, the Sweeney team was on the defensive from the beginning: at no point in the debate or during the split was it able to gain the initiative. In the opening moments of the struggle, however, no one knew what approach Sweeney would take.

During the period of the New Unity Partnership and before the formal appearance of CTW, Sweeney took no programmatic or theoretical initiative. At this point, his main goal was to persuade the Carpenters Union to return to the AFL-CIO, so he did not engage in open debates with McCarron, or for that matter with the New Unity Partnership. In late 2003 and early 2004, as the rhetoric from the unions that would later form CTW became more heated, the AFL-CIO offered little response. The Service Employees International Union and its allies had relatively uncontested space in which to articulate their views. However, Sweeney was able to arrange the equivalent of a cease-fire in the name of organized labor, putting its emphasis on the November 2004 general elections. SEIU broke the cease-fire twice, both times in a curious manner, offering a different rationale each time.[2] Nevertheless, the cease-fire basically held.

Following the November election, Sweeney took an important step by calling for an open debate and inviting all parts of the trade union movement—including individual members—to offer their thoughts on the future of organized labor. According to the AFL-CIO, the call for debate produced significant results: "The response was incredible—23 extensive proposals came from national unions, 40 from state federations and central labor councils, three from AFL-CIO trade departments, five from Constituency Groups, two from Executive Council committees, two from community partner organizations and 20 from academics and other individuals. Through an open website (www.aflcio .org/ourfuture), rank-and-file union members submitted nearly 7,000 comments and recommendations."[3] This level of participation was quite an accomplishment for a movement with no history of significant open debate. But despite this flurry of proposals, neither side spoke directly to the other's concerns. Participants issued position papers but generally received no replies. Individuals and organizations offered opinions and suggestions, but the leadership generally didn't indicate whether it had factored in the suggestions when it formulated new positions. What should have been a debate quickly became an occasion for both sides to maneuver for position.[4]

Sweeney was unable or unwilling to seize control of this contest. He was incapable of—or unwilling—to harness the energy coursing through the union movement to focus a debate in productive directions. Taking advantage of this opportunity would have required an entirely different approach toward struggle than Sweeney was used to. He would have needed to put forward a new vision for the movement while engaging the affiliates, the central labor councils, the state federations of labor, and the other components of the broader labor movement in a mass debate about the future. When various parties attempted such an approach, they did so without any involvement of the Sweeney team and saw their proposals tabled at the AFL-CIO Convention.One such attempt—a proposal by the American Federation of Government Employees (AFGE), Communications Workers of America, American Postal Workers Union, and International Federation of Professional and Technical Engineers (see appendix A)—was significant for several reasons. First, it called for stepping back from a split. It did not foreclose the possibility of a split in the future, instead suggesting that the leadership had not fashioned the preconvention period to surface the real and most significant issues facing the union movement. Second, the proposal called for a broad and deep debate, engaging virtually every level of the formal union movement. Third, the proposal identified some of the key strategic and organizational questions that confront the movement. The proposal did not deny the structural questions facing organized labor, but it did not take them as the starting point for the debate. In fact, it called for starting with a discussion of the actual global and domestic situation. Fourth, the proposal identified an end point to the debate, sending a clear signal that it was not a stalling tactic. Fifth, it demanded that forces commit to the process and avoid prejudging the outcome. Those who concluded that fundamental, unresolvable differences still afflicted the organization after the debate could walk away.

Finally, the proposal demanded a great deal of the top leaders of the union movement. It demanded a significant amount of their time and attention, pushing them to move beyond their normal manner of operating. The CTW forces ultimately rejected the proposal, declaring that it was too late. One union within the CTW declared that the proposal would be acceptable as long as John Sweeney stepped down first. Whether this declaration reflected the CTW position or only the view of the union presenting it is unclear. In any case, this response clearly sought to sabotage the proposal.

When CTW boycotted the convention and later began the process of disaffiliation, the AFL-CIO top leadership apparently concluded that the proposal by the AFGE coalition was no longer relevant. Ironically, whether the debate ended in one labor federation or several, the AFGE coalition proposal would have been a good guide for clarifying issues and developing the strategic and organizational conclusions necessary to drive a twenty-first-century labor movement. Instead, the proposal was tabled and has received no public discussion since the convention.

In the lead-up to the AFL-CIO Convention, the CTW forces had the initiative. Though AFL-CIO loyalists (along with some uncommitted forces) increasingly expressed anger about the perceived arrogance and factionalism of the CTW coalition, as well as its apparently cavalier attitude toward the implications of a split, CTW was generally able to set the terms of the debate. At each moment, Sweeney had to react to CTW, and he was never able to change the media's perception that the debate was between those supporting organizing (CTW) versus those wanting to focus on political action (Sweeney). In effect, the media described a debate between the vibrant SEIU and UNITE HERE!, on the one hand, and the aging Sweeney, on the other.[5]

In April 2005, the Sweeney team offered its view of the issues facing organized labor and proposed solutions. The document it released, *Winning for Working Families,* was noteworthy for several reasons.

- Contrary to the CTW allegations, the officers made an explicit connection between politics and organizing: "The narrow losses of Al Gore in 2000 and John Kerry in 2004 made it plain that the American labor movement's growing political effectiveness could not compensate for its loss of membership density."[6]
- The proposals in the document, which included suggestions for organizing, mobilizing, and launching political action, differed only slightly from those of the CTW coalition. The primary differences centered on the state federations and central labor councils.[7]
- The officers did not believe that a fundamental reworking of trade unionism was necessary.
- The document paid slight attention to membership education, though, interestingly, it called this process "informing."
- The statement presented an extensive list of reforms introduced during the ten years of the Sweeney administration but left out any evaluation of what had worked and what had not worked.[8] Thus, the list of accomplishments, regardless of the writers' intention, came across as an attempt to dismiss criticisms of the Sweeney years. The document did not discuss why the union movement is in its current state (aside from stating that the Bush administration is out to get unions and workers), nor did it discuss what role a national labor center or federation should play in the twenty-first century.

Taking these points together, *Winning for Working Families* reads like a "me too" rather than a self-criticism, challenge, or polemical response. More than anything, it seems to reflect Sweeney's consensus-building style. It *might* have worked (depending on how one defines "worked") had all the CTW forces committed to struggling for principled unity and had an independent voice emerged from among the affiliates arguing a strong, coherent, and visionary response to CTW. Neither event materialized. Leaving aside the AFGE coalition proposal—which falls into a different category—and including even the American Federation of Teachers' thought-provoking entry into the debate, most of the (anti-CTW) responses boiled down to the following points:

- The union movement is in trouble.
- The union movement needs politics and organizing.
- Forced mergers do not work.
- The AFL-CIO needs to commit greater resources to politics and organizing.
- The affiliates must have a greater role in the future and must have a say in plotting the direction of the AFL-CIO.

None of the responses acknowledged the depth of the crisis or called for the level of discussion and membership involvement that were necessary to get to the roots of the problem. Only the AFGE coalition proposal encouraged a thoroughgoing evaluation.

In general, Sweeney's approach seemed to indicate a continued hope that differences could be resolved quietly, and largely behind closed doors. In the face of provocations by members of the CTW coalition, Sweeney remained relatively quiet. Even after the split, during a critical debate about CTW participation in the state federations and central labor councils (ultimately resolved via the introduction of so-called Solidarity Charters), Sweeney allowed his opponents to portray him as the bad guy who opposed labor unity. He had great difficulty articulating a message of labor unity and labor advancement even though he seemed concerned about not coming on too strong against CTW (perhaps hoping to bring it back to the fold). Thus, instead of either allowing the state federations and central labor councils to handle the question of local union affiliation on their own for the moment or opting for quiet diplomacy and focusing on developing a forward-looking approach to the direction of the AFL-CIO, Sweeney appeared to be paralyzed and reactive.

Instead of inaugurating a major campaign or even implementing the sort of debate that the AFGE and other unions were calling for, the AFL-CIO leadership seemed to disappear behind a veil of silence at the 16th Street NW headquarters, while everyone waited and waited . . . for *what*?

CHAPTER 16

LEFT BEHIND

One cannot discuss the unfortunate lack of debate and the split in the AFL-CIO without focusing some attention on who was *not* included. Within the staffs and top leadership of at least several of the Change to Win unions, an internal discussion, if not debate, had taken place for some years about the nature and scope of organizing, the role of a national labor federation, forms of political action, and the structure of the union movement. This debate had not spread to the base in any significant manner. Although the rank-and-file members did read or hear presentations about discussions at the leadership level, they played no major role in the development of positions or directions for the unions. Communication traveled one way, from the top to the bottom. Only a certain level of feedback traveled up.

Though the Service Employees International Union had issued a pronouncement in 2004 stating that it might leave the AFL-CIO, many of its local union leaders did not believe that the union would take such a step. Only in 2005, when the call came for local unions to vote (at the level of their executive boards) on the possibility of disaffiliation did it become apparent that a crisis was unfolding.

SEIU and the Teamsters made a point of getting material about the impending split to their local unions. SEIU had a PowerPoint presentation that covered the basic issues: declining union power, shrinking density, anarchic and archaic union structures, the need to build industrial power through a reorganization, and other points. The presentation was not particularly impressive, though it was consistent with the messages coming out of headquarters. More important, it was not part of a comprehensive education process to provoke debate and further insight. Rather, it was a means of moving the message of the union. This approach fit with the leadership's lack of interest in developing an internal educational program, because it reflected the notion that education was simply a matter of informing members of the views of the leadership.

The presentation was, in many respects, symptomatic of the entire approach toward the internal discussion and the split. First, it relayed certain basic facts about the declining power of unions. Second, it identified some of the problems in the way unions are organized. Third, it suggested the need for a new course of action. It offered nothing particularly novel, but the most interesting aspect was what it did not offer. Specifically, the presentation did not ask the viewer (presumably a member) to consider the implications of a split, think about alternatives, or suggest a proper role for unions. Thus, members were more like spectators at a sports event than participants in a social movement.

Other unions circulated information through mailings to local unions (the Teamsters sent CTW material to all locals) or through websites. The extent and sophistication of this information varied from union to union. No union, however, conducted a public debate about the issues at stake, though some central labor councils sponsored debates. The case of the United Food and Commercial Workers union is, in that sense, quite a sad one but one worth examining.

The 2003–04 Southern California grocery strike was one of the most remarkable events in recent labor history. The strike and lockout by seventy thousand UFCW members started as a strike against Vons/Pavilion (owned by Safeway). Ralph's and Albertson's, in an interesting display of business-to-business class solidarity, chose to lock out their employees (also members of UFCW), and the companies agreed to share monies earned during the period of the strike and lockout.

In the background of this event was Wal-Mart. The pressure that Wal-Mart placed on the market through its low prices and nonunion workforce led the grocery companies to decide that the best way to compete was to cut $1 billion in labor costs. They hoped to reach this goal through cuts in health benefits and pensions and through the creation of a two-tier workforce. The decision of the companies to create a united front against the UFCW was significant, undermining and eventually defeating the UFCW's effort to focus on one company and make it an example.[1]

Despite significant support from the Los Angeles County Federation of Labor and the San Diego Central Labor Council, both of which rallied union and community support and recognized the significance of this struggle for the Southern California union movement, the UFCW's strike failed. Reportedly, the Teamsters, who had initially supported the picket lines, refused to make a long-term commitment to support the strike. More important, the UFCW suffered from its own mistakes, which included inadequate strike preparation, little outreach to community-based allies in advance of the strike, and little coordination with the central labor councils. This lack of preparation was a recipe for disaster. Yet, for reasons having almost nothing to do with the work of the UFCW, the strikers received an immense amount of public sympathy and support. Commentators have suggested that this support stemmed from community identification with the workforce (recognizing the workers not as faceless personnel but as the individuals with whom people interacted every week) or resentment of perceived attacks on the workforce. Whatever the reason, the UFCW did not adequately organize and capitalize on community support. In sum, the UFCW leadership failed to rise to the occasion and to turn the latent and active support in Southern California into a movement for justice. The combination of faulty leadership and massive employer resistance sank an effort that could have been a subregional analogy to the Teamsters' strike against UPS in 1997, when the public's identification with the strikers' issues completely isolated UPS. The grocery-strike debacle would have been even worse without other unions' show of solidarity and without the support of the San Diego Central Labor Council and the Los Angeles County Federation of Labor, a fact that did not seem to enter the discussions of a UFCW withdrawal from the AFL-CIO.

The Southern California grocery strike coincided with a major leadership change in the UFCW. Longtime president Douglas Dority was stepping down, to be replaced by Secretary-Treasurer Joseph Hansen. Hansen, a former participant in Richard Bensinger's Elected Leader Task Force[2] (and thus a contemporary, if not a colleague, of key CTW leaders), was viewed as a quiet reformer who was open to change in the UFCW, which was encumbered by a conservative bureaucracy.

On taking office, however, Hansen appeared, at least initially, to be unfocused and quite conservative in his approach toward change in the UFCW (albeit with a sincere concern for membership growth through organizing). In connection with the AFL-CIO turmoil, Hansen began sending signals in 2005 that he had differences with the AFL-CIO. His concerns lacked specificity (though they reportedly had something to do with disagreements with Sweeney and Chief of Staff Welsh about strategy concerning Wal-Mart and the allegedly condescending treatment of Hansen and the UFCW by AFL-CIO staff). Despite these issues, it did not appear, at first glance, to put Hansen solidly in the CTW camp. In fact, at around the same time that he was beginning to criticize the AFL-CIO, the SEIU and UFCW—separately—began exploring campaigns in response to the growth of Wal-Mart. Tension had emerged between these two unions, given that Wal-Mart had traditionally been considered part of the UFCW's jurisdiction. Why SEIU decided to take on this campaign rather than support UFCW was and remains unclear, but the tension between the two unions became apparent to most observers.[3]

The decision to ally UFCW with CTW was apparently Hansen's alone. The executive board's decision to authorize Hansen to pull the UFCW out of the AFL-CIO reportedly had opposition. One board member made an impassioned plea to remain in the AFL-CIO, but despite this protest, and despite knowledge that some of the most politically important locals in the union opposed withdrawal, Hansen pulled the UFCW out. No significant debate took place within the UFCW, and we would not be surprised to learn that many UFCW members still do not know that their union has withdrawn. Nevertheless, in the words of one UFCW leader (speaking to us off the record), local unions in the UFCW were prepared—despite serious reservations about the wisdom of withdrawal—to defer to Hansen and mute their reservations. This decision is the latest example of a traditional and reactionary union-movement protocol, which calls for local union leaders to remain silent as long as the top leaders leave them alone. In this case, as long as Hansen did not bother the local unions, the local union leaders were prepared to let Hansen create his own sandcastle.

Speculation continues about why the UFCW withdrew. Financial issues may have played a role. Both the UFCW and the Teamsters have been under serious financial constraints, so withdrawing from the AFL-CIO would have reduced expenditures significantly. Undoubtedly, frustration with Sweeney (and his staff) was a contributing factor. The support that UFCW received during the Southern California grocery strike would seem to have been sufficient illustration of the need for union unity. In light of what we now know about last-minute negotiations before the split, the UFCW may not have intended to withdraw but found itself, along with several other passengers in the CTW van, unable to swerve at the final moment.

Much has been made of the use of websites and blogs in the weeks and months leading to the split. Andy Stern deserves credit for kicking off the Internet exchange through the creation of his blog. Other blogs and websites soon followed. As we have noted, the AFL-CIO website alone logged some seven thousand comments by individuals, not to mention many more from labor organizations. This technology clearly brought the drama closer to local activists than would have occurred otherwise.

Nonetheless, the submission of comments, suggestions, or proposals works only if it is part of a larger process that factors these views into a final decision or outcome. The circulation of varied points of view is meaningless if no one's position changes as a result, and, as we have seen, little did change in either side's core arguments, except insofar as the Sweeney team attempted to compromise with CTW, and after the split, attention was given to the state federations and central labor councils. CTW's positions and tactics altered only slightly during the period leading to the split, as is evident from its rejection of the proposal by the AFGE coalition. CTW's substantive comments did not seem to affect the underlying positions of affiliates—such as CWA—that were aligned against it, though various documents indicate that they did affect the positions of the AFL-CIO officers.

Thus, the reality is that neither side solicited the views of the average member, or even the average local union activist, on the future of the union movement in a way that assured members their views would have an impact. The provision of information about the issues at stake was, fundamentally, no different than mailing out a union newspaper or magazine.

Leaving aside the AFGE coalition proposal for a moment, let us consider what steps the leaders could have taken:

- Each national or international union could have developed an internal education program to solicit members' views and promote debate, using the written positions of the various parties as the starting point.

- Central labor councils and state federations could have organized at least one public debate on the issues and then followed up with small group discussions. Use of computer technology could have enabled long-distance interaction. Indeed, the AFL-CIO could have required state federations and central labor councils to organize such debates.

- AFL-CIO Constituency Groups could have organized debates, either in conjunction with central labor councils and state federations or on their own.[4]

- Labor studies programs could have organized roundtable discussions and debates to examine the issues at stake. Major scholars could have contributed valuable commentary on the debate.

- The national AFL-CIO could have encouraged leaders from other international labor movements to participate in special sessions to offer their observations.[5] College and university labor studies programs could have taken advantage of this opportunity to promote external observation and analysis of the strategic dilemmas facing the U.S. and global union movements.

- The establishment of computer chat rooms could have fostered discussion at all levels in the union movement.

- Unions that were considering withdrawing from the AFL-CIO could have organized plebiscites to engage members not only on the technical question of withdrawal from the AFL-CIO but also on the future of the union movement.[6]

No one appeared to be considering such steps. If anything, people at all levels of the movement appeared to be afraid that real debate might take place. Organizations that are living either in denial or in absolute dread choose to ignore the issues confronting them, even when their existence is at stake. As the AFL-CIO Convention approached, central labor councils, state federations, and Constituency Groups recoiled from the idea of taking positions against a split and in favor of a debate. Thus, one might ask what is new in the "new unionism" that each side is now promoting?

Beyond exploring the basic democratic critique of the two sides' failure to involve all members in a discussion about their own future, one needs to look at who was included and who was not. Racial and gender exclusion has a long and ignominious history within the ranks of organized labor. Even in the 1930s, perhaps one of the high points for organized labor in the United States, the contributions of women and people of color were largely at the grassroots level and received little attention from the leaders of the movement. The movement of the 1930s was largely, though not exclusively, led by white men. The progressive social movements that have emerged or in some cases been revitalized since then have had a delayed impact on organized labor. The chief officers of AFL-CIO unions today are almost exclusively white men, as are their seconds-in-command. Although the AFL-CIO under Sweeney made a concerted effort to diversify the AFL-CIO Executive Council, the decision makers were nearly always, though not exclusively, white men. In the affiliates, increased diversity did not necessarily bring more inclusion, at least in decision making. SEIU, which has a fairly diverse executive board, has increased the number of women in decision-making roles, but the record for people of color is not exciting.

In the period of the AFL-CIO split, discussions, until very late in the game, largely took place among white male union leaders. This fact highlights a major problem in the movement itself. Despite Andy Stern's frequent (beginning in 1996) proclamations that the union movement was *too male, too pale, and too stale,* the distribution of power had changed very little in the nearly ten years between the time he began making this point and the time of the split.

The principals in the presplit discussion also largely ignored the AFL-CIO Constituency Groups, despite the fact that these groups had members from both the CTW and anti-CTW camps.[7] Though the key players contacted some of the leaders of these Constituency Groups, they did so late in the game, and then only to garner their opinion or support. These organizations were treated as if they were on the margins of the union movement, despite the fact that they had offered suggestions for the future of the union movement and had ideas about how it should be organized.

In 2003, tensions erupted between leaders of several Constituency Groups, on the one hand, and SEIU, on the other, about an effort that had been under way to establish a new AFL-CIO–sponsored political action committee under the leadership of Steve Rosenthal, a former AFL-CIO political director. In a presentation to the AFL-CIO Executive Council about the committee, Rosenthal inexplicably chose to insult the Constituency Groups publicly by deprecating their effectiveness in voter education and mobilization. The problem was not so much that he had criticized the Constituency Groups but that he had appeared to write off the groups entirely. Rosenthal, however, was and remains a close friend and ally of SEIU's Andy Stern and Secretary-Treasurer Anna Burger. Rather than intervene to address the criticisms that the Constituency Groups offered, Stern and Burger either did nothing at all or defended their longtime friend, thus strengthening skepticism about the intentions of these labor reformers in matters affecting unionists of color.

One of the striking features in the unfolding drama of the split was how little enthusiasm the discussion, particularly the CTW effort, elicited among women members and members of color. African American leaders, including some in the CTW camp, had a dramatically different attitude toward the discussion and the split than they had had during the Sweeney campaign for the AFL-CIO presidency ten years earlier. In contrast to their curiosity and excitement in 1995, their tone was one of cynicism and fatalism. Comments such as "white folks will do what white folks will do" were not unusual among leaders of color. And within the Constituency Groups as a whole, comments such as "this debate has nothing to do with us" were common.

The damning component of this situation was people's fear of verbalizing these concerns. Even elected local union leaders who were displeased with the direction of the AFL-CIO, their respective affiliates, or the CTW coalition were reluctant to voice their views openly, fearing that a public display of opinion might bring an unfavorable, if not hostile, response.

Contrary to the cynics' belief, the presplit discussion—particularly the CTW's views on union and federation structure—had everything to do with women and members of color. Consolidation of unions, if not mitigated by other structural changes and shifts in power relations, tends to place power in the hands of whites generally and white males in particular.

One of the less-acknowledged contributions of the Congress of Industrial Organizations in the 1930s and 1940s was the emergence of union leaders of color.[8] Before the rise of the CIO and its commitment to racially just unionism, African American leaders (that is, leaders of Black America) tended to arise from the middle strata and thus were primarily lawyers, doctors, educators, ministers, and sometimes businesspeople. The working class was largely missing from these ranks; many people could not envision working-class people as leaders of Black America.[9] The CIO helped promote Black leaders, who proceeded to shape developments in the union movement and often became community political leaders.

The leaders of local unions, and indeed the leaders of national and international unions, have the potential to do much more than lead alliances of bargaining units. They can, and in many cases do, serve as community political leaders and become a voice for workers throughout their communities. A well-known example is the late Coleman Young of Detroit, a former UAW member and leader of the National Negro Labor Council who went on to become mayor of Detroit. The late congressman Charles Hayes of Chicago rose within the Packinghouse Workers (which later became part of the UFCW) and became a noted community leader after achieving eminence as a union leader.

Such community leadership can go beyond name and position to shape both the perceptions and the reality of power. Individual union women and union members of color may achieve leadership positions within the union movement, and enjoy the accompanying titles and salaries, but they must have real power—the power to close the deal rather than go to someone else. Without this power, they will generally be incapable of becoming community political leaders. Further, without this power, they will be incapable of creating the community coalitions or blocs necessary to build power for working-class people at the community level. The rush toward organizational consolidation, regardless of the intentions of its architects, removes the opportunity for leadership advancement and also removes the positions from which women and people of color can exert leadership outside the traditional arena of collective bargaining. Thus, the CTW theory of building industry or sector power overlooks another realm of power—at the community political or geographic level—that is undermined by organizational consolidation. We explore this type of geographic power in the final section of this book.

Many of the issues that received no attention in the period leading to the split were critically important for women and people of color. For example:

- *Racial and gender discrimination within the workforce.* With the exception of references to diversity, the discussion contained precious little analysis of the role of the union movement in championing struggles against racial and gender discrimination. What sort of union movement and what sort of union politics are necessary to ensure that the union movement becomes an arm of the struggle for racial and gender justice?

- *Unemployment.* The union movement seems to rest content with the official unemployment figures. Yet, as the National Urban League demonstrates every year with its *State of Black America* report, a *hidden* unemployment index exists that is rarely, if ever, addressed in official discourse. In these statistics are the workers who are compelled to work part-time or who have given up looking for work. The AFL-CIO discussion did not touch on this problem. Neither side offered solutions to the current hollowing of cities and the class cleansing under way in major metropolitan areas.

- *Organization of the South and the Southwest.* Though unions discussed the need to organize the South and the Southwest, they had little to say about how to accomplish the task. Neither CTW nor the Sweeney camp attempted to glean historical lessons from post–World War II efforts to organize in the South and Southwest or to note the failure of many unions to even consider organizing in these regions. Yet the failure to organize the South and the Southwest has a deep impact on African Americans, Latinos, and Native Americans, who make up a high proportion of the population in those areas.

Though the main players in the discussion may have been white males, the stakes were and remain high for women and people of color in the union movement. These groups' tendency to write off the debate as irrelevant was more a statement of alienation and powerlessness than one of disinterest. Indeed, as the AFL-CIO Convention approached, many union members began to believe that the leaders of CTW had made up their minds to split and that the views of people at the base mattered little, if at all. Unfortunately, all indications suggest that their perceptions were correct.

Ironically, in the immediate aftermath of the split, SEIU secretary-treasurer Anna Burger, the new chairperson of the CTW coalition, declared that the debate was now over. Perhaps in her mind and the minds of other CTW leaders, even in the minds of the AFL-CIO leaders, it was indeed over. Yet, though the split completed the structural change, the two sides had actually settled little in political and strategic terms. This fact should surprise no one, because a true debate never took place; the membership saw only the mirage of a debate, which appeared for a brief moment and then quickly vanished.

PART FIVE

THE WAY FORWARD

Social Justice Unionism

We come marching, marching,
    unnumbered women dead
Go crying through our singing their
    ancient cry for bread.
Small art and love and beauty their
    drudging spirits knew.
Yes, it is bread we fight for—but we fight
    for roses, too!

Caroline Kohlsaat and James Oppenheim,
"Bread and Roses," 1912

CHAPTER 17

THE NEED FOR SOCIAL JUSTICE UNIONISM

In many respects, the U.S. trade union movement is akin to a tire with a slow leak. You can walk out to the car in the morning, notice that the tire is low, and go to a gas station to add some air. All day the tire may look fine, but overnight it loses air and is low again the next morning. If it is not actually flat, you may decide to refill it and keep driving. Then one day the tire has a blowout, destroying, in one catastrophic moment, not only the tire but potentially the car and driver as well.

Those who advocate organizing new members into existing unions as *the* solution to the crisis of U.S. labor are essentially refilling a slow-leaking tire. This stopgap measure is certainly better than not taking action, but it is, at best, a temporary repair of an underlying problem. To draw out the metaphor a bit more: depending on the nature of the puncture, the slow leak may be repairable, or deep-seated structural damage may necessitate a new tire.

The conclusion we have drawn, based on the analysis presented here, is that the current framework of U.S. trade unionism is so fundamentally flawed that a new framework is needed. With that new framework will inevitably come new organizational structures, but forging new structures without *defining the moment* and *defining the framework* would simply create new problems. This situation has become obvious even to reformers within the existing structures, whether the CTW Federation or the Sweeney team at the AFL-CIO.

As exemplified by both Stern's reference to Irish tripartism and Sweeney's nearly uncritical support of the Clinton administration and the Democrats, the principal faces of U.S. trade unionism have misanalyzed the moment. They have concluded

- that there is a wing of U.S. capital with a strategic interest in partnering with labor
- that the U.S. state is a neutral vessel that can be filled by either side—capital or labor—and thus can serve a historical role as arbiter
- that the U.S. labor movement and the trade unions are essentially one and the same
- that pragmatism needs to be the guiding philosophy of the union movement
- that the demands and needs of the working class can largely be reduced to the bargaining and institutional demands of the trade unions
- that the members are largely the objects rather than the subjects of change

In sum, given the framework shared by the two sides, the split in the AFL-CIO was a pointless exercise that has neither repaired the tire nor recognized that it must be replaced.

A need exists for an alternative framework for trade unionism—which we call *social justice unionism*. Elements of this framework have already been formulated and put into practice. Nevertheless, social justice unionism has not yet come together as a coherent program with the requisite solid underpinnings of theory and practice. The remaining sections of this book set forth the key elements of this framework.

THE INEVITABILITY OF CLASS STRUGGLE

The inevitability of class struggle is a useful starting point. Arriving at a precise definition of class struggle is particularly important, because the notion of class struggle has been perverted over the years in the U.S. trade union movement. Class struggle and trade union struggle are not necessarily the same thing. Trade union struggle is a subset of class struggle. Class struggle emerges from a simple dynamic: in a society with a social surplus and a division between those who produce and those who make decisions, a struggle inevitably occurs over that surplus. Insofar as the surplus ultimately results from the uncompensated labor power of workers and those workers—whether working or rendered "redundant"—have no say over the disposition of that surplus, an antagonism develops between those who possess the means of distributing that surplus (and thus hold power) and those who do not: those with the means to distribute the surplus ultimately control society's means of production, distribution, and exchange.

Class struggle, then, is not something that can be turned on and off: it can, however, take various forms, depending on the leadership of the contending sides. It can also be influenced by conditions external to the society in which it occurs. Class struggle, in other words, is not a situation in which workers or unions create "problems" but a social interaction resulting from the nature of a class society.

Class struggle is built into the fabric of all societies that have classes. It is not just a matter of what does or does not take place in a particular workplace or set of workplaces. It also involves who can live in what sections of a city, who is exposed to toxic wastes, who gets access to what sorts of education, whose votes are counted in elections, and who pays attention to greenhouse gases.

Class struggle interacts with, is influenced by, and influences other social struggles. Class does not act alone in an abstract economic relationship. Though additional, independent forms of oppression are at work within a capitalist society, such as race and gender, these forms regularly overlap with class. By way of example, race often becomes, in the words of Dr. Manning Marable, the prism through which issues of class are seen in the United States, given the strength of white supremacy and racism in U.S. society. Class is often viewed as secondary to race, given the totality of racist oppression. Black or Chicano workers may perceive their treatment to be the result of race or nationality rather than an outgrowth of class oppression. Class struggle *within* Black America, then, can be perceived as a conflict between those who are "genuinely" African American and those who have "sold out" to whites.

Race oppression and gender oppression both exist independently of class oppression—gender oppression, for example, goes back thousands of years through various modes of production—but they are also affected by issues of class. The exclusion of a sector of the female population, particularly white females, from much of the formal workforce toward the end of the nineteenth century marked a remarkable convergence of issues of race (the notion that real women were white women and that they had a special place outside of the workforce), gender (the notion that men were the breadwinners and women the competitors), and class (efforts to establish social control over the entire workforce and introduce changes in the production process).

For these reasons, twenty-first-century unionism cannot view class oppression simply as an economic concept that exists in isolation from other forms of oppression in capitalist society. Race and gender are not just grafted onto class division in capitalist society. The interrelationship of these forms of oppression means that twenty-first-century unionism must advocate for consistent social justice rather than restrict itself to narrow employer-employee relations.

Not only does class go beyond employer versus employee; it is also about more than bargaining units, collections of bargaining units, or even sectors of the economy. Class speaks to the relationship of individuals and groups of individuals to the production process and power. As such, twenty-first-century unionism must recognize that struggles beyond the workplace are as legitimate as struggles within the workplace—and we are not speaking only of political or legislative struggles. For instance, the battle over the reconstruction of the Gulf Coast in the aftermath of Hurricane Katrina since 2005 is a class and racial struggle. The vastly different ideas for a rebuilt Gulf Coast reflect class and racial politics. For that reason, the union movement not only must seek to provide relief for the hurricane victims but also should position itself at the center of this struggle for justice. A struggle of this magnitude has implications nationally and is as worthy of solidarity as any collective-bargaining battle—if not more so.

From this perspective, one must be critical of the response of both the AFL-CIO and CTW to the Katrina disaster. Though both federations provided extremely generous material support to the evacuees and have been active in rebuilding, neither federation approached the Katrina crisis as a *Katrina political moment*. The Katrina disaster was less a natural disaster than a political and economic one, the result of years of neglect and of a neoliberal approach toward economics that drained the public sector of the resources necessary to defend the people of New Orleans. Katrina pointed up which segments of the city's population counted with those in power and which ones were irrelevant.

Assuming agreement with this analysis, Katrina should have been (and should still be!) the occasion for a direct assault on neoliberal economics and the racial and class bias evident in the entire crisis. By defining Katrina as a political moment, we suggest that the reconstruction period should be a time for organizing workers around the country to identify what failed on the Gulf Coast; who is to blame; and what must be done, not only to save the evacuees and other survivors but to rebuild the Gulf Coast on behalf of working people and people of color. Thus, it can be an organizing project necessitating the enlistment of state federations, central labor councils, and Jobs with Justice chapters, as well as their allies. This project must assist in organizing the evacuees and other survivors, particularly helping them create their own organizational vehicles to define their futures and the future of the Gulf Coast. It should be no less than a national campaign. But organized labor has opted for a different approach.

Another issue around which there should be a call for action is the forced redundancy of millions of workers. The union movement has largely ignored this development or treated it as a matter for United Way action. It has not, to any great extent, explored the possibility of organizing and uniting with the structurally unemployed. During the first stages of economic restructuring in the late 1970s and early 1980s, some unions, such as the United Electrical, Radio and Machine Workers of America and the United Auto Workers, experimented with various forms of unemployment councils. By and large, however, these projects did not last, though while in existence, they were able to service the immediate interests of former members displaced from jobs because of so-called deindustrialization.

The further growth in the number of the unemployed and the partially employed has sparked little interest in the union movement. Certain experiments, such as the AFL-CIO's Working America (see below), speak by and large to workers who are not in collective-bargaining situations. Yet the union movement offers little to unemployed workers, particularly those who are structurally unemployed or underemployed. Work to aid these workers, to the extent to which anyone has taken it up, has largely fallen to worker-center–type organizations. Chuck Turner, a Boston city councilman and longtime progressive and activist, has convened supporters and allies to take up the specific question of organizing the unemployed. This work is precisely the type the central labor councils and state federations should be supporting. These organizations' failure to reach out to the unemployed and underemployed speaks to a separation within the working class that could lead to intraclass struggle as the battle unfolds for diminishing resources (health care, housing, education).

LABOR-COMMUNITY ALLIANCES VERSUS
STRATEGIC POLITICAL BLOCS

Although forces on the left have nearly always sought to link labor and community struggles, not until the mid- to late 1980s did the notion of building labor-community alliances enter the mainstream.[1] In general, such alliances have taken several forms: tactical alliances to tackle specific issues, mechanisms for asserting general platitudes about the importance of the community (and sometimes, by implication, the importance of uniting with the aspirations of communities of color), or groups espousing a concept of "community unionism."[2] Every so often, however, an alliance shows hints of a different approach.

At the tactical level, the most common approach has been for unions to seek the support of community-based organizations and institutions for organizing or contract campaigns. The examples of this approach are numerous. Local 26 of the Hotel Employees and Restaurant Employees Union (HERE, now UNITE HERE!) in Boston developed near-legendary contract campaigns in the 1980s in which it set out to win, and received, substantial community support. Under the inspiring leadership of the enigmatic Domenic Bozzotto, not only did Local 26 achieve leadership of the progressive wing of the union movement, but also its members came to be seen as champions of the community. Local 26 actively reached out to gain the support of community leaders, and it generally framed its struggles to emphasize social justice rather than put forth a litany of bargaining demands. In the late 1980s, Bozzotto broke new ground when he struggled for and won a rental and housing fund enabling Local 26 members to gain financing for housing deposits or down payments (this move, by the way, necessitated statutory changes that were themselves difficult to win but were eventually instituted). From this action came the Union Neighborhood Assistance Corporation, which works on issues of housing and predatory lending.[3]

Most labor-community work by unions has never been as visionary as the work of Local 26, whose scope narrowed during the 1990s.[4] Although positive results have come out of this work, such as Local 26/HERE or UNITE's successful organizing (with community support) of K-Mart distribution centers in Greensboro, North Carolina, alliances generally do not go beyond conducting outreach and perhaps creating a community advisory committee with lists of endorsers of a union effort. Upon completion of a campaign, they usually lie dormant until the next campaign.

The responsibility for addressing the difficulties in building union-community partnerships does not rest on unions alone. In the mid- to late 1980s, District 65 of the UAW embarked on an ambitious effort to organize child-care and human service centers in Massachusetts. Though the campaign had great vitality, it ran into very particular and peculiar resistance within communities of color, where many directors of nonprofit agencies saw the union as an antagonistic force. In an odd turnabout, agency directors (and personnel) who might be otherwise progressive (and in some cases left leaning) openly opposed unionization. This position seemed to reflect concerns about power and control in their respective agencies and their perception that unionization would threaten their power. Despite efforts by UAW's District 65 to build partnerships with a number of these directors and to focus on the benefits of establishing a common front to obtain greater funding for child-care and human service agencies in the Commonwealth of Massachusetts, many of these directors balked. Their opposition to or coolness toward the idea of unionization weakened the organizing campaigns. Some agency directors played upon skepticism about the objectives of the union—even this historically progressive union—to undermine the notion that agency workers not only had a right to organize but that unionization could strengthen the hand of the community.

On the union side, some union-community initiatives have been positive exceptions to the usual ineffective alliances and are thus worthy of some attention. Such initiatives include Jobs with Justice; the Stamford, Connecticut, "Geo" organizing campaign; and Justice for Janitors (the SEIU effort to organize janitors). Jobs for Justice and Justice for Janitors have both been initiatives that focused on the rights of workers who are either already in unions or are in the process of unionizing.

Jobs with Justice, having emerged from the Kirkland years as a center of more advanced unionism, entered the Sweeney years with a question hanging over it. Given the Sweeney interest in revamping the central labor councils, did a need exist for an organization—JwJ—that took on many of the roles of a CLC? The Sweeney administration decided to support JwJ, though it never formally answered this question.

JwJ is a unique labor-community organization in that it is composed of labor activists who may or may not be in unions. Although some community-based organizations participate in JwJ and work alongside it, one cannot describe JwJ as a union-community coalition. This observation is not a criticism; it is merely a statement of fact.

In effect, JwJ is a mass organization through which labor activists can operate outside their local unions (if they happen to be in one). It is not, however, an organization like the North Carolina–based Black Workers for Justice, which is open to both union and nonunion workers, but plays an active role in both workplace-based and community-based struggles. JwJ focuses largely on the question of workers' rights and within that framework, on workers' rights at the workplace.

JwJ can continue to play this important role, as well as continue to serve as a training ground for new activists, and promote militancy, organization, worker education, and solidarity (including by supporting other workers on strikes or in organizing campaigns). JwJ has, since its inception, aimed to put in practice a new and vital form of unionism.

Justice for Janitors is equally impressive and visionary, having taken on the corporate (and ethnic) reorganization of the building services industry with innovative approaches. Nevertheless, its work has been equivalent, in many respects, to that of HERE's Local 26 in that it committed itself to a substantial community outreach effort, including a campaign to win over community-based leaders. Many people came to see JfJ as an arm of the immigrant-rights struggle in the United States, particularly in light of the demographic changes in the building services industry. Yet JfJ largely failed to address the ethnic implications of the reorganization of the janitorial industry (the removal of African Americans). To the extent that any union has addressed this displacement, SEIU has committed itself to an organizing effort among security guards, a workforce with a large African American presence. This development is important, though it faces some of the same limitations that JfJ does, in that it is a largely union-driven campaign and is not part of an ongoing alliance with community-based organizations.[5]

The Stamford, Connecticut, organizing effort was different from these other campaigns. As part of the AFL-CIO's "geographic organizing initiatives," which were based in part in central labor councils, the Stamford project (led for most of its existence by Jane McAlevey) began framing the work of the union movement within the larger context of community economic development. Thus, the Stamford project not only focused on unionization but also pushed for housing for the workers who could no longer afford to live in Stamford. In 1999 and 2000, the AFL-CIO cited the Stamford project as a model for a possible program of "labor-community strategic partnerships" within the larger context of community economic development. The idea was to assemble various union-based resources to help organize specific geographic areas. In other words, the program would pump up the Stamford model and focus on areas in which unions were conducting significant organizing efforts. This initiative, though quite vocally supported by the AFL-CIO's executive vice president, Linda Chavez-Thompson, collapsed because of changes in the AFL-CIO's Organizing Department in early 2000 and the strategic paralysis that befell the AFL-CIO after George W. Bush captured the White House later that year.

In the political arena, labor-community alliances have largely been tactical, with unions identifying and working for specific candidates but not gathering forces to pursue a longer-term strategic effort. In the early 1990s, some unions experimented with a program called Labor/Neighbor on the West Coast that sought to organize members for political action in their respective neighborhoods. This program was less about organizing communities than about building a union political organization in the communities. It could have been used much more widely, but the myopia of the union movement relegated it to election season, as is common for such projects, and prevented the long-term building of a political organization in the communities.[6]

A final form of community involvement is union participation in charity work, which is what many trade unionists believe community outreach to be. Two examples immediately come to mind. Every year, the AFL-CIO sponsors Martin Luther King Weekend, during which trade unionists gather—originally in Atlanta and later in a rotation among other cities in the South—both to commemorate the life and work of King and to participate in educational programs and community outreach programs. For example, some building trades unions do repair work in the community, in a one-day version of Habitat for Humanity's homebuilding program. The leadership describes this work as a means of increasing the visibility of the union movement in the community as well as improving the image of the movement. As we have seen, the union response to the Katrina disaster has been much the same. Union members gathered food, clothing, and money to support the victims of the storm and organized volunteers to help the victims meet their immediate needs.

Though nothing is wrong with such charity efforts, they are either one-shot deals or short-term efforts, so they do not build movements. They can also come across as "photo ops" to improve a union's image rather than as part of an overall initiative. Instead of strengthening the battle for social justice, they inadvertently reinforce the idea that the union movement is an outside force or institution that stands apart from the struggles that workers face every day.

We see a need for a different approach that addresses questions of both class and power. In this approach, *labor-community* is not the correct dichotomy. A better one would be *union-community,* but it, too, is not sufficient for a social justice framework. *Workplace-community*—designating a relationship between workplace-based and community-based organizations—is perhaps most useful. This distinction is important, but it is not the most important.

To the extent that labor speaks about matters of class, it should not see itself as separate from the community. The term *labor* should denote forms of organization with roots in the working class and with agendas that explicitly advance the class demands of the working class. In that sense, a community-based organization rooted in the working class (such as a workers' center) that addresses class-specific issues is a labor organization in the same way that a trade union is. To push the envelope a bit more, a trade union that addresses the interests of only one section of the working class (such as a white supremacist craft union) deserves the label *labor organization* less than does a community-based organization that assists the unemployed or the homeless.

In this view, labor organizations should set their sights on achieving power that enables them to advance the interests of working people. If one accepts this proposition, a genuine labor movement would advance the notion of a *social-political bloc* whose goal is to achieve power. This power goes beyond bargaining power—whether in a specific workplace or even within a specific industry—to confer political-economic power in society as a whole. This concept is not the same as the idea of limiting organized labor to supporting specific candidates that the leadership brings before it. Rather it calls for building strategic relationships between and with key *progressive* social, political, and economic actors, some of whom may be within the working class and others of whom may be outside it but have agendas that overlap in fundamental ways.

This approach essentially defies current trade union practices in forming alliances and taking political action. Indeed, it has the following central premise: *if class struggle is not restricted to the workplace, then neither should unions be.* The strategic conclusion is that unions must think in terms of organizing cities rather than simply organizing workplaces (or industries). And organizing cities is possible only if unions work with allies in metropolitan social-political blocs.

How, then, does one organize a city? The Stamford project gives a clue to the possibilities, yet it is merely a prototype. Organizing cities calls for practicing *class politics:* identifying individuals and forces within the working class that have sufficient common cause to unite. To borrow an idea raised by the South African Left, we must delineate the minimum bases for unity to accomplish a set of objectives that strengthen the power of the working class. This larger objective requires organizers to think very broadly about who needs to be in the same room to craft a strategic plan. Many efforts stumble on this step. Too often, unions and other progressive formations focus only on groups they happen to like working with, have a history of working with, and feel comfortable working with—rather than on who should be in the room if they are to accomplish their objectives.

Recent experiences of the Black Freedom Movement illustrate this point. In the aftermath of the Katrina disaster, confusion was rampant within the movement about the best way to respond to the catastrophe and its implications. The National Association for the Advancement of Colored People, under the then-new leadership of Bruce Gordon, convened a Black leadership meeting at Howard University in September 2005. The meeting turned into a gathering of the "usual suspects." Though a very broad list of suggested participants had been offered (including a list by one of us, Bill Fletcher, Jr.) that incorporated not only the traditional Black leadership but also Black leftists of different stripes (including but not limited to nationalists and Pan-Africanists), meeting planners either ignored nontraditional forces or excluded them outright. They gave no reason for this exclusion, though one can guess that these forces were simply outside the leadership's comfort zone. In the absence of the Left, the discussion focused more on the interests of the Black business community than on the need to build a movement to address the Katrina moment. In other words, any attempt to develop a comprehensive strategic orientation was impossible given the glaring absences in the room. Comfort, whether personal or organizational, overrode strategic necessity, limiting the ability of the conference to accomplish its goals. In a similar fashion, the trade union movement regularly finds ways to exclude the very people with whom it needs to work.

Therefore, the first step in building a progressive labor community social-political bloc is to gather the forces together. This process involves more than issuing an invitation. It calls for building trust among people and groups that may not feel they have a basis for trust or that may not have worked together before.

Within the working class are a number of relatively new organizations and movements associated with so-called workers' centers, as well as other independent workers' organizations. These groups are often ignored by the established union movement, and some of them have written off the established movement as archaic. Yet many of these formations—for example, the northern Virginia–based Tenants & Workers United, the Miami Workers Center, the New York–based Chinese Staff and Workers' Association, the Philadelphia Unemployment Project, the Boston-based City Life/Vida Urbana (CL/VU)—have deep roots within sections of the working class that are relatively untouched or ignored by official trade unionism. They are often the poorest of the working class, and in some cases, the most marginal. They rarely have much power in the workplace, attempting instead to have an impact at the community level. For the 88 percent of the U.S. workforce that is not in unions, these organizations offer a way to organize to advance their own interests. The organizations can also provide cultural and language bridges between communities that have been denied access to civic participation or traditional unions. This capability is particularly useful for workers' centers established in immigrant communities of color. The *centros* provide a safe haven for working people seeking to develop skills for coping with civic society and for organizing for power in the community or in the workplace.

With the changes in the economy and the shift in the types of manufacturing and service industries, not to mention the increase in the number of the structurally unemployed, these groups' work is all the more important. It offers an opportunity to forge a *labor movement* rather than simply a trade union movement.[7]

The nontraditional organizations above have established significant niches in various sections of the working class. Tenants & Workers United has developed significant work among largely Latino immigrants in northern Virginia; the Miami Workers Center has done important work among the African American poor in the highly segregated and repressive city of Miami; the Chinese Staff and Workers' Association has long had a foothold in New York among Chinese restaurant workers; CAAV (founded as the Committee Against Anti-Asian Violence) has a project to support domestic workers in New York City, a largely immigrant workforce; the Workplace Project in Long Island, New York, has organized immigrant workers and pursued many claims for back wages and reports of poor working conditions; and in Los Angeles, the Labor/Community Strategy Center (LCSC) works with the poorest sectors of the working class, initiating, for example, an unusual mass organization known as the Bus Riders Union to address inequities in transportation funding and services in Los Angeles County.

The second piece of this approach of organizing cities is to return to the notion of unionism as a force in pro–working-class economic development. Thus, it requires union leaders to think about the various struggles and demands of specific sections of the working class, such as the demand for affordable housing, as well as find ways to generate decent-paying jobs. The union movement can support this project in ways that were first described by economist-theorist Randy Barber in the book he coauthored with Jeremy Rifkin in 1978, *The North Shall Rise Again.*[8] Barber and Rifkin suggest that unions direct vast pools of pension-fund money to promote economic development. The AFL-CIO has programs—such as the Housing Investment Trust—that can serve as allies in such work. The main point, though, is to advance unionism as one tool for strengthening the working class, its living standard, and its power.

The principal vehicles for advancing such class politics could be coalitions that we call *working people's assemblies*. The idea is a simple one: to gather together working-class–based organizations that have an interest—objective and subjective—in formulating a working people's agenda. The agenda would need to begin at the local level (city or county) before expanding outward. It would need to focus on the issues particular to working-class people in the target area, identifying the key issues as well as strategies for addressing them. Such strategies could combine self-help initiatives, such as industrial cooperatives and housing cooperatives, with efforts to take programmatic demands to government, through mass action and electoral politics. For example:

- *Industrial cooperatives.* The modern trade union movement has largely ignored the possibilities of industrial cooperatives. In the nineteenth century, co-ops were a key part of movements such as the Knights of Labor. The working people's assembly in an area might either create a committee to initiate a cooperative (conducting the research, raising the capital, identifying markets, hiring a labor force) or pressure a government body—municipal, county, or state—to start a quasi-public economic development venture (particularly in geographic areas or parts of the economy that the private sector has abandoned).[9]

- *Electoral challenges.* Contrary to the practice of many leftist and progressive initiatives, a basis of unity for working people's assemblies should *not* be participants' attitude toward a particular established political party (or, for that matter, toward a minor political party). Each assembly—which would constitute a united front—would need to establish the appropriate organizational vehicle for implementing its decisions. Upon adopting a program, the assembly might begin to construct a political organization that can follow through on the agenda. We believe that this type of organization would likely be a *neo-Rainbow* effort.[10] In other words, it would not be a political party but would be a political organization capable of running candidates for office either within one of the existing parties (most likely the Democrats) or in an independent effort. Such an endeavor would go beyond efforts such as the Labor/Neighbor program of the San Francisco Central Labor Council. Rather than create a union political operation, it would create a pro–working-class political *organization*.[11]

Organizing cities, then, would be a comprehensive, multilevel effort. Rather than have one union concentrate on multiple workplaces or launch a multiunion organizing effort (such as the AFL-CIO's failed 1980s Houston organizing project), this approach would bring together labor forces for a multiyear effort focused on a set of clear strategic objectives. The three-decades-old community-based organization City Life/Vida Urbana illustrates some of the elements of this approach. The organization has been working to win collective bargaining for tenants in the city of Boston. Under its banner, tenants' associations would have a right to bargain on behalf of their members. Through a formation called Community Labor United, efforts have been under way to bring together union activists and City Life/Vida Urbana activists. Some unions, for instance, have supported the CL/VU legislation on tenant collective bargaining. Some unions, such as SEIU, have reached out to CL/VU to gain its support in organizing efforts (such as campaigns to organize security guards), and discussions have taken place about areas in which the unions could provide reciprocal support.[12]

As important as these initiatives are, conceptualizing this work within a working people's assembly could raise its strategic ambitions and level of unity. CL/VU's work, then, could be part of a *joint concentration* of progressive forces in the Boston metropolitan area. The assembly could call on other organizations, including trade unions, to provide technical, financial, moral, and personnel support to its efforts. Those efforts could parallel multiunion organizing efforts within the Boston metropolitan area. Rather than have the timing of these efforts appear to be a coincidence, participants in the working people's assembly could share demands and show real (rather than symbolic) solidarity.

To create a strategic bloc, working-class organizations need to see that their interests, objectives, and identities coalesce. Rather than have each struggle move ahead on its own, the bloc would aim to build coherence among progressive forces, thereby transforming a series of tactical alliances into a social movement. The ultimate aim, of course, would be to construct a nationwide strategic bloc. To achieve this transformation, a neo-Rainbow-type formation would be essential. The movement must be grounded within the working class. The question is whether unions could play more than an ancillary role in building such a movement.

RACE AND GENDER

The post–World War II union movement has largely been unable to develop a politics that truly addresses issues of race, gender, and labor, apart from making superficial or rhetorical gestures. A few exceptions exist, such as several Left-led unions purged by the CIO during the Cold War era, in the late 1940s and early 1950s. Union leaders who emerged during the era of the Vietnam War, the civil rights movements of people of color, and the women's movement have tended to be more sensitive to issues of race and gender than have their predecessors, but this sensitivity has not necessarily or mainly translated into consistently antiracist and antisexist practice. We suggest that the union movement's acceptance of the Gompers paradigm, combined with anticommunism, has limited its ability to understand not only issues of race and gender but, more generally, the need for consistent democracy.

As we have seen, race and gender are not sideshows to the alleged real story of class (which itself is too often understood in narrow terms). The oppression of women is thousands of years old and certainly precedes capitalism. Race is a sociopolitical construct created in the aftermath of the English invasion of Ireland that later took on notions of color with the European invasion of the Western Hemisphere and the introduction of the African slave trade. The tendency to define people by race largely stems from a drive to establish and maintain social control. Both race and gender have been successfully incorporated into and influenced by the development of modern capitalism. Thus, capitalism would not exist without issues of race and gender. Though these issues may play out differently in different places, they are part and parcel of the system.

If this conclusion is correct, and we obviously believe that it is, the consequences for a union movement are profound. A prominent white union leader told one of us that s/he does not know what an antiracist practice is or why s/he should advance such an idea. This comment, which the leader claimed was an effort to play the devil's advocate, nevertheless spoke to a troublesome inclination. Even union leaders who have emerged from earlier struggles and count themselves as progressives tend to collapse all struggles into economics and to believe that a militant economic struggle is sufficient to unite the working class and build working-class power in the United States. The assumption is that the working class stands apart from issues of race and class. Despite the fact that history demonstrates the folly of this view, its proponents often state it without apology.

For example, the Change to Win Federation, at least as recently as the writing of this book, has shied away from issues it sees as divisive—usually in the name of "growth." Growth—increased membership in organized labor—has become the altar at which everyone should pray. However, we have heard this song before.

During the 1930s and 1940s, the CIO had two distinct tendencies in dealing with matters of race and gender. One approach, favored by unions such as the United Steel Workers of America, was to organize all workers in a given plant without challenging patterns and practices of racial and gender discrimination in the workplace. Thus, though every worker's living standard rose as a result of unionization, racial and gender differentials remained. At the other end of the spectrum were the Left-led unions such as the International Longshore and Warehouse Union and the Packinghouse Workers, which saw a duty to challenge, in particular, racist discrimination (albeit not always consistently). The prevailing CIO message, against which the Left struggled, was that growth alone should drive unions' agendas. According to the labor pragmatists, growth would change the dynamics, creating the conditions for resolving all outstanding questions affecting specific segments of the working class. Yet growth did not lead to resolution of those questions, even though it did improve the living standards of most unionized workers. In fact, the CIO's failure to follow through on its promise, compounded by the purging of the Left-led unions, laid the foundation for the emergence of Black caucuses and networks—and later the formation of caucuses and networks among other oppressed groups. And these groups challenged the racism, and complicity in racism, of the movement's leaders.[13]

A twenty-first-century union movement must begin with recognition of one point: the working class divides along lines drawn by the oppressions built into capitalism. These divisions lead some theorists to believe—incorrectly—that the United States has no working class but rather a series of identities fighting for recognition (and often fighting only against the specific form of oppression they face).

Divisions within the working class are linked to larger social divisions. Divisions on racial lines are not simply divisions within the working class but a component of a larger set of societal racial divisions. As a result, people's social and political identification tends to cross class lines because of the all-round nature of special oppression. For example, African American and Chicano workers might identify with other things African American and Chicano, respectively, because of the scale and scope of racial oppression. Women workers might identify with issues that affect women who are not of the working class (though this process is complicated).

This does not mean, crudely, that "everyone has it rough." Rather it means that class cannot be understood in a linear fashion. One cannot, for instance, inoculate oneself against racism and sexism or overlook the experiences that one has had as a member of a group that has known racial or gender oppression. Such experiences inform one's existence in general but also the way in which one perceives other components of reality—in this case, class.

In turn, oppressions such as racism and sexism become battlegrounds to unite workers in the larger challenge for power, or they become battlegrounds in the intraclass struggle over resources (given the manner in which capitalism allocates the social surplus). They also potentially become battlegrounds in the reshaping of society.

Because class consciousness is directly affected by how one understands and acts upon other oppressions, such as race and gender, not to mention economic oppression, a linear or overly economic view of class can create an illusion of unity. In other words, reducing workers' experience to their economic reality in the workplace or, for that matter, in the street can conceal the impact of other oppressions on their consciousness and reality. Workers can come to believe that by ignoring those other realities, they can all march off together. Such a view, as we have seen throughout U.S. history, is disastrous. The union movement largely ignores the fact that capitalism engenders competition and that the system promotes and absorbs divisions such as race and gender as a means of maintaining social control. The leadership of organized labor fails to confront this reality not because of stupidity but because of awareness of the consequences of addressing it: leaders have a deep-seated fear that addressing the all-too-apparent divisions will antagonize whites or men.

If the working class is already divided, then the strategic question for the union movement and all labor activists must be how to bring about the highest degree of unity. The twenty-first-century union movement not only must reject the Gompers paradigm of anticommunism and empire but must embrace *consistent democracy.*

To the white union leader who does not know what an antiracist practice looks like, one could answer as follows: *antiracist practices are those that champion consistent democracy.* In other words, in an anti-racist movement, a union leader would rise to leadership by championing struggles that go beyond one industry or sector and, for that matter, that look beyond economics. Fighting for consistent democracy is essential to build the strategic political blocs we describe above.

Unions' struggle for consistent democracy could take several forms:

- active struggles against racist and sexist employer practices in the workplace, such as differentials in working conditions, pay, access to employment, and promotions
- opposition to religious persecution, such as that against Muslims since 9/11
- support for on-site child care or employer-paid child-care programs
- support for federal funding of education coupled with educational reform (taking this function out of the hands of the states)
- support for national health care
- support for secure voting rights and for reforms in voting procedures to open up the process
- support for affordable housing
- opposition to the persecution of immigrants and support for the rights of immigrants
- advocacy of a democratic foreign policy

Many other possibilities for action could join this list. Some unions, particularly Left-led unions, have historically made a practice of advancing such demands. Nevertheless, the pull toward a narrow Gompers-style emphasis on economics is strong and has led many a union leader to assume that common economic demands are the surest way of establishing unity.

The union movement's approach to race and gender has at least two other elements, one external and the other internal. Externally, unions have failed to make common cause with independent social movements, many of which demonstrate that race and gender cross class boundaries. Many legitimate multiclass movements of people of color and of women have focused on demands and issues that are both specific to their groups (and their fights for freedom) and central to the pursuit of genuine democracy. These movements have often been ahead of organized labor in advancing social agendas. Thus, an interesting sort of tension can develop, in part because many union leaders believe they stand at the helm of the most advanced progressive social movements. In the 1950s and 1960s, for example, the civil rights stage of the Black Freedom Movement regularly advanced demands for democracy that outclassed nearly everything emerging from the trade union movement.

Even more important, the demands raised by these independent social movements can be at odds with the demands and practices of U.S. trade unions. When, for instance, Black, Puerto Rican, and Chinese workers and their community-based allies demanded the desegregation of the building trades unions in New York from the early 1960s onward, they were essentially making a demand for democracy and, by extension, a demand for a different sort of trade union movement. Unions should have broken ranks at this point, and progressives should have led their unions to support the communities calling for desegregation. Such support should have been both moral and material. Rarely, however, did unions step forward in this way. Instead, the bulk of the union movement, in the name of "labor solidarity," either remained conveniently silent or found ways to ally with the racist building trades. This struggle or set of struggles would have been legitimate grounds for a split within organized labor.

Another occasion on which a union failed to see potential in an external movement was the legendary and notorious (and devastating) 1968 teachers' strike in New York. In this classic example, the United Federation of Teachers (UFT; an affiliate of the American Federation of Teachers)—then under the leadership of Albert Shanker, a right-wing social democrat—took a hard-line position against efforts by the African American and Puerto Rican communities to gain community control of schools. Narrowing its view to issues of seniority and ignoring the racial discrimination that had kept African American and Latino teachers out of the school system for years, the UFT struck, in effect, against the communities of color, against the freedom movements. In many respects, relations between communities of color and the UFT (specifically Black-Jewish relations) have not fully recovered from this battle. The bulk of organized labor failed to break ranks from the UFT and failed to appreciate the significance of the African American and Puerto Rican demands for community control of the schools.

Therefore, the unions must reconceptualize their relationships with other progressive social movements. The demands that these movements generally raise are not tangential to economic demands but rather speak directly to the question of consistent democracy.

The internal element of unions' engagement with issues of race and gender is whether they have the will or the mechanisms to recognize race and gender oppression. The practice of U.S. trade unionism since the mid-1980s has illustrated the tension between diversity and inclusion. In large part because of the struggles of the 1950s, 1960s, and 1970s, the traditional trade union leadership faced new pressure to open its ranks to women and people of color. Demands for greater diversity came from organized caucuses or formations, such as the Coalition of Labor Union Women, the League of Revolutionary Black Workers, and the USWA Ad Hoc Committee. In addition, pressure came from the outside, including but not limited to lawsuits accusing unions of exclusion. In either case, during the 1990s, the trade union leadership and staffs began to become more diverse.

In the recent past, some backsliding has occurred. One reason is that many of the staff positions that went to women and people of color did not confer sufficient power or allow these staffers to exert influence on the real decision makers. Though the balance sheet differs from union to union, staff members of color have rarely found themselves in positions of real power and authority. Those who have had power have largely been those in unions run by leaders of color. Certainly, these individuals in largely white settings were not necessarily figureheads. Rather the power was often drained from their positions once they assumed them.[14] Most often, women and people of color have difficulty gaining access to powerful staff positions in the first place. A case in point is the staff position of national/international organizing director. As of late 2006, only one national/international union had a Black organizing director. How can this be possible in the beginning of the twenty-first century?

Elected positions are a bit more complicated because, by definition, elected leaders are chosen by a membership. Yet the formality of this selection process should not confuse anyone. First, many "elected" leaders within the union movement gain their position through the assistance of someone currently occupying that position or of someone else in authority. The recent history of the Communications Workers of America is instructive. Progressive leader Larry Cohen assumed the presidency of CWA after years of anticipation, and a shakeup followed, along with the emergence of new leaders. The new leadership grouping is almost all white. Despite the opportunity to recruit and develop leaders of color, the culture of the organization apparently took over, changing the cast of characters in various positions but not the types of people usually promoted into these jobs. In some unions, the situation is quite blatant and embarrassing, with the promotion of family members creating an almost monarchical succession.

A complicated issue is at play in matters related to elected union office, one that haunts all electoral politics in the United States: how many whites are willing to vote for individuals of color, and how many people of both genders are willing to vote for women? The union movement has an uneven record in this area, speaking volumes about the lack of internal education about inclusion.

A twenty-first-century union movement must recognize several facts:

- The working class is divided and must be united, but unity cannot be based solely on common economic demands and must join people together in a struggle for consistent democracy.

- The union movement has an obligation to build and support working-class leaders of color and women leaders who can be influential within their respective independent social movements. It must recognize that such individuals have independent power and constituency bases and thus must have independent authority.

- Diversity is important, but *inclusion is fundamental*. Thus, union leadership—at both the staff and elected levels—must mirror the membership. Women and staff members of color must also have opportunities to hold positions of real authority, not just the positions they have traditionally held, such as civil rights and women's director positions. Full inclusion is not only a moral position but also a pragmatic necessity: whites cannot know the experiences of workers of color any more than men can know the experiences of women. Whites can be allies of people of color, and men can be allies of women, but they must do so in a spirit of partnership rather than condescension.

- The movement's organizing strategy must incorporate and coordinate with social movements of color, incorporate sectors that have large numbers of women and people of color, and validate sectors that are primarily centers for women workers, and therefore receive short shrift, such as domestic work, home care, and child care.[15]

CHAPTER 18

THE NEED FOR A GLOBAL OUTLOOK

Transformation will occur when the labor movement thinks and acts both globally and locally. All of the data available indicate that unionization provides the most consistent means for workers to improve their economic welfare.[1] But what about the rest of the workers, the majority of working people (now 88 percent) who do not have unions? The union movement succeeded in the past because unions were able to manifest the aspirations and hopes of most working people and consequently earned the mass support of working-class communities. Unions were "schools of democracy" in which working people could learn how to build their power where they work and often learned to fight for the equal rights of all workers, regardless of their race, gender, sexual orientation, disabilities, immigration status, and nationality. This class-based perspective of unionism informed unionized workers about the importance of building power for working people in their communities.[2]

The union movement needs to make some critical changes to ensure its own future. From a leftist perspective, the future of the union movement lies in a combination of renewed internationalism and the ability of local union movements to transform themselves. Today 70 percent of the union movement's resources are tied up in local unions, which is the level at which workers and their communities interact with the union movement every day. People have long recognized that the only structure in the union movement that can blend the various interests and cultures of unions with the culture and interests of local communities is the central labor council. We join with other scholars and activists in believing that the shift from business unionism to social justice unionism requires a dramatic cultural, ideological, and structural transformation in and of the U.S. union movement, and that change will have to come from local bases of activism informed by global realities.[3] Thinking and acting globally and locally will change unions and communities simultaneously.

When a progressive movement culture in the unions captured the hopes and aspirations of working people, union and labor "movements" were built, such as the Knights of Labor in the late nineteenth century and the CIO in the 1930s and 1940s. Industrial organizing, driven at its height by a center-Left alliance in the CIO, inspired hope for workplace democracy, broad-based democratic reforms, a social safety net, gender and racial equality, and an end to grinding poverty. Similarly today, a union movement that reflects how global forces affect workers in their communities and effectively combats neoliberal globalization at the local level (and unites with others to resist it globally) will improve workers' lives and enable unions to reclaim their place as the basic institution of working-class people.

TRADE UNIONISM STAGE SOUTH

Despite the fact that several unions have abandoned use of the term *solidarity,* apparently because of feedback they received from focus groups, we find the term not only politically valuable but analytically useful, because it describes a particular practice that organizations, social movements, and other groups undertake to establish common cause in their efforts. An interesting and problematic view of international working-class solidarity began to emerge in the U.S. union movement several years ago. This view, which was apparently shared by the future members of Change to Win and the Sweeney leadership in the AFL-CIO, identifies three forms of solidarity: Cold War solidarity, pragmatic solidarity, and a third form we call "altruistic solidarity" (helping weaker movements with educational programs and in some cases resources).[4] None of these approaches assumes that U.S. unions have much to learn from or to emulate in the union movements of the Global South. None acknowledges that support for other movements—whether they are union movements or other forms of justice movements—is essential to achieve solidarity within the U.S. union movement.[5]

The U.S. union movement has emerged from a tradition of Cold War trade unionism. This tradition has characteristically viewed other nations' trade unions with arrogance and condescension, even when U.S. unions have been able to do good work with these non-U.S. organizations. The tradition has also involved destructive interference in other countries and their labor movements. And Cold War unionism has clouded the ability of the U.S. union movement to understand responses in the Global South to emerging neoliberal globalization.

The Global South is, of course, not a monolithic bloc. Within it are countries that have pursued economic and political policies often at odds with global capitalism (for example, China before 1976 and Cuba), countries that have undertaken a form of national capitalism (such as South Korea, India, and China after 1978), and more classic neocolonies (such as the Philippines, Kenya, and most of Central America). Clearly, some countries fall between these categories or reside at the nexus of them.

For reasons rooted in Cold War geopolitics, the United States has supported the economic development of certain countries more than others. It has done so in Japan, for example, by relieving the country of the burden of developing a large-scale military and creating favorable trade agreements, and in this way, it has been able to position the country to place needed resources into industrialization and large-scale economic development. In countries with more distorted development, such as Indonesia and Nigeria, foreign investment has helped expand the size of the working classes. These classes, however, have often been unbalanced, with significant investments in particular sectors, such as the petrochemical industry, being unmatched in other sectors. This unevenness can lead to polarization within the working class. Nevertheless, one can reasonably say that the world has witnessed a process of proletarianization over the last forty-plus years. This process has taken place in the shadow of the expansion of capitalism in the farming sector (and in many cases the displacement of farmers, which has encouraged migration into urban slums or to other countries).[6] In turn, particularly during the past decade, we have seen the expansion of the informal sector, the sector of the workforce not tied into the official economy (such as unregistered businesses or workers paid "under the table").

The response to neoliberal globalization in the Global South has been mixed, with class often determining people's responses. Neocolonial elites have embraced neoliberal globalization, as one would expect. In some cases—for example, contemporary South Africa—ruling groups formerly associated with national liberation movements have also embraced neoliberal globalization but have had to navigate complicated relationships with the United States to avoid total subordination. As Greg Albo has noted, relations between the major capitalist states today hover between competition and cooperation.[7] This statement also describes the relations between the G-8 countries and many of the lesser capitalist countries such as South Africa and Brazil. Discussions, for instance, about South–South relations and an alignment between China, Brazil, India, and South Africa often reflect the desire of the national ruling groups of the Global South to strengthen their position in relation to the United States, but they do not fundamentally challenge neoliberal globalization.[8]

At the grassroots, however, significant challenges have emerged. Time and space do not permit an exhaustive examination of these efforts, but several general observations apply. First, the collapse of national populist projects beginning in the late 1970s has created a space in which new transformative movements are attempting to grow.[9] The struggles for national independence and national liberation from the 1940s through the 1970s created formal or informal national united fronts in which various social forces subordinated themselves. The inability of the national populist projects to evolve into fully transformative projects (in large part because of their acceptance of the parameters of existing capitalism), combined with the end of the Cold War, threw these movements into chaos. The leading elements of most of these countries rejected, formally and informally, noncapitalist directions and embraced neoliberalism. This change in fundamental direction alienated parts of the movements that had hitherto worked directly with the leading organization or party of the national populist project.[10]

Despite accepting some form of neoliberal globalization, ruling elites in the Global South have, by and large, been able to maintain links, however illusory, between their projects and those of their nations. This posture has created significant challenges for social movements, which want to warn their fellow citizens that these elites are in fact betraying the national project.[11]

Second, class, gender, ethnicity, and the environment have become critical issues in the Global South and thus are providing the bases for significant social movements. The struggle against outside control originally subordinated and marginalized many questions of social justice. Now, however, the crisis of national populist projects in the Global South has opened the door for these issues to emerge. The global reorganization of capitalism and the production process is also having a major impact. Increased participation of women in both the formal and the informal workforce, albeit often in gender-segregated conditions, is part of this transformation.[12] In some cases, these issues have been skewed or co-opted by the right wing. Cases in point include the ethnic conflict that led to the Rwanda genocide and the rise of right-wing Christian and Muslim fundamentalist movements that have challenged the status of women.[13]

By the same token, positive developments have taken place, including the mobilization of the Venezuelan poor by Hugo Chavez and his movement (which spoke to the crisis of the political party system in Venezuela), the vibrant trade union movement and poor people's movements in South Africa, and a burgeoning underground women's movement in Afghanistan.

Third, vibrant trade union movements have emerged in the Global South that have had significant social impacts. In Nigeria, South Africa, Brazil, South Korea, and India (the list is not exclusive), large-scale trade union movements have galvanized other social movements. Labor theorist Peter Waterman generally describes these labor movements as forms of "social movement unionism"—that is, activist movements that mobilize members to challenge the status quo of labor-capital relations.[14] Each of these movements has a visible Left presence that is sometimes very well organized and other times much looser.

Fourth, even in countries with vibrant labor movements, the absence of a broader social movement allows organized labor to backslide toward standard labor-capital relations. Under neoliberal globalization, workers are under nearly constant attack by capitalist forces. Though these attacks are national in nature, the subtext is always international. In the face of vibrant labor movements, the protectors of capital tend toward a combination of repression (sometimes violent) and co-optation (specifically, insistence on respectable labor-capital relations and conformity to established standards).

South Africa provides an illustration of this point. The country has three main labor federations, two of which—the Congress of South African Trade Unions (COSATU, the largest of the federations) and the National Council of Trade Unions (NACTU, the smallest of the federations)—emerged directly from the antiapartheid struggle under explicitly left-wing leadership. These two federations have different ideological roots but retain much in common. They have participated in activities ranging from strikes to mass marches while leading, coalescing with, and depending on other social movements.

With the democratic victory and end of apartheid in South Africa, these labor federations faced an entirely new situation. With the African

National Congress's (ANC's) assumption of power in the 1994, 1999, and 2004 elections, the strategies and tactics employed against the apartheid regime no longer applied. Nevertheless, the conditions facing the South African working class have remained difficult, particularly in light of the application of neoliberalism to South Africa. The ANC-led government has promoted the European-inspired "social partnership" model, in which labor, capital, and the state are independent partners that must collaborate in the interests of economic development. The government has set up institutions, such as the National Economic Development and Labour Council (NEDLAC), to coordinate and organize this relationship.[15]

This scenario has several problems, not the least of which is the fact that this model is collapsing in Europe. Second, the model does not mesh with the neoliberal approach to economics because it essentially obstructs the objectives of capital. For this reason, such corporatist notions have no place in a neoliberal environment. Third, this corporatist strategy raises questions about the role of other social forces, including nonunion working-class–based organizations. This last point has been a hot-button issue in South Africa. Though the unions are a significant force in South Africa (representing approximately 50 percent of the workforce), unemployment in the country ranges from 30 to 50 percent, and working people face issues in their communities that are just as important as those in the workplace, such as the need for electrification and drinkable water. Thus, a need exists to define the relationship of the trade union movement—particularly COSATU—to the social forces that have emerged to address these issues and to determine how the union movement will respond to these issues in and of themselves. Finally, the model assumes that the capitalist state is a neutral institution through which labor and capital compete. This assumption can lead to deadly consequences.[16]

Not surprisingly, the South African federations coming out of the revolutionary national democratic revolution—COSATU and NACTU—are under considerable pressure to be "legitimate" and "respectable" institutions. During the antiapartheid struggle, these movements defined their respectability and legitimacy in terms of their mass bases and the struggle against the white minority regime. Now that the country has Black majority rule, however, the situation is more complicated. COSATU, which has active alliances with both the African National Congress and the South African Communist Party, finds itself at odds with the prevailing economic approach of the government. Yet it and other social movements must decide whether to press the ANC government for social transformation or to define their role in more traditional trade unionist terms.

As with the National Postal Mail Handlers Union (though on a much greater scale), which we discussed in chapter 6, various echelons in the South African union movement are under pressure to accommodate to standard patterns of labor-management relations. Along with this pressure come certain enticements and comforts for union leaders that can create distance between them and the rank and file. This matter has generated great controversy in South Africa.

Yet unionism in South Africa remains highly political, a fact that some U.S. trade unionists find both confusing and unsettling. The political discussions within COSATU and NACTU are more extensive and more sophisticated than any discussions taking place within the U.S. union movement. Grappling with some of the same questions that face U.S. unions, both South African federations, to different extents, are attempting to define the challenges facing the movement in their country during this era of neoliberal globalization. Whether they will be able ultimately to resist the sirens of neoliberalism and bureaucratism is not yet clear.

EMPIRE

> No doubt one is a wretched plebeian harassed by debts and military service, but, to make up for it, one is a Roman citizen, one has one's share in the task of ruling other nations and dictating their laws.
>
> **Sigmund Freud,** *The Future of Illusion,* 1927

Missing from the lexicon of U.S. trade unionism is a six-letter word: *empire.* This word, in association with U.S. foreign policy, is so explosive that it is normally avoided in polite company within the union movement. When it comes up in official U.S. trade union circles, a silence falls, as if the listeners had stumbled across a blank spot in a recording.

The notion of *empire* carries implications that the bulk of the U.S. trade union movement would rather avoid. The most important one is that movement actions do not take place in a vacuum. Every action, or failure to act, has consequences, as does every issue the union movement chooses to emphasize or ignore. U.S. organized labor's silence on questions of empire has made the movement largely complicit in the actions of the U.S. government on the international stage. This collusion has come at great cost, both domestically and internationally. Yet the bulk of organized labor would rather see matters of U.S. foreign policy as irrelevant to the union movement. Absent is a willingness to ask fundamental questions, such as (1) What do we think about U.S. foreign policy? (2) Why is the United States hated overseas? (3) Should the United States support governments that crush workers and farmers? (4) What would a democratic foreign policy look like? (5) What is international working-class solidarity?

Although union leaders frequently cloak their acceptance of U.S. foreign policy in patriotism, something far deeper and more troubling is at work: *acceptance of empire*. The U.S. trade union movement has come to accept the legitimacy of the U.S. de facto international empire and has decided that such an empire is not inconsistent with democracy. As such, it is caught in a fundamental contradiction between the notion of international working-class solidarity and silence about or support for empire. The failure to question empire has many roots, not the least of which is the high standard of living in the United States, as well as the employment relationship that many workers have with the U.S. military and corporations doing business overseas. In the realm of military production, a disconnect often exists between workers' production and the policy implications of what they produce. Workers making missiles, military aircraft, and other weaponry often focus on the job at hand and do not inquire about how these products will be used. Military production that serves to strengthen the role of U.S. capitalism internationally not only results in the deaths of thousands but also redirects capital, technology, and labor away from socially useful investment. Nevertheless, workers who play a direct or indirect role in military production are encouraged or trained not to think through the implications of the products of their labor.

The point is not to make people feel bad about their jobs but to encourage people to consider the consequences of their actions or failures to act. To the extent that the trade union movement is silent about military production or silent about the social costs of multinational corporate activity in other countries, the union movement and its members become complicit in empire, regardless of their intentions. Such complicity can often cause inaction or prompt unions and their memberships to defend unconscionable activities, all in the name of saving jobs.

As we have said, the U.S. trade union movement's attempts to understand globalization have resulted in a one-sided analysis that recognizes only the activities of multinational corporations. The tendency has been to look at globalization in terms of the ability of corporations to move around the world, outsourcing jobs and downsizing workers. Though this element is certainly an important aspect of neoliberal globalization, the phenomenon is much broader than this analysis suggests.

The best response to the reorganization of global capitalism is for the international working class to forge solidarity across borders. Moreover, it requires the unity of workers with others—not just workers—who are falling victim to neoliberal globalization. Insofar as the trade union movement (and the labor movement more broadly) does not advance a constructive alternative to neoliberal globalization, it opens the doors to right-wing nationalist movements that pose as anti-imperialist but are essentially fascist, including, on the extreme wing, the militia movement in the United States (and, internationally, groups like al-Qaeda).

The trade union movement treats neoliberal globalization as simply a matter of corporations and economics. When, however, the United States intervenes elsewhere in the world—as it has in Iraq and did in Central America in the 1980s—the union movement is often paralyzed and cannot respond because its leaders view governmental foreign policy as separate from the aims and objectives of trade unionism (unless the policy is blatantly procorporate, and even then, unions often tolerate the U.S. position). The union movement generally considers foreign policy on the narrowest of terms—for example, by focusing on the North American Free Trade Agreement—rather than considering its impact on democracy, self-determination, and human rights. Thus, U.S. unions view foreign-policy issues in light of their effect on an identifiable group of U.S. workers or, in more enlightened moments, their impact on U.S. workers in general.

Because of this narrow view, the global justice movement in the United States has grown up largely separate from the trade union movement. Though the Seattle demonstrations against the World Trade Organization in 1999 showed that unity is possible, this unity was short-lived, and the movement was unable to integrate its lessons in theory or practice. As such, the Seattle effort was an example of tactical unity rather than strategic convergence. This fact is not surprising given the serious disagreements within the AFL-CIO about the nature of the World Trade Organization.

Neither the AFL-CIO nor the CTW Federation has consistent views on the international situation. As we have noted, CTW has so far taken no position on the Iraq war. Under the leadership of SEIU, its approach to international affairs seems to combine case-by-case analysis with the viewpoint of a trade association. This view does not differ qualitatively from that of the AFL-CIO. Traditionally, the AFL-CIO has been reluctant to take any position on international affairs that might challenge U.S. foreign policy, unless the policy has affected workers represented by one of its member unions.

Given this history, a critical need exists for a new unionism that embraces a new (for the United States) type of international solidarity. For the sake of argument, we call this new unionism *social justice solidarity*. Another form of solidarity, pragmatic solidarity, has gained popularity in the United States, particularly under the leadership of SEIU (though the union certainly did not invent it). As we have pointed out, however, this form of solidarity has a "corporate" outlook in the literal sense of the word (rather than in the sense of a "corporation") in that it looks for shared interests to maximize the respective power of each union or union movement in an interaction. As such, each side cooperates on the basis of its immediate material interests. No larger view informs this type of solidarity; it forms around the needs of the moment. Both sides treat each agreement akin to a business decision, rather than see their activities as part of a larger struggle for power and against a common opponent.

Social justice solidarity begins with an important assumption: that unions are workers' organizations engaged in class struggle (whether they like it or not) rather than corporations (regardless of the legalese). Thus, *solidarity*—a term we continue to insist upon—grows out of common interests at both the tactical *and* the strategic levels (which presumes that workers across borders have common strategic interests). Though we cannot assume that a union will necessarily have an ideological commitment beyond its commitment to the common struggle of workers, social justice solidarity looks at solidarity as a relationship rather than as a specific action. This relationship will inevitably change over time, but the commitment to common struggle and mutual respect will not.

Some of the best U.S. examples of social justice solidarity were in the mid- to late 1980s, when U.S. unions stood together against the apartheid regime in South Africa and in opposition to U.S. intervention in Central America. Today social justice solidarity is evident (albeit inconsistently) in the slowly developing fight against Wal-Mart's antiworker activity. Yet social justice solidarity is at best a minority tendency within U.S. trade unionism. Clearly, a view we might call "empire consciousness" continues to dominate the outlook of much of the U.S. trade union movement, and empire consciousness is antithetical to social justice solidarity.

The meaning of social justice solidarity is clear in the words of a noted Colombian trade unionist, who stated, "The most important thing that North American activists seeking to support trade unions in Colombia can do is to work to change U.S. policy towards Colombia, especially its emphasis on military and police aid."[17] Colombian workers are asking that their fellow workers in the United States look beyond common economic concerns in uniting with them. Instead, workers around the world are asking U.S. trade unionists to make a leap to social justice solidarity by addressing a wide range of issues, including:

- immigration and the rights of immigrant workers who cross borders seeking a livelihood (often because their nations' economies are in disarray because of interference by countries of the Global North)

- economic decisions by corporations of the Global North that render the economies of entire regions—for example, the Caribbean—unstable

- political repression and abuse of human rights, such as the actions faced by workers in countries like Swaziland and Burma/Myanmar, who may not have a common employer

- support for regional trade alliances in the Global South that strengthen workers' position and improve their nations' abilities to achieve genuine self-determination

- opposition to illegal wars of aggression, such as the current one in Iraq, as well as opposition to threatening behavior by the U.S. government toward countries that will not accept U.S. direction

- unity against neoliberal globalization and its impact in the United States and abroad

- unity against common employers and against the policies of governments that undermine democracy and workers' rights

This level of solidarity goes beyond one-shot agreements between partners; it requires principle-driven strategic pacts. What principles should drive social justice solidarity? At the head of the list are nonaggression among nations, national self-determination, workers' rights, human rights, and recognition of the need for a common global agenda—demonstrating at least a minimum level of unity—for the dispossessed.[18]

—

CHAPTER 19

REALIZING SOCIAL JUSTICE UNIONISM

Strategies for Transformation

PUTTING THE LEFT FOOT FORWARD

The irony of the current situation is that the U.S. union movement must become part of a new labor movement. To do so, unions must move left; they have no alternative.

The Gompers compromise unfolded as national capitalism, and later imperialism, took hold in the United States. The bulk of the U.S. movement (excluding the Industrial Workers of the World and other forces that followed them on the left) did not see a close connection between the imperial adventures of the United States and the development of U.S. capitalism. Production largely took place in the United States, though businesses had foreign investments. At least through the end of World War II, however, overseas investment focused largely on obtaining raw materials and new markets rather than on relocating U.S.-bound production. Rubber to make tires, for instance, came from Brazil and later from Asia, but the tires were produced in Akron, Ohio, and other production centers in the Global North.

This situation has fundamentally changed, which is why we argue that the material basis for international working-class solidarity is greater than at any point since the development of capitalism. Nevertheless, the existence of a material basis does not ensure success. Moving from the general recognition that international solidarity is a good idea to its realization will require changes in ideological orientation as well as practical programmatic steps.

To bring social justice trade unionism into existence, we must change not only the leadership of existing organized labor but also the relationship between the existing trade union movement and other progressive social forces (for example, workers' centers, independent unions, and progressive social clubs). Such change will not happen in the absence of a conscious Left force, as we have seen in the Change to Win Federation, which lacks Left leadership and a left-wing orientation. Despite having some outstanding leaders, CTW remains trapped in a Gompers-style view, albeit one that is dressed up in twenty-first-century stylings.

Do unions therefore have to become left-wing organizations? At the risk of avoiding the question, we offer the following answer:

- Unions, as united fronts of workers, develop a set of real-world politics and practices through both external and internal struggles. They are not, however, political parties.

- The Gompersian perspective has failed, even in CTW's revised form. It cannot explain the current reality of the class struggle, and any answers it may try to provide are fundamentally dead ends.

- The predatory nature of U.S. capitalism, both at home and across the world, is forcing workers and their organizations to make some tough choices based on a stark reality: capital has eliminated the possibility for significant capital-labor cooperation. The ramifications of the end of the so-called social contract that had been established in the 1940s—because of the victories of workers combined with the dominant position of U.S. capitalism—have largely been denied by the bulk of the leadership of organized labor. Their approach continues to hold out hope for a return to an earlier understanding.

- Unions cannot replace political parties or other sectoral social movements. Nor should they conceive of themselves as special interest groups. In attempting to represent a class of people—literally— they should act in their members' and potential members' interests in multiple arenas. No arena should be immune to unionism.

Having asserted that the union movement needs to move left, we need to define "left." The Left embraces a critique of capitalism that recognizes the system's inability to meet the objectives of human rights, workers' rights, environmental justice, and other issues. For unions, moving to the left means pushing the envelope to expand worker control over the workplace and the work process and to expand democracy beyond its formal limits. Unions need to recognize that democracy is not simply a matter of multiparty elections but truly embraces the rule of the people. The Left is the force that expands democracy—or fights for its expansion—against those forces, including but not limited to corporations, attempting to narrow the public sphere. A Left-led union movement must be prepared to fight for every reform that strengthens the working class and other sectors of society subject to oppression.

If the union movement is to shift further to the left, the left-wing forces within the movement must achieve organizational coherence. One of the biggest mistakes leftists made in the 1980s was to assume that they could influence change through individual action. Rather than seek the development of a genuine left-wing presence in organized labor, individual leftists often shifted their politics and their practice to become acceptable to the existing labor movement. At that point, for many such individuals, being on the left became little more than a wink to acknowledge one's past affiliation; it did not signify adherence to a current belief system or practice.

MOVING TOWARD SOCIAL JUSTICE UNIONISM

Though we could easily devote an entire book to ideas for winning the U.S. trade union movement to social justice unionism, in this section, we offer suggestions in two areas: the key steps necessary to advance a practice of social justice unionism for the twenty-first century and the vehicles necessary to move that practice forward. In addition to the working people's assemblies and social-political blocs we have already mentioned, below are suggestions for other areas of change.

Union Transformation

As we have pointed out, most of today's unions have been shaped by the Gompers legacy and anticommunism. Unions are not necessarily becoming either less or more democratic, but they are evolving. The early movement under Gompers generally combined decentralized authoritarianism with racism and sexism. National and international affiliates were highly autonomous, as were the local unions.

The purge of Left-led unions strengthened a corporate culture within the official union movement that discouraged creativity, democracy (particularly dissent), and any broad sense of class struggle. Though clamor for union reform emerged in the late 1980s in the face of crisis and reached a fever pitch in 1995 with John Sweeney's election as president of the AFL-CIO, the reformers did not envision a full transformation. In the early to mid-1990s, the notion of union transformation focused on retooling existing unions to make them more effective *organizing machines*. Even then, divisions existed among the advocates of transformation, who formed two camps one might call *technicians* and *reconstructionists*.

The technicians considered union reform largely a technical matter calling for straightforward steps such as changes in leadership or the introduction of new tools or approaches to growth. The reconstructionists, in contrast, considered transformation of the organizations as a whole, looking at fundamental changes in the way the unions conducted their business.

Though the technicians and the reconstructionists had significant differences, they shared certain ideological precepts that no one challenged. Nevertheless, any changes that have taken place have largely been under the hegemony and leadership of the technicians. Ideology and worldview, such as SEIU's, have no formal and explicit role, though the ideological orientation of SEIU has been changing since the split in the AFL-CIO (in ways that many reformers did not anticipate).[1]

To bring about social justice unionism, union transformation must take a very different shape. Reformers must see transformation not merely as a matter of technique but as a campaign of purpose and objectives. The relationship between the member and his/her union must fundamentally change.

Union transformation must begin with the notion that the union has to build a broader labor movement as part of the process of introducing progressive change. Such change is not only a domestic matter—one of wages, hours, and working conditions—but also an imperative to improve the lives and power of working-class people. These goals in turn call for reevaluating the structure and functioning of the union, looking at everything from internal education to organizing targets, the union's relationship to various political actors, and international solidarity.

Advancing a practice of social justice unionism requires an intense process of strategic planning and so-called power analysis. This process needs to focus on matters of class struggle, taking as the starting point the state of the working class generally and, specifically, the state of the working class represented by the relevant union(s). Such an examination does not presume that unions are the only or main player when considering the state of the working class in a particular context. (Activist-theorists Anthony Thigpen [from Los Angeles] and Richard Healy [Washington, D.C., and Boston] have helped raise awareness of these important tools of analysis as instruments for struggle.) On a movement-wide scale, the AFGE coalition proposal was attempting to promote this sort of thinking and orientation (see appendix A).

The next step is to examine how the union currently operates and to explore ways to structure it so that it can advance the objectives identified in the earlier analysis. This step is complicated. Given that the union is, except in so-called right-to-work states or under agency shop or fee-paying agreements, a nonvoluntary organization of workers with often vastly different points of view, real transformation cannot be imposed from the top.[2] Thus, a process must unfold to win a political mandate from the membership for social justice unionism. Many leftists elected to office have assumed that their election signals the members' endorsement of a Left agenda, but members may have simply been endorsing the individual or the slate or registering opposition to the other side. Achievement of a membership mandate is a more complicated process because it must win over a significant portion of the membership to a new approach. Genuine membership education must be a major component of this process.

Transformation is a long-term effort and has no shortcuts. Effective and inspiring leadership may bring about changes and victories, but it does not necessarily lead to lasting change. Not until a significant portion of the membership embraces the new style of unionism can reformers say a union is on the road to social justice unionism. Consider, for example, the late Machinists president William Wimpisinger, who was an open democratic socialist and a friend of many a progressive cause but oversaw a union with a complicated, if not ignominious, history in matters of race. Wimpisinger was elected not because he was a socialist or because members wanted to transform the International Association of Machinists into a socialist-led union. He was elected largely *despite* his politics and because he was a "good trade unionist." Moving a union toward the embrace of social justice unionism ultimately calls for bringing about internal cultural and political change. And for this change to occur, reformers need to win a mandate for change from the members.

Transformation challenges the thinking and practice of the union on issues of race and gender. It requires concrete steps to shift power and power relationships within the locals, central labor councils, state federations, and ultimately the national labor federations. Placing visionaries in key positions is only one step in the process; the overall organization must turn its attention to the often-ignored or disenfranchised sectors of the workforce and of the wider population. When Karen Nussbaum was the director of the AFL-CIO Working Women's Department, she repeatedly pointed out that the union movement is the largest organization of women in the United States. Yet, she noted, the union movement did not act as such, and it has still not oriented itself toward women. As part of its transformation, the union movement must become a vehicle through which oppressed groups, such as women and people of color, can advance their demands for freedom. This approach contrasts with the current tendency to look at these groups simply as several constituencies among many.

Public-Sector Unionism in the South and Southwest

In the 1960s and early 1970s, some interesting experiments in health-care and public-sector organizing began to emerge in the South. Led mainly by Local 1199 of the National Union of Health and Hospital Workers and the American Federation of State, County, and Municipal Employees, these efforts—such as the famous Memphis sanitation workers' struggle involving Dr. Martin Luther King—fused economic struggles for workers' rights with political struggles for Black freedom.[3] These efforts petered out, and an incredible opportunity to reshape southern organizing was lost. The union movement has never replicated this effort.

The public sector in the South and the Southwest offers interesting opportunities to link electoral activism, community-based work (including demands for reforms in the public sector), and workers' rights. It provides a means to organize African American workers and communities (and increasingly Latino immigrant communities) in the South and Chicano and Native American workers and communities in the Southwest.

Yet, if carried out in traditional trade unionist ways, an organizing effort in these regions will inevitably fail. In contrast to the AFL-CIO's discussions of southern organizing in 2000, any new efforts in the South must recognize the centrality of the African American struggle, the newly emerging struggles of Latino immigrants, and the role of community-based organizations. With this focus, organizing departs from traditional union organizing, instead following along the lines of the organizing-cities concept and becoming a political-geographic project that embraces a variety of forces. To achieve this objective, unions cannot simply call upon their traditional allies to show up and wave; they must engage with these allies in formulating a coherent strategy. In the South and Southwest, they can draw upon the African American, Latino immigrant, and Chicano and Native American movements. The pursuit of workers' rights, then, has to go beyond institution building in the unions and become a movement for social advancement and transformation.

Nonmajority Unionism

Nonmajority unionism is the theory and practice of building a union among workers regardless of whether the union can officially conduct collective bargaining with an employer. Normally, the union builds its membership and operates in a workplace in which it has not yet achieved the 50 percent-plus-one vote necessary to be certified as the bargaining representative for the workers.

Various unions have experimented with nonmajority unionism. Unions organizing in the South—particularly in the public sector, which provides no right to unionize, and in high-tech industries—have undertaken organizational efforts that go beyond the scope of traditional trade union activities.

Though nonmajority unions have operated in one form or another since the beginning of unionism, national interest in this concept revived in 1990 with the publication of an essay by Clyde Summers, "Unions without Majority—A Black Hole?"[4] This article suggested that the union movement explore new and creative ways of organizing and providing representation, particularly using Section 7 of the National Labor Relations Act. Summers's comments generated a great degree of interest, particularly among activists working in right-to-work states. A more recent article explores the application of this concept to collective bargaining.[5] Such articles supply the theory to back up the experience of organizations such as North Carolina's Black Workers for Justice, South Carolina's Carolina Alliance for Fair Employment, and the Mississippi Alliance of State Employees/Communications Workers of America Local 3570.

With the passage of the Wagner Act in the 1930s, most unions chose to focus on achieving the 50 percent-plus-one votes necessary to receive National Labor Relations Board certification, which enabled them to engage in formal bargaining. Though activists in the South and Southwest faced risks in building unions that had nonmajority status (due to right-to-work laws), or that could slip into this status, their concerns were not elevated to the national level for discussion and strategizing for a long time, a fact that speaks volumes about the state of organized labor. This neglect persisted even during the Sweeney years at both SEIU and the AFL-CIO. While Sweeney was president of SEIU, he supported certain nonmajority union experiments, such as Local 1985 of SEIU (the Georgia State Employees Union). However, the development of nonmajority unions in other portions of the South was not central to the SEIU's growth strategy. During the Sweeney years at the AFL-CIO— including during the tenure of Richard Bensinger as organizing direc-tor—no special efforts took place to explore nonmajority unionism as a movementwide strategy for growth, particularly in the less-hospitable geographic and industry sectors.

To succeed, nonmajority unionism requires significant commitment by the parent union—in the form of subsidies. The idea of constituting an organization with no guaranteed dues checkoff and, more than likely, a fluctuating membership without external support is untenable.

The local union must also align itself with the idea of social justice unionism, functioning as a component of a movement. Thus, it must not only provide technical resources for members but also adopt a con-tinuous organizing mode (organizing both internally and externally). Examples of this approach include Local 1985 of SEIU in Georgia and CWA's work in Mississippi and Texas. These efforts, however, are only incompletely tied into a significant organizing effort in their respective states; the unions largely operate apart from other social movement organizations and activists (except when those organizations and activists can help advance the objectives of the union itself).

Redefining Worker Control of the Unions

The matter of internal democracy has haunted the union movement since its inception. The issue is not limited to who should have the right to vote. It goes to the heart of how the organization operates.

In recent years, unions have increasingly moved toward organiza-tional consolidation. Local unions are merging into other local unions, becoming regional institutions and losing their local flavor. National/ international unions are merging, often in ways that defy any straight-forward explanation. For example, if through consolidation, a local union crosses state boundaries and its members number in the tens of thousands, how can a member become sufficiently well-known to run for office or to influence the organization in other ways? In fact, consolidation tends to distance the organization from its members. This situation is unfortunate, given that consolidation is not the only way to accumulate resources and mount a united front against a common employer.

The United Auto Workers and the Teamsters have maintained local unions with roots in particular communities while facilitating regional and even nationwide bargaining through joint bargaining councils that bring together local unions under collective-bargaining agreements. The local unions, being local in fact as well as name, enable members to make many decisions directly rather than through representatives, thus facilitating more direct democracy at the lowest level of the union structure. SEIU, in contrast, has built a structure of statewide consolidated unions. Some SEIU jurisdictions facilitate organizing within a labor market such as building services (janitors)—Local 1877 in California is one example—whereas others, such as Local 668 in Pennsylvania, appear to be nothing more than amalgamations of unions. In statewide locals like 668, the local chapters have limited decision-making power and policies, and the power to allocate resources is in the hands of representatives at the state level. In other unions with similar structures, the average member has virtually no avenue for participating directly, and dissidents in particular have no way to create opposition to the incumbent leadership. Our experience also shows that getting statewide bureaucratic organizations like consolidated unions to respond to local political situations—for example, by providing financial support for a local political campaign or by passing local Solidarity Charters—is a slow and difficult process.[6]

The SEIU model, which many unionists hold up as the only approach to organization, is certainly not the only solution to problems of competitive markets and aggressive employers. The UAW and Teamsters, by mandating joint bargaining councils, have demonstrated this fact. Many unions already have such institutions, and an organization can constitutionally mandate common bargaining among unions dealing with the same employer. Such a proposal is no less efficient, at least theoretically, than a forced merger. A forced or even a voluntary merger can create culture clashes, including clashes growing out of geographical differences.[7]

On a different front, too many unions either smash factions within the union or otherwise undermine the ability of members to express dissent. Contrary to the idea that factions inhibit democracy and create chaos, noted scholars Judith Stepan-Norris and Maurice Zeitlin, in a remarkable study of Left-led unions in the 1940s, came to exactly the opposite conclusion.[8] They found that a competitive political atmosphere in unions can strengthen an organization's democratic culture as well as increase members' enthusiasm about participation.[9] Insofar as members see the union as an organization apart from them, they will treat it as such.

As part of a cultural change, social justice unionism would promote debate and referenda. In general today, decisions within unions are currently made at the top, whether the top is the leadership of the national/ international union or the heads of local or regional bodies. Leaders regularly make decisions without membership consultation, the assumption being that the members, by voting in these leaders, have given them a mandate to do as they see fit.

Instead, unions could move toward a system of internal dialogue followed by membership votes. These debates and votes could determine which political candidates the union will endorse or what the union's stand will be on a question of U.S. foreign policy. Such an approach would be dramatically different from the experience in most unions today. Thus, it would require a dramatically different approach toward membership education.

What's the Point of Member Education?

A look at the budgets of most unions and union bodies reveals that membership education is not a priority. The programs that come closest to membership education are those at the George Meany Center/National Labor College, building trades apprenticeship programs, and training programs on specific union skills. Though unions have periodically launched efforts to expand the conception of education—for example, the AFL-CIO's Common Sense Economics program—most of these programs have been short-lived and underfunded.

What is membership education? It is not a PowerPoint presentation, though PowerPoint may play a role. Membership education is largely conceptual and secondarily technical. It aims to provide a framework that members can use to analyze their experiences and guide actions in their own interests. Thus, it deals with the big picture. It does not start and end with tips on how to handle a grievance or even how to organize. It needs to begin with certain basic concepts: What is a union? How do employers operate, and why do they seem to have the upper hand? What is capitalism, and what are its impacts on workers in the United States and overseas? What role do race and gender play in the workplace and in the larger society? From such a conceptual base, education can move to specific skills building or more in-depth conceptual education.

Membership education is about recognizing and developing leaders. Thus, it should encourage members to question, express differences of opinion, and debate. To the extent to which the leadership of a union fears debate, the organization will stagnate.

Membership education, however, must be in the lifeblood of the union. It cannot sit on the margins and be called upon only when an internal problem must be settled. A prototype for good integration of education was the Construction Organizing Membership Education and Training (COMET) program, introduced into the building trades in the early 1990s to promote understanding of the conditions causing the unions in the building trades to lose strength. COMET was a path-breaking program, though it did not go far enough in tackling one of the most problematic aspects of the history and practice of the building trades: race. Nonetheless, it raised people's consciousness and demonstrated the immense possibilities for membership education.

Too many unions see membership education, if they think of it at all, as a means of communicating the message of the leadership to the membership. To the extent to which education programs perform this function, they promote cynicism. Membership education is not value neutral, but it needs to encourage the dialogue and debate necessary for participants to take ownership of the ideas that emerge. If members strongly disagree with the direction of the leadership, the union is better off if leaders find out this fact in the course of education rather than in the midst of a struggle. This open approach to member education not only recognizes the existence of different points of view within the union but also reveals contradictory ideas within the minds of many members. Thus, a member who is strongly anticorporate may also be a right-wing populist and hold racist ideas. Another member may be a staunch fighter against racist harassment but oppose affirmative action. We cannot expect consistency. The union educator's job is to help provide a framework for members to sort out their ideas and contribute to a consistent union message while struggling to win over workers to the theory and practice of social justice unionism.

Central Labor Councils

One of the most intriguing ideas to emerge in the early part of the Sweeney administration was the notion of recasting central labor councils as *central workers' councils*. Unfortunately, this notion was never acted upon despite ongoing discussion among CLC leaders. This concept would not simply have introduced a semantic change. The thinking was that the central labor councils needed to open their doors to organizations other than unions.

Social justice unionism would take this notion of central labor councils as a starting point and then rethink the overall roles of CLCs, moving beyond the ideas of the Union Cities program and even the New Alliance program. Reforming CLCs would be complicated, however, given that national and international union bureaucracies are ambivalent about the councils, preferring to relegate them to a supportive role in specific projects the unions designate.

Thus, a struggle must unfold over the future role of the central labor councils. Labor councils should reconstitute themselves as the local representative bodies of working people. As such, they should be in the forefront of workers' struggles for economic justice and democracy.

The Sweeney administration attempted to shift and broaden the focus of the central labor councils, though it was willing to push the envelope of reform only so far. Yet one can think of myriad possibilities for central labor councils in an era of social justice unionism. The Los Angeles County Labor Federation re-created itself by building on the Union Cities organizing initiative, the living-wage movement, and the immigrant-rights movement. The federation set down roots in the immigrant community and linked the immigrant community and the African American community. These links translated into political power for all participants. The King County Central Labor Council in Seattle, at the time led by Ron Judd, was an active player in the anti-WTO mobilizations in 1999. These two initiatives are examples of excellent work, but the CLCs can push the envelope further:

- Working people's assemblies should, in fact, be a principal object of the central labor councils, with the CLCs serving as a major organizing center to move the process.

- CLCs could open their doors to other working-class organizations, thus shifting from a council of unions to a council of working-class organizations. The CLCs could be a vehicle for mutual support and coordination, as well as for joint campaigns.

- CLCs could play a major role in regional economic development, representing the point of view of the working class in economic development projects that are already on the books as well as advancing new projects that are proworker and propeople—such as the Boston-based Dudley Street Neighborhood Initiative.[10]

- Political action, always central to the CLCs, could be expanded. For example, CLCs could expand the Labor/Neighbor model into a permanent organization centered on specific communities. The Labor/Neighbor program began as an organization constituted by union members, but CLCs could expand the program's reach to include other neighbors who support the organization's political agenda. Ultimately, the union movement must think about the social-political bloc that must be built, and that bloc must be a neo-Rainbow-type organization. Labor/Neighbor programs can contribute to the development of such blocs as well as to the development of a neo-Rainbow organization (or series of such organizations).

- Labor councils must function independently in their jurisdictions and not be subordinate to any national or international union. Mandatory affiliation of local unions must be enforced to ensure that labor councils have sufficient resources. Labor councils should receive additional funding from state federations or the AFL-CIO based on their planned or achieved actions and on the populations or growth projections of their jurisdictions.

- Labor councils should be able to forge links, even across state lines, to facilitate multiunion or geographically larger campaigns.

- Central labor councils could incorporate Jobs with Justice chapters as full affiliates. Thus, JwJ could assist in CLC planning and provide support, and CLCs could encourage local unions to recruit member-activists to join JwJ.

These actions represent a break from the notion of CLCs as clubs or trade associations. The CLCs would become the hub or prime mover of working-class activism within specific geographic areas.

The Role of the National Labor Center or Federation

Before the split within the AFL-CIO, the role of the national labor center or federation was a topic of considerable discussion. However, no one addressed the questions raised by the coalition headed by the American Federation of Government Employees (see chapter 15).

National labor federations in the United States have typically been loose-knit organizations. Their first priority is to represent the interests of the affiliate unions.[11] Each affiliate, operating within the Gompers perspective, defines its existence and its interests largely by its own constituency.

National labor centers tend to be shaped not only by their affiliates but also by the major struggles in their respective countries. In South Africa, for instance, the Congress of South African Trade Unions has considerable influence over its affiliates, not because of bureaucratic measures but largely because of its roots and leadership role in the anti-apartheid struggle. COSATU's leadership, in other words, was earned, not legislated.

National labor centers are shaped, by implication, by ideological decisions as well. Thus, a national labor center that largely seeks to speak for and represent the working class may operate differently than one that acts more as a commercial trade association.

The debate over the role of organizing in the AFL-CIO was not only a turf war but also a debate about vision. The central question should have been whether the AFL-CIO—as an institution—could and would undertake organizing in areas in which the affiliates were inactive. Thus, the AFL-CIO might have undertaken organizing in cities, such as Los Angeles under the Los Angeles Manufacturing Action Project, or in underserved regions, such as the South and Southwest, to build the presence of labor. It could also have broadened the scope of organizing, as it has in Working America, but also organizing the unemployed and underemployed.

The restriction of the AFL-CIO to politics—which is a false claim, actually—was the decision of the affiliates rather than of one leader. Efforts to involve the AFL-CIO directly in organizing, including geographic organizing projects as well as the Organizing Fund (a fund set aside to match affiliate commitments to major organizing campaigns), have largely failed, not mainly because of the AFL-CIO leadership but because of affiliates' perceptions of these projects and ambivalence about an AFL-CIO role. As we have noted, some of the affiliates most critical of AFL-CIO organizing efforts were those that, in 2005, criticized the AFL-CIO for its lack of commitment to organizing.

Defining national labor centers' roles in the realms of politics, organizing, policy, and other matters must begin with discussion and debate between the leaders of the affiliates. Moreover, the first step in defining these roles is to analyze the situation on the ground to determine what is needed.

We believe that in addition to coordinating organizing efforts and initiating experimental organizing efforts where affiliates may not currently be involved, a national labor center in the United States can play a major role in developing an independent political organization, coordinating membership education programs, and uniting with other national labor centers in addressing global capital (and U.S. foreign policy). It should also help position the union movement as part of the larger labor movement.

VEHICLES FOR TRANSFORMATION

The ideas we advance here are antithetical to the current practice of trade unionism in the United States. Though we have highlighted specific activities that give us hope for the future, the reality is that an alliance of the pragmatists and the traditionalists still holds hegemony over organized labor. Moreover, though the trade union Left has allies on the outside—for example, in the workers' center movement—the Left must recognize that it begins from a position of weakness in attempting to bring change to the trade union movement.

Since the 1980s, various unions, particularly those committed to growth, have been willing to hire some leftists in various positions, including prominent positions. Nevertheless, this activity looked more like the recruitment of gunslingers than like a sea change in trade unionism. Leftists have had a certain amount of room to maneuver as long as they have not strayed outside the Gompers/anticommunist worldview. Although Red-baiting has decreased significantly, particularly since John Sweeney took office, no existing union or formal labor body is consistently practicing social justice unionism (including social justice solidarity).

This situation presents a strategic problem. In view of the weakness of the political Left in the United States, which is made up of small organizations with limited influence and large numbers of unaffiliated individuals, many individual leftists and their allies have chosen to be loners, doing the best they can as individuals within the union movement. Some other individuals and groups of individuals have taken an alternative, more activist path—for example, by advancing workers' centers or other independent organizations, often in opposition to the existing union movement.

The next step, which is risky because of the U.S. trade union movement's intense discomfort with dissent, is to build a movement linking those inside and outside the trade union movement who embrace a vision of social justice unionism (under whatever name). This movement must explicitly be part of building a new labor movement, not by ignoring the existing one but by transforming it—organizationally and politically. Not only will this transformation require a fight for leadership but it will need to introduce a new practice of *labor unionism*—one that has as much to say to the unemployed worker as it does to the assembly-line worker, as much to say to women as to men, and as much to say to people of color as to whites. It must also be truly internationalist or global in its outlook and practice. At a moment when right-wing populism and various forms of economic isolationism have a base within the working class and the middle strata of U.S. society, a critical need exists for a movement with a global perspective that situates U.S. workers' struggle in a broader context.

Oddly, had the struggle within the AFL-CIO between 2003 and 2005 been about these issues, then even if the split had still occurred, it would have had a qualitatively different look. The separation would have stemmed from fundamentally different visions of the relationship of the union movement to the rest of the working class both in the United States and in the rest of the world.

Given that the issues of the split have not been settled—indeed, few debaters even addressed them—the time has come to advance the debate, whether the leaders are comfortable with the discussion or not. What good are leaders who have no followers?

CONCLUSION

Neoconservative cultural strategies have played a major role in pounding the cultural terrain of the U.S. working class. An increasing sense of alienation and hopelessness has moved U.S. working people from a notion of democracy that promoted civic and collective participation to one that promotes individual behavior.[12] Studies indicate that voluntary associations in the workplace and community can act as "schools of democracy."[13] Unions can operate as models of democracy that reflect the importance of citizenship, duties, responsibilities, and rights. But to do so, they must militate against neoliberal market-based notions of democracy. Unionism today, as in the past, requires activists to confront a bewildering array of community cultures that often interpenetrate and play themselves out in terms of class, race, gender, sexual orientation, and immigration status—and that inevitably determine the success of the union/labor movements. Union cultures are not homogeneous, nor should they be. What is required for the revitalization and growth of the union/labor movement is a compelling set of articulated values (such as inclusion, militancy, class politics, and internationalism) that are institutionalized at both the national and the local levels and that are reflected in broad-based governmental policies and decisions. A political project of this nature would permit the union movement to create intersections with progressive social movements and transcend the divisions between working people. The political front created by such a project would produce the leverage to take on the state and demand broader political reform and changes in labor laws.[14] Such a project should be cultivated and allowed to blossom in hundreds of local venues, unencumbered by the restrictive cultural filters imposed by "pure and simple business unionism." This project would also require the Left to reconstitute itself in a visible institution, beginning in a network and ultimately taking the form of a political organization or party that transcends the lines dividing labor from other social movements.

Traditional unionism has typically focused on a limited goal: redistribution of some of the social surplus away from corporate profits and into the hands of workers. Even the New Voice's 1995–96 rallying cry, "America needs a raise," speaks to this limited goal. However, from a leftist perspective, this approach raises two major questions. First, is this goal systematically attainable in the long run, especially if increasing the workers' share interferes with capital accumulation? Specifically, unless we are actually challenging profit accumulation and the distribution of the social surplus, we will, at best, find ourselves in a situation in which certain sectors of the working class can or try to carve out a favorable return for themselves, at the expense of other workers, by maintaining exclusiveness. In this way, they can take a bigger cut of the wage allocation, while other workers, in the United States and abroad, must take less.

Second, and following from the previous point, is social equality achievable under capitalism, or should the working class (and the union and labor movements) plan to challenge capitalist institutions, including the fundamentally exploitative character of the wage relationship? We have found that even union leaders who consider themselves socialists believe that raising socialist issues is wildly idealistic and impractical. They put off these questions to the indefinite future, believing that they need to win more power or organize more workers before raising these issues. However, because they are losing power rapidly rather than gaining it, their struggle for organizational survival has taken precedence. We suggest that keeping the higher goals in mind is a prerequisite for winning real power. As long as unions operate solidly within capitalism, accepting its basic rules and premises as permanent, they may be marching to their doom. The current crisis should lead unionists not to narrow our vision but to broaden it.[15]

Our conclusion about the future of unions is not as unconventional as one might think. A provocative piece in the German magazine *Spiegel* forces readers to consider such an idea.[16] Writer Gabor Steingart, completing a review of globalization, soberly concludes that unions in the Global North are dead—that is, that they can do nothing to regain the power they once held. Looking at the situation through the glasses of Gompersism, Steingart is probably correct. There is no exit. Only by adopting an approach that begins with an entirely different set of assumptions can we hope to see the renaissance of a labor movement in the United States.

Thus, a piece of our conclusion—which for some will be unsettling— is that a Left, anticapitalist analysis and a reconstituted Left are essential for the renewal of labor and the reconstruction of trade unionism. Try as some may to erase the role of the Left in the successful historical moments of U.S. (or even global) trade unionism, their effort will fail. A rigorous analysis of the current situation needs a Left framework, and the movement needs the inspiration of a Left vision.

One development that has changed the interpretation of leftist, anticapitalist theories is the change in the international situation. One of the major critiques of the Communist Party during the Cold War was that the party allegedly served as a fifth column for the Soviet Union. With the demise of the USSR and the movement of the People's Republic of China away from socialism, we argue that though the left wing has been influenced by both these international experiments in socialism, the Left alternative now developing in the United States must be internationalist in perspective and promote the interests of all workers, not just U.S. workers. Today's globalized capitalism permits the rebuilding of the international Left on a much broader front than was realizable in past decades. Evidence of this trend appears in the growing popularity of the World Social Forum and, within the Americas, the recent rise of leftist and center-left governments in Brazil, Venezuela, Uruguay, Argentina, Chile, and possibly other countries south of the Rio Grande in the near future.[17] The growing interest in Left alternatives to global capitalist orthodoxy is directly attributable to the wider array of international social movements aligning themselves against imperialism and against powers seeking to create global empires for the benefit of the world's corporate elite. We hope that this book will be a useful guide to those seeking to reconstitute such a Left and to build a globally conscious social justice unionism in the United States.

A PROCESS FOR ADDRESSING THE FUTURE OF U.S. ORGANIZED LABOR

July 13, 2005

Dear Brothers and Sisters:

There is universal agreement that the labor movement needs to change.

Obviously, there is not universal agreement on how either the AFL-CIO or its affiliates should change in order to adapt to the new environment and build the strength needed to confront our many challenges.

We all want our movement to grow in numbers and strength in order to secure the promise for workers and their families to secure decent jobs, a decent standard of living, and a government that supports their inspirations.

There have been many excellent ideas offered by thousands of union members and unions about reform. The two most prominent sets of proposals are thoughtful frameworks but lack specificity on "how" the ideas would be implemented. The labor movement needs not only ideas, but a blueprint for successful implementation.

Sadly, it seems clear that the two most prominent proposals are not so divergent as to justify a split in the labor movement. The ideas for change have much in common.

We submit that we should put our collective energy into the creation of more understanding and the integration of these proposals, rather than focusing on what divides them.

No one has all the answers or a single solution to what reforms are needed to make the labor movement successful. Our dialogue should not be about who will be the President of the AFL-CIO, rather it should be about the heart and soul of the labor movement. It should be union leaders engaging in a real process of dialogue aimed at analyzing our environment and devising the strategies that will produce success for our members.

The debate needs to also be about a compelling vision for the future of workers in the USA, not to mention the rest of the world. It needs to be a debate about what sort of strategies work in the face of dramatic changes in the economy, including the way that work is done, and the fact that growing numbers of people are not working in the formal economy at all.

We have attached for your consideration a proposal that describes a process that we hope will lead to serious analysis, dialogue and reform. It is meant to build acceptance for change and the strategy which may follow. Creating a local roadmap for a revitalized and strengthened "labor movement for the 21st century" is worth our time and energy.

The process will be time consuming for union leaders, but all of us must be willing to commit the time and energy together.

The process would provide:

1. the opportunity for real analysis and sharing of critical data;
2. a true consideration of voices from the grassroots;
3. the time needed to develop real reform recommendations from the union leadership; and
4. a special convention—which would approve, modify or create reforms by majority vote.

Instead of coming out of this convention bitter and divided, adopting this process gives us an opportunity to demonstrate our seriousness about creating a new labor movement. Imagine being able[,] one year from now, to announce with pride our new 21st Century strategy instead of the bitter headlines of today.

Breaking apart should be an action of last resort. We owe it to our predecessors and we owe it to members to give this our best effort. We respectfully request our brothers and sisters to endorse this or a similar process as the right reform proposal for this convention.

In Solidarity,
John Gage, President, American Federation of Government Employees
William Burrus, President, American Postal Workers Union

Morton Bahr, President, Communications Workers of America
Gregory J. Junemann, President, International Federation of Professional & Technical Engineers

A PROCESS FOR ADDRESSING THE FUTURE
OF U.S. ORGANIZED LABOR

Introduction

There is universal agreement that changes are needed in the labor movement to deal with our changing environment. Obviously, there is not
universal agreement on how the labor movement and the AFL-CIO
should be changed to adapt to the new and future terrain.

Central to the resolution of the immediate conflict within the AFL-
CIO is the establishment of a process to identify and debate the fundamental issues facing organized labor in the USA. The outcome of such a
debate cannot be predetermined, but a process can be put into place
that creates the appropriate environment for a constructive and creative
exchange. The process proposed here would launch a nine month discussion that will include leaders and members of the union movement
in addressing many of the issues before us and will ultimately result in a
special convention of the AFL-CIO at which point recommendations
will be ratified by majority vote and commence to be implemented.

Objectives

- Understand the terrain on which US trade unionism is today operating.
- Identify key issues that must be resolved in order to renew trade
  unionism.
- Identify structural reforms necessary in the union movement that
  will help to advance trade unionism.
- Build a healthy and advanced consensus among the leadership of
  organized labor around a path for forward motion.
- Integrate the various layers of the union movement into this discussion.

Step 1: A resolution at the July 2005 Convention

- A resolution that calls for the immediate commencement of a
  process to accomplish the above objectives.

- Such a process is aimed at unifying and advancing the US union movement.
- Such a process will be led by an independent facilitator or facilitators and will include current Executive Council members and representatives of key State Federations and Central Labor Councils.
- Such a resolution will call for a special convention of the AFL-CIO to resolve and implement the recommendations of this process by majority vote including any necessary changes to the constitution.
- The resolution will include the details found below.

Step 2: Multi-part process

- Part 1 should last approximately 5–6 months and is primarily oriented towards the top leaders of the union movement.
- Part 2 takes these discussions and opens them up for broader movement-wide debate culminating in a special convention of the AFL-CIO.
- Other parts involve specific actions.

PART 1

- Commitment of Executive Council members to meet three (3) days per month for at least five (5) to six (6) months.
- Facilitated discussion.
- Meeting should include: (a) Executive Council members, (b) representatives from key State Feds and Central Labor Councils. Union staff, either from the AFL-CIO or from affiliates should be absent from meetings.
- Meetings are discussions, which should flow from the issues facing the meeting.
- The role of the facilitators should be to engage the group.
- The first meeting should begin with an overview of the global and domestic situation facing workers with the aim of identifying whether there is a common analysis of current reality. If there are differences, those differences should be identified rather than hidden or ignored.
- An agenda of issues should be agreed upon in advance that this process wishes to address. The following include some issues for consideration but the list should not be limited to these:

- Does the AFL-CIO have a role in organizing? If so, what? What happens in cases where no affiliates are organizing (e.g., in a region or sector) but organizing needs to take place? Is there a need for an Organizing Fund?
- Does the AFL-CIO have a role in politics? If so, what? What have we learned from our activities in the last several Presidential elections? What about Congressional elections and local elections?
- In the 21st century, what is expected from a national labor federation, national labor unions, state federations, central labor bodies, and other affiliated groups? How can they be organized to maximize effectiveness?
- How do we enhance communication and outreach in order to send a clear message on behalf of the labor movement as well as to offer a compelling vision which will attract the vast majority of working people in the United States?
- Do changes in (domestic and/or international) economic organization and/or the US state necessitate changes in the forms of union organization, including but not limited to the AFL-CIO? How can we organize millions of workers from whom an employer based union is not within reach in a short term?
- How should issues of jurisdiction be handled?
- Does size matter in terms of unions? Should unions be encouraged to merge? If so, under what terms? If not, what does that mean for the union movement?
- What should the Executive Council of the AFL-CIO look like in terms of (a) numbers of members, (b) representation of women and people of color, (c) role, (d) size of unions?
- Should there be a smaller committee of the Executive Council, i.e., an executive committee, that works with the Officers or should the Officers organize themselves differently?
- What is the role of US unions vis a vis the ICFTU [International Confederation of Free Trade Unions], the Global Union Federations, individual unions, national labor centers? How do we address the changing world situation?
- How should US organized labor approach US foreign policy? Are there any grounds that are off limits?
- Each gathering should identify which agenda items will be covered. Preparatory material will be offered in advance. Where

appropriate, debates can be organized between contending positions that are then followed by small group and large group discussions.

- At the end of the five months, a report would be developed for circulation summarizing agreements, outstanding issues and areas of firm disagreement. This report would include the specifics on how reforms would be implemented.

- This would provide the basis for **Part 2.**

PART 2

- In order to transform the union movement the discussion needs to be moved downward to the base. This can be done in a planned way.

- The report or discussion document from Part 1 would be circulated broadly.

- Affiliates, state feds and central labor councils would commit themselves to moving the discussion within their ranks.

- The objective of the discussion would be to engage union activists particularly, but union members more broadly, in a dialogue about the issues raised and the proposals advanced.

- Local debates and discussions would be organized. Recommendations would be solicited.

- Within sixty days reports and recommendations would be forwarded to the facilitation team which would summarize the information. The summary would be provided to the members of the Executive Council.

PART 3

- A special Executive Council [EC] meeting would be held to review the reports from the field as well as further exchanges that may have taken place among the EC members.

- Where approved by a majority of the EC, resolutions would be drafted for the Special Convention.

- Where there is no majority support for a particular proposal, it will be up to individual affiliates to draft their respective resolutions for consideration before the Special Convention.

PART 4

- A period of not less than thirty days for review by affiliates would be scheduled between the time of the special EC meeting and the Special Convention.

PART 5

- Special Convention of the AFL-CIO held and moves on the resolutions by majority vote.
- Celebration of the resolutions and the 21st century AFL-CIO.
- Implementation and renewal begin!

CONSTITUTIONAL RESOLUTION
FOR AFL-CIO CONVENTION

Submitted by the American Federation
of Government Employees

WHEREAS it is crucial to the vitality of trade unionism immediately to identify and forthrightly engage the issues facing organized labor in the United States and world today and in the opening decades of the 21st century, undertaking such identification and engagement in a manner which promotes trade union solidarity, BE IT RESOLVED, that Article XIII be amended to add the following "Section 4—Special 2006 Convention":

"(a) Notwithstanding any other provision of this Constitution, by September 1, 2005, the AFL-CIO will commence a process to identify, investigate, debate, and formulate recommendations regarding the fundamental issues confronting trade unionism and ultimately to formally adopt recommendations to resolve these issues at a Special Convention in 2006;

"(b) The specific objectives of the process will be to: (1) understand the terrain on which US trade unionism is today operating; (2) identify key issues that must be resolved in order to renew trade unionism; (3) identify structural reforms necessary in the union movement that will help to advance trade unionism; (4) build a healthy and advanced consensus among the leadership of organized labor around a path for forward motion; and (5) integrate the various layers of the union movement into this discussion.

"(c) The process to accomplish the above objectives will be aimed at unifying and advancing the US union movement, will be led by an independent facilitator, and will include current Executive Council members and representatives from key State Federations and Central Labor Councils. Process participants will meet at least three (3) days per month for at least five (5) to six (6) months in undertaking this process. The process will to the extent possible follow the format and steps found in the following document entitled 'A Process for Addressing the Future of US Organized Labor,' herein incorporated by reference.

"(d) A Special Convention will be called for two (2) days, pursuant to Article IV, Section 3 of the AFL-CIO Constitution, not earlier than September, 2006, or later than November, 2006, solely for the purpose of considering the report resulting from the above process and moving resolutions therein or resulting from the report, including proposed constitutional amendments, adoption of which shall be by majority vote of those present and voting."

USING RACE, CLASS, AND GENDER ANALYSIS TO TRANSFORM LOCAL UNIONS

A Case Study

Fernando Gapasin's case study of a local union's transformation provides a useful example of how race, gender, and class interpenetrate. This analysis can help activists grapple with the challenge of transforming unions. Other versions of this study have appeared in *Race, Gender and Class* and *Social Justice*.[1]

Historically, union leaders have viewed racial and gender diversity as a problem that hinders cooperative action, the formation of labor unions, and the maintenance of class unity within unions.[2] Progressive scholars generally agree that corporate leaders understand how racial and gender fragmentation affects the U.S. working class and use these divisions to advance their class interests.[3] As we have pointed out, inclusion is fundamental to union transformation. We offer this case study as a concrete example of this point. It shows how a local union can use race, gender, and class analysis to help it grapple with the challenges of self-transformation.

This study followed a local union in the public transportation industry from 1970 through 1992. During this period, the local changed from a 124-member private-sector union, made up mostly of white male bus drivers, into an 1,800-member multiracial, mixed-gender, multioccupational local. The two decades covered by the study saw tremendous economic, political, social, and ideological change. The period was marked by militancy, with a rank-and-file movement for democracy unseating an incumbent president who had been in power for twenty-five years. During this period, the local's formerly all-white leadership gave way to minority leadership.

This study suggests that demographic changes in the workforce set objective conditions for fragmentation to occur, but the decisive variable in building working-class unity is the subjective factor of *class-conscious leadership*. Class-conscious leaders are those who understand the United States to be a social system divided by class relationships, with the primary division being between the working class and the capitalist class. These leaders understand that the system of dominance is not simply one of capitalist domination over the working class, but also one of a system of domination through racial and gender privilege. In other words, as we have attempted to show in this book, within classes are structures and cultures of domination by which white males have a privileged position over racial minorities (women and men) and white women. In addition, white men and women share a favored position over racial minorities (women and men) in the U.S. social system.

TRANSIT UNION LOCAL 299

Local 299 of the Transit Union (a pseudonym for the purposes of the study) was first organized in 1902 as a streetcar workers' craft union. It remained a small union of 120 or fewer members for the next seventy-two years. It did not begin to grow until several developments—the rising price of fossil fuels, concerns about the environment, an expansion of electronic manufacturing, and the financial collapse of privately owned mass transit—forced the passage of both federal and state legislation supporting publicly owned mass transit in the mid-1960s. As a result, the Transit District was formed in 1972. The district was created locally, but the enabling legislation was moved at the state level.

In 1974, a movement began in the Chicano community to stop federal funding until the Transit District complied with affirmative action regulations. In 1972, the employees of the transit agency were mainly white males; the entire workforce was approximately 10 percent minority and 4 percent female, in a community with a 40 percent minority population. The white-run Transit District admitted it was not in compliance with the terms for receiving federal money, and during the next three weeks, it hired hundreds of minorities and women, who became members of the white-led Local 299 of the Transit Union. The agency attracted people from all over the country, even college-educated people, because the pay was high and the requirements for getting a job were minimal. In just over a year, minorities became more than 35 percent of the union, and women accounted for more than 24 percent. Just as significantly, by 1976, more than 80 percent of the union members had less than two years' seniority. The stage was set for a clash between high- and low-seniority union members. As the issue of federal funding reveals, race and gender became important political issues for public mass transit and for Local 299.

The massive influx of new hires presented complications for transit management, which did not welcome the shift from a homogeneous workforce to a highly diverse workforce. According to a former assistant personnel manager, management sought to avoid and then resist affirmative action from the beginning. Transit management had repeatedly asked him how to avoid affirmative action requirements. The reasons management cited for not wanting to hire minority workers included the fear that women could adversely affect bus operations because they get pregnant and the belief that many minority workers were just "not up to snuff."

Transit District management was forced to hire minorities and women, but as the agency's 1977 Equal Employment Opportunity report showed, few if any minorities and women were hired or promoted into professional or skilled areas. Minorities and women were hired into the lower-skilled classifications and then kept there by management. At first, the union did not fight this segregation of workers and in fact contributed to the alienation of minority and women union members by failing to integrate the new members socially into the union. The following statements illustrate the union leadership's attitude toward minority and women workers during this period. As one twenty-year veteran Latino bus driver revealed in an interview, "They [Local 299 leadership] didn't want us. I used to hang around and listen to them union leaders. They thought all minorities came from the welfare line and that we were lazy. They didn't associate with us much. They hardly told us anything."

One Black maintenance worker with twenty years' seniority stated, "Hell, I had my BA, but my foreman, then a union officer, would not treat me with any respect. He would give the white guys jobs that I could do. He barely spoke to me. He seemed to think that all I was good for was cleaning buses. I just kept my mouth shut, did my job, and waited for my chance."

Similar tension existed between women and the union leaders. For example, a retired woman, an information service representative (ISR) who was active in the union until her retirement, describes her social integration into the union in the following way:

> It was clear to me that [the president] really didn't care about us ISRs. . . .
>
> Lots of us [women] from here used to go to union meetings. Sometimes twelve or twenty of us would go. They'd go because I asked them to go and others would go because they were pissed off and thought they could get something done. Joni would go to lots of union meetings and state her mind. [The president] would tell her she was out of order and tell her to sit down. I think that's one of the reasons she went to management and why she doesn't like the union so much.
>
> There was another time, I had to go up to the new union office. . . . [The president] and two or three other board members were sitting around . . . I felt real uncomfortable there. The place smelled like cigar smoke and their attitude seemed like they had some kinda secret they didn't want the rest of us to know about. It didn't feel like a very friendly place for a woman to be.

Another retired woman bus driver, a veteran of twenty-two years of service, explained her first impressions of the union leadership during the early days (1974) of the Transit District:

> It was clear to me that it was an old boys' network type of union. [The president] ran the show for however long he ran it. The most flagrant violation for me was when we were being forced to work thirteen-hour days, that was the nail on the head and I was pregnant at the time. And I went to him and told him we can't do this. He said, "You have to. It's the law." And he was lying through his teeth. It was an outrageous lie. . . .
>
> Oh, he [the president] was in with them [management]. I felt he was in with them. . . . And, you know, [the president] had been the head of a ninety-nine-member local and all of a sudden he had six hundred members to deal with and we were a ratty-looking bunch of people. I mean we were outrageous. We were the most mixed group of people. It was fun. [The president] was part of the old boy network. He didn't know how to deal with women on the job.

The failure to integrate the new hires might have been the result of the tightness of the incumbent leadership and the number of high-seniority union members. The high-seniority members of the union had endured tremendous hardships during the 1950s and 1960s. Because of low ridership and the economic weakness of the privately owned transit system, public transit in the county was constantly in danger of going out of business. This situation threatened the existence of Local 299, and the membership kept the system going on "baling wire and glue." The members of Local 299 during the 1950s and 1960s were among the lowest-paid workers in the entire industry. They also endured two major strikes during the 1960s. Facing these external threats to the union, the members developed close social ties. For example, one veteran bus driver said, "A lot of us were related and we all lived in the same city. In those days [1950s and 1960s] everybody knew each other; we went places together. We ate at each other's houses. Our kids played together. Not like it is nowadays." As an organization, Local 299 was unaccustomed to integrating such a large number of "new" people.

Using racial formation and social encasement perspectives, we argue that the incumbent leadership during this period did not recognize that the influx of minorities and women required them to reassess their preconceptions of women and minority workers. Indeed, the incumbent union leader's comments about "those welfare recipients and those people"—references to minority workers—causing problems in the union were not different from management's saying that minority workers were not "up to snuff."

The incumbent union president had demonstrated tremendous leadership during the hard times before the formation of the Transit District and had worked closely with management and politicians to create the new agency. He had gained the respect of his members, management, and local politicians. Unfortunately, he continued to rely on his old networks, and he had very little dialogue with the new hires. Incumbent union leaders, encased in the pre–civil rights "racial and gender projects," attributed disunity in the union to "those people," welfare recipients, and "those women who were taking jobs away from men." In addition, because the majority of the members were white male bus drivers, the president's philosophy of making decisions based on what was good for the majority of the membership led to the practical disenfranchisement of most nondriver occupations and minorities and women. Because his leadership was "color-blind," the president made few, if any, affirmative efforts to mentor, train, or prepare minorities and women for union participation and leadership. In fact, as the examples show, these members were often discouraged from participation. This "color blindness" would also affect future leaders of Local 299.

In 1975, the cleavages around race, gender, and occupation became clear in the struggle for shop-floor representation and improved driver safety. These two issues led to the downfall of the incumbent union leadership.

Shop-floor representation was a demand of minority members and those in nondriver occupations. Bus drivers were 70 percent of the union. Maintenance and ISRs made up the other 30 percent. Many jobs in the maintenance section—for example, janitorial services—were filled by the recent influx of minority workers. Racial minorities accounted for 49 percent of maintenance workers in 1974 and only 10 percent of bus drivers. According to one Chicano maintenance man with twenty-two years of seniority:

> We all started to go to the union meetings because we didn't have a representative at the yard and we didn't like the way we were being treated. . . . We went to the union meeting and demanded that we have elected shop stewards. [The president] told us that the bylaws did not require that anybody but the officers be elected and if we wanted shop stewards he would appoint them. We wanted to choose our steward. We didn't want one of his cronies. And besides he would probably pick a bus driver to represent us.

A group calling itself the Third World Caucus emerged for a short time. It had the explicit goal of training caucus members (then mostly minorities) in union skills. These workers wanted to learn how to run meetings, handle grievances, and eventually run the union.

The issue of shop-floor representation was soon overshadowed by membership concern for driver safety. Despite critical reports by agency mechanics and other maintenance experts, the Transit District purchased experimental buses and a fleet of old buses. Several experimental buses caught fire, and one bus, as the press thoroughly documented, burned down to its frame on a busy highway. The old buses caused longer-term problems as well, with hundreds of bus drivers suffering industrial injuries because of "hard steering"—a fact that received a lot of press coverage. The problem was particularly severe for women bus drivers. Most of the buses required forty to fifty pulling pounds to turn the bus. The stress of turning the steering wheel caused arm, shoulder, neck, and back injuries.

From the perspective of the new hires in 1974, many high-seniority bus drivers had little concern for driver safety. One bus driver explained, "Those old guys were used to driving buses held together with baling wire . . . they would drive anything to keep the system going." When this driver went to the union meeting to raise concerns about driver safety, the older drivers told him, "Real men don't worry about that sort of stuff."

The movement to improve driver safety merged with the existing rank-and-file movement to win shop-floor representation. Many white people joined the Third World Caucus. Whites soon became the majority, and conflict with racial implications soon emerged in the rank-and-file group. The minorities and many white women within the rank-and-file movement emphasized the need to train themselves to become union leaders and to build a strong union from the bottom up. The white males, many of whom were college educated, gave precedence to getting rid of those "dumb guys" (the incumbent leadership) and replacing them with qualified people—themselves. Certainly, if the definition of "qualified" people included only those who had a college education or had held a union office, it excluded many minorities and women from leadership. As one of the minority founders of the Third World Caucus said, "Some of us became 'gofers.' I wanted to learn how to be a unionist. I didn't want to be a 'gofer,' so I quit."

In the absence of a plan to develop, mentor, and train minority and women leaders, the racial and gender divisions in the local persisted. The reflection of these divisions in occupational imbalances continued to ghettoize minority and women members within the union.

In 1976, the incumbent president resigned from office, and in the next few years, the white male leadership of the rank-and-file movement was elected to union office. By 1980, all but two members of the twelve-member executive board were white. All were bus drivers. In the early 1980s, driver safety, "hard steering," and representation for nondriver occupations continued to divide the union. Maintenance workers, led by Chicanos within their ranks, issued a call to decertify Local 299. They argued that because Local 299 was a bus drivers' union, they would be better represented by a mechanics' union. Although race was not an explicit theme in the decertification effort, minority maintenance workers pointed out the lack of minority union leadership on several occasions.

During the late 1970s and early 1980s, hiring surges doubled the size of Local 299. The new hires during this period included more class-conscious activists and workers with experience in the civil rights movement and the labor movement. These activists prevented workers from working in unsafe conditions. They fought management's disciplinary and promotional policies, which discriminated against minorities and women. And they combated one of management's most common tactics: if a worker complained about working conditions, management blamed another worker for the problem. Most of these activists saw their day-to-day interclass conflicts with management and the intraclass tensions between workers as part of a national and international socio-economic/political/historical struggle. Thus, they were able to frame issues like reduced governmental transit funding and privatization in the national and global struggle for fair wages and decent working conditions. In other words, these activists were able to "think globally and act locally."[4]

The class-conscious workers based their strategy on their recognition that the union was fractured by race, gender, and occupation. They understood that a change in the union bylaws to base the leadership structure on occupation could help heal the divisions. Because a disproportionate percentage of the minority and women union members worked in nondriver occupations, occupational representation could improve the chances of minorities and women to be elected to union office. However, the maintenance people first had to help the bus drivers resolve their problems with hard steering. A political alliance between maintenance and bus drivers was necessary to achieve the two-thirds vote to pass bylaw changes. The nondriver occupations constituted only 30 percent of the union.

The plan had five stages and took three years to implement. The first step was to create an organizational base within the union. The organ for change was the Maintenance Advisory Committee (MAC). The second was to recognize MAC. The third step was to communicate victories and discuss the plan. And the final two steps were to institutionalize occupational coalitions and to educate and mobilize for the bylaws change.

The absence of maintenance representation on the union's executive board was the rationale for creating the Maintenance Advisory Committee. The executive board and the membership approved the concept. MAC was structured so that each of the seven maintenance locations would elect one MAC representative. The committee met once a week to discuss "maintenance issues." The chair of MAC rotated once a month, and the person in this position also attended the executive board meetings to aid in the passage of MAC resolutions and monitor the proceedings of the executive board. MAC representatives, on their own time, also attended all meetings between union members and management that dealt with maintenance issues.

To accomplish the second step of achieving union visibility, MAC members realized that if the plan was to succeed, MAC had to develop a reputation for getting things done. At first, MAC took on small issues that were important to mechanics. For instance, it fought for and achieved access for tool trucks at all maintenance facilities. MAC took on and won issues such as clean air in the shop, dust-free brake lathes, emergency eye washers, uniforms, and equitable distribution of work.

The first interoccupational issue that MAC won was defeat of a management-imposed "quality circle" program. MAC developed a broad-based program that educated all Local 299 members and other county unions about the dangers to unionism of a management-imposed labor-management program. Local 299 members voted down and refused to participate in the management program despite the fact that the program had the support of the union's executive board.

To create a bridge between bus drivers and maintenance, MAC began to meet with the union's safety committee to seek a solution to the hard-steering problem. Management argued that a fix would cost too much money and that the union mechanics did not have the skills to carry one out. MAC assembled a "think tank" of mechanics and came up with a cost-effective plan for fixing the hard-steering buses. With some help from the local press, management was forced to accept the plan, and over the next year, the Transit District eliminated hard-steering buses. To communicate the plan and inform members of MAC's achievements, the committee produced a newsletter called *Maintenance Outlook*. A network of members whose work required them to go to various work locations distributed the newsletter every two weeks. MAC could distribute special notices anywhere in the Transit District within eight hours (much of this activity was before computers and e-mail).

MAC representatives also became the union stewards for their work locations. On a shop-by-shop basis, MAC was able to institutionalize interoccupational coalitions by creating work-site grievance committees. The membership approved the plan to consolidate all stewards, regardless of occupation, at the various work sites because this step would facilitate stewards' training and the handling of work-site problems. Every week, the work-site committees brought together rank-and-file leaders from all the occupations within the union. The meetings not only brought together people in different occupations but also increased the day-to-day interaction of different races and of men and women, thereby uniting them around work concerns. For instance, one of the rank-and-file leaders who emerged was a Black nationalist, and the other was a white man whose father had been a national leader in the Ku Klux Klan. Both had worked at the Transit District for several years but had never spoken to each other. They came together because they both wanted better representation of their occupations in their union. Later they were also on the same side in opposing quality circles, opposing discrimination against minorities and women, and supporting affirmative action plans for maintenance. The activists, through the MAC plan, created structures in the union that enabled rank and filers to get mentoring and training. The activists also helped create a new view of the possibilities for the rank and file within the union. As one African American MAC representative said:

> We [MAC] started education, going to school, reading, and finding out how to do this. Never rely on one person. . . . We started to rely on you [class-conscious worker] and you said no. You said everybody has to know, go look it up, here's how you do it, that is how I started learning the law. Actually, remember how you told me, why don't we go down here [a law library] and I'll show you how to look up the law. And see, I learned that in MAC. We all started taking labor studies, reading in general, understanding. That is power. Besides hanging together and partying on the weekends . . . MAC had a plan. Nobody was afraid to fight in MAC.

The work-site committees became the basis for internal and external union support work and political campaigns. Some 90 percent of the union executive board members over the next ten years were active members of these early work-site grievance boards.

Finally, the union executive board formed a bylaws committee to draft the changes to the existing union constitution and bylaws. The bylaws committee included people from all occupations. MAC representatives and friends were part of the committee. The proposed changes were extensive and aimed at further democratizing the union and achieving occupational representation on the union's executive board and negotiation committees. All of the intraunion coalitions built over the past three years were pulled together, and a marketing plan was created to "sell" the bylaws changes. The opposition forces within the union argued that these changes would reduce the efficiency of service for union members and that the bus drivers would lose control of the union. When the vote took place in 1983, the bylaws changes passed by the necessary two-thirds majority. The margin of victory was twenty-four votes.

AN ANALYSIS OF THE LOCAL 299 EXPERIENCE

To avoid the errors that come with reducing all issues to matters of class, successful strategies must consider the multiple identities of the workforce. In this section, we talk about the intersection of race, gender, and class in the action at Local 299. We recognize that this intersection includes complicated divisions within each category. For instance, clear divisions exist between white women and women of color, between racial minorities, and between workers in different occupations. This case study involved many of these complex interrelations. To understand the intersection of race, gender, and class, we discuss the categories separately below and then examine how they intersected into a common strategy at Local 299.

Race

The terms *racial project* and *social encasement* are useful for our analysis of racial dynamics: "A racial project is simultaneously an interpretation, representation, or explanation of racial dynamics, and an effort to reorganize and redistribute resources along particular racial lines."[5] *Racial projects* provide meaning for race within particular social structures and everyday experiences. *Social encasement* is the total effect of social structures and racial projects on an individual worker's world outlook toward race.

One can define race in various ways. A Social Darwinist defines race as a biological characteristic, which thus creates an unalterable set of physical, mental, and behavioral attributes.[6] In this perspective, one race of human beings can be genetically superior to another; for instance, Black people can be more intelligent than whites because of a genetic predisposition. Another view of race defines it within a particular social, historical, and political process. This definition assumes a complex set of social meanings that constantly change under the influence of contending social, economic, and political forces. This view sees no biological basis for distinguishing between human groups by race.[7]

If race is such a divisive force and is so difficult to define, should we simply dispense with the idea? Should we strive to be a color-blind society and ignore racial differences? Michael Omi and Howard Winant explore this question in *Racial Formation in the United States:*

> A more effective starting point is the recognition that despite its uncertainties and contradictions, the concept of race continues to play a fundamental role in structuring and representing the social world. The task for theory is to explain this situation. It is to avoid both the utopian framework which sees race as an illusion we can somehow "get beyond," and also the essentialist formulation which sees race as something objective and fixed, a biological datum. Thus we should think of race as an element of social structure rather than as an irregularity within it: we should see race as a dimension of human representation rather than an illusion. These perspectives inform the theoretical approach we call racial formation.

> We define *racial formation* as the sociohistorical process by which
> racial categories are created, inhabited, transformed, and destroyed. . . .
> First we argue that racial formation is a process of historically situated
> *projects* in which human bodies and social structures are represented and
> organized. Next we link racial formation to the evolution of hegemony,
> the way in which society is organized and ruled. [8]

From this theoretical perspective, race is a matter of both social
structure (or social systems of human interaction) and culture (or the
values, norms, and behaviors of a society). This view attempts to understand the concept of race as an interaction between these two dimen-
sions. Race is an integral component of social structure (for example,
class society), but efforts to explain racial inequality as only a product
of social structure cannot explain its patterning and persistence over
time and in the absence of difference in social structure. However, to
explain race as culture based, as ethnicity theory does, does not explain
racial economic stratification.[9]

Numerous racial projects are operating and contending for dominance in the United States. In the 1960s, the civil rights movement, in
particular the Black Freedom Movement, radically changed the structure and the culture of race relations in the country. The Black Freedom
Movement of the 1950s and 1960s transformed racial politics from blatant coercion to the beginnings of democratic inclusion. Though the
racial project did not achieve its goal of full inclusion, it did usher in
sweeping political and cultural changes. New organizations formed.
New political norms and new collective identities also emerged. This
racial project challenged past racial practices and stereotypes and introduced a wave of social reform that extended democratic notions beyond
the issue of race.[10]

The ethnicity theory of race argues that assimilation is the solution to
racial conflict. Belief in this theory held multiracial coalitions together
during the high point of the civil rights movement. Since the passage
of the Civil Rights Act of 1964, a neoconservative racial project has
emerged that denies the significance of race. Taking equality under the
law as the basis for assimilation, the neoconservative racial project
argues that all races are now equal under the law. Therefore, those races
that suffer persistent social and economic inequality do so because of
individual shortcomings and certainly not because of inequalities in
the "system." This view justifies notions such as "reverse discrimination." It leads to "color-blind" race politics and noninterventionist state
policies. Such policies stand in contrast to the liberal interventionist

state policies, such as affirmative action, that emerged from the civil rights movement.

At Local 299, several racial projects were apparent. The incumbent leadership of the 1960s was encased in a racial project that identified racial minorities as "welfare recipients" or as "lazy." The union culture—including members' values, norms, practices, rituals, customs, and behaviors—was forged during a twenty-year period of adversity by a small group of white male bus drivers who lived close to each other.[11] This culture valued "toughness," such as the ability to drive any vehicle, and questioned the masculinity of any male who complained about unsafe conditions. The white bus drivers separated themselves from the racial minorities at work and made important union decisions at a bar called Sam's Log Cabin instead of at union meetings. As one Latino veteran bus driver said, "They [union leadership] didn't want us. . . . They hardly told us anything."

After the massive influx of new hires in the 1970s, new white leaders replaced the old white union leaders. Although racial minorities were almost one-half the union, their position in the union leadership did not improve. The views that "We're all one working class," or in this case, "We're all bus drivers," negated the inherent privilege of white male bus drivers. Because the leadership did not recognize that the existing organizational culture defined race in hierarchical terms, it did not recognize the importance of training, developing, and mentoring minority leadership and did not see the need to restructure the organization. Thus, the new white union leaders, unable to step outside of their social encasement, repeated the racial errors of their predecessors.

Gender

The case study reveals that the union "didn't feel like a friendly place for a woman to be." Management didn't want to hire women in the first place because they would miss work and because they got pregnant. Some of their male coworkers would accuse them of "taking jobs from hard-working men who needed the jobs." The organizational culture valued "manliness" and discouraged participation by women.

Unions in general have historically been at odds with working women. During the nineteenth century, many unions forbade female membership, and although formal prohibitions were lifted early in the twentieth century, unions as a whole had little interest in organizing "women's work" until the 1970s.[12] Today, although women are more than one-third of the union membership in the United States, only 9 percent of the top leadership in AFL-CIO unions are women. At the local union level, especially in the public sector, some unions have a higher percentage of women in leadership—for example, 40 percent in the Service Employees International Union and roughly 50 percent in the American Federation of State, County, and Municipal Employees. Despite these numbers, men lead most local unions, even in industries with a high percentage of women.[13]

Studies show that the most pervasive roadblock to women's activism in unions has been women's prescribed roles as homemakers and child rearers.[14] In this case study, women activists also had to overcome a male-dominated union culture that had values, norms, practices, rituals, customs, and behaviors that worked against women's participation in the union. According to veteran women union members, the old white male leadership of the union didn't care about representing the female-dominated occupations of the union like the ISRs, as we saw in the earlier quote by a woman retiree. The union leadership paid little attention to protecting the rights of the female occupations, as evidenced by the small amount of contractual language dedicated to the protections of workers in those occupations. Bus drivers had twenty-two pages of protections, maintenance had eight pages, and communications (ISRs, Dial-A-Ride, and systems monitors) had one and a half pages.

The tough-guy values of the white male bus drivers fell hard on male bus drivers who cared about safety and even harder on women. As we have seen, women suffered a disproportionate number of industrial injuries because of the need to exert fifty pounds of pull pressure to turn some of the buses. The union leadership prided itself on keeping the system going and paid little attention to driver safety.

Because of the difficulty of breaking into the good old boy network or even participating in the real decision-making process, white women activists and racial minorities began to create alternative forms of organizations within the union. Activist white women were the first white people invited to join the Third World Caucus, which became the base for the internal opposition to the incumbent union leadership in the 1970s.

Homemaking and child-care responsibilities, a male-dominated union culture, and a lack of training, mentoring, and access to networks were roadblocks to women's achievement of union leadership positions.[15] Because some occupations had a much higher concentration of women, the union's structure of governance (at-large elections) placed women at a disadvantage if they sought election to union office. Researchers have found that because women are often concentrated in occupations classified as women's work, they will not have ready access to leadership positions unless unions change their governance structures.[16] In this case, people in the women-dominated occupations (communications) formed a coalition with those in the occupations with a high percentage of minorities (maintenance) to redo the union's governance structure and achieve occupational, racial, and gender representation in the union's leadership.

Race and Gender

The restructuring of Local 299 increased racial minorities' chances of being elected to leadership positions and virtually guaranteed that at least one woman would be elected to union office. After the first election under the new structure, the executive board membership was 50 percent racial minorities (African American and Mexican/Chicano). Before the restructuring, four women had been elected to the executive board: one African American woman and three white women. After the restructuring, four white women were elected to the executive board. The African American woman served two three-year terms. Since 1987, no woman from a racial minority has served on the union's executive board. Minority women have twice attempted to win union office but lost on both occasions.

The election of the four women before the restructuring stemmed from their involvement in the first reform movement, which gave them visibility. In the first election after the restructuring, two of the women ran for reelection: one lost her election bid, and the African American woman won reelection. Three out of four of the women elected since then have benefited from the guarantee of a seat to the communications section. The woman who was elected to the nonoccupational, at-large seat enjoyed the support of the local union's women's caucus, which formed in the late 1980s. The women's caucus was predominantly white women. Minority participation and leadership of the caucus ended in 1991.

A closer analysis might suggest that although the earlier reform movement became dominated by college-educated white males, at least initially it included women, especially white women. The network created during the first reform movement facilitated the growth of a social network that included more women.

A critical look at the second reform movement, which led to the restructuring of the local, reveals that the hub of the network, MAC, was predominantly males from several racial minorities. The committee's activism centered on achieving occupational representation and increasing minority involvement. Although the restructuring created a "woman's seat" on the executive board, the social-political network created by the second reform movement was predominantly minority male. This group of reformers paid little attention to the recruitment, training, and mentoring of minority women.

After attending a women's training conference sponsored by the international union, minority women started a women's caucus in the local union. In two years, 1989 to 1991, the women's caucus broke into factions, and involvement by minority women ended. Minority women presently play little if any role in the governance of the union.

Angela Harris (1995) cautions against the notion of a monolithic "woman's experience" that stands apart from other facets of life such as race and class. Harris quotes Smith College professor Elizabeth Spelman on this point: "The real problem has been how feminist theory has confused the condition of one group of women with the condition of all. . . . A measure of the depth of white middle-class privilege is that the apparently straightforward and logical points and axioms at the heart of much of feminist theory guarantee the direction of its attention to the concerns of white middle-class women."[17]

This case study and the research of others suggest that not only is there no monolithic woman's experience, but also that there is no monolithic African American experience, no monolithic Chicano experience, and obviously no monolithic working-class experience. Thus, the only way one can hope to create an effective strategy for working-class unity is to understand the intersection of these facets of working-class life and how they play out in U.S. society.[18]

Race, Gender, and Class

How should one understand the issues at work in the reform movement in Local 299? In the United States, one's position in society reflects one's relationship to a structure of class, racial, and gender dominance. At the risk of oversimplifying, let us use an organizational analogy for society. Whoever is in the center of this organization (society) determines how the organization defines itself. For the majority of U.S. history, this core has comprised rich, white, Anglo-Saxon males. In organizations, as one moves away from the core, one has less influence on how the organization defines its values and behaviors.[19] In the United States, the range of power—that is, the ability to make the organization (society) do something—extends from the rich, white, Anglo-Saxon male at the core to the poor, immigrant, minority female on the margins. Power emanates from the core and moves outward. Because the boundaries between levels of the organization are porous, the core is not immune to the influences of those outside of it, even those out on the margins.

The shouts or screams of people on the margins may reach the ears of the more powerful people near the core. For the core to act, however, the screams and shouts have to be very loud or come from coalitions of voices. Within any organization or society are multiple voices, but the voices are not equally loud. The voices of those in the core are the loudest. Though those in the core may hear interjections from the margins and even allow changes to occur, they are the ones who ultimately interpret and frame the response for the whole organization, and they are also the ones with the power to reinterpret the values and behaviors of the organization. As they define the values and behaviors for the organization, they define their personal values as well. And they base these definitions primarily on existing definitions. Thus, the starting point of change within the core comes from existing values within it, encasing the people at the center in what they create. As a result, they are both recipients and beneficiaries of the decisions and values emerging from the core.

The organization values created at the core become the norm—that which is normal—and all else becomes "other."[20] Thus, when someone says that a behavior or value is "human nature," he or she defines what is normal. However, within the analogy of the organization, what is normal for a rich, white, Anglo-Saxon male has greater power in the organization (society) than do the values and norms created on the margins. Therefore, the U.S. working class faces a complex system of domination that affects the entire structure and culture of American society. Although this system has other components, the three main intersecting points of contention are race, gender, and class. Clearly, the working class is not in the "core" of this society. One's race and gender define one's relationship to the core values and norms. For instance, white men or women who define racism in extreme terms, perhaps seeing it as exclusive to groups like the Ku Klux Klan or the Nazis, would not see their own more subtle discriminatory acts as racist. A working-class white male who identifies with the values and norms of the core might dismiss more subtle acts of racism or sexism as normal or as human nature. He might innocently dismiss such acts with statements like "You know how men are."

People who are closer to the core might derive some short-term benefits from the system of domination that favors rich, white, Anglo-Saxon males. Not only does this system confer obvious economic benefits, as economic theorists have pointed out, but it also provides other structural and cultural outcomes that benefit white people in general. As immigrants from eastern and southern Europe came to the United States in the late nineteenth and early twentieth centuries, conflicts arose between recent immigrants and those who had immigrated a generation or two before (so-called natives). These "border skirmishes" between whites were resolved over time through the process of assimilation, not exclusion, as is the case with most racial minorities.[21]

The U.S. "melting pot" obviously melted for whites more easily than for people of color. By seeing U.S. culture as simply a mixture of different cultures, one could conclude that the United States lacks its own, unique culture. To view U.S. culture as no culture (that is, as color-blind) opens the door to defining racial minority cultures as "other" cultures. If "other" cultures exist in the United States, then what is the normative culture against which one should measure other cultures? The unique U.S. culture was created by whites, who have underwritten oppression and domination of racial minorities since the beginning of colonial expansion.[22] For instance, U.S. pioneers assumed a norm of private property. This norm justified their appropriation of land that they assumed had no owner—and then justified their protection of their private property from others, like the Native Americans. The subjugation of Blacks and the extermination and expropriation of Native Americans and Mexicans had racial justifications that left ideological imprints on the people of the United States. Racial theories like so-called scientific racism and quasi-racial theories such as Social Darwinism place white people at the top of the racial hierarchy. From the earliest days of the Republic, white people owned the property and controlled the government. Ideological props like Social Darwinism supported this structure. U.S. culture thus reflected values, norms, and behaviors favoring white people and maintained a social structure that continued the relative privilege of white people over racial minorities. By extending this analysis to the U.S. union movement, we can see why some union leaders view ethnic, racial, and gender diversity as "problematic." Their view flows both from their definition of "differentness" and from their encasement in whiteness, a unique structure and culture that U.S. history has shaped in their likeness.

The racial project of whiteness has helped create a false sense of oneness among European Americans.[23] Whiteness is a construct that helps to create the illusion that Irish and Slavic steelworkers have more in common with white robber barons like Carnegie and Frick than with Black steelworkers. Whiteness is a hierarchal construct that creates white-skin privilege and dark-skin and gender oppression. It is a racial project that permits white people to blame immigrants and racial minorities for economic woes instead of creating strategies and building coalitions against the corporate and governmental leaders who favor economic exploitation over social and economic justice.[24] Moreover, whiteness links white people together who have nothing in common but their skin color, and it divides trade unionists and other workers who have economic, social, and political reasons to unite.

Therefore . . .

To succeed, union strategies require rigorous examination of the intersection of race, gender, and class. Union leaders must critically examine the union's governance structure and organizational culture. Most important, union leaders have to be self-reflective and force themselves to examine their own social encasement so that they can break with the racial project of whiteness.

NOTES

PREFACE

1. Ellen Dannin, in *Taking Back the Workers' Law: How to Fight the Assault on Labor Rights* (Ithaca, N.Y.: ILR Press/Cornell University Press, 2006), offers a strong argument that the main problem with the NLRA is not the statute itself but the judicial interpretations of it going back to the 1930s. While we agree with much of this analysis, substantive parts of the act, particularly in light of the Taft-Hartley amendments, make it problematic from the standpoint of workers.

INTRODUCTION

1. Jerry Tucker, "Big Labor Split Now Seems Certain: Four of Six 'Change-to-Win' Unions to Boycott AFL-CIO Convention," *MR Zine*, July 24, 2005, http://mrzine.monthlyreview.org/aflcio2005.html.

2. See www.changetowin.org/for-the-media/press-releases-and-statements/change-to-win-coalition-submits-amendments-for-afl-cio-convention.html.

3. Nathan Newman, "United Farm Workers Joins Change to Win Camp," *TPM Cafe*, July 23, 2005, www.tpmcafe.com/story/2005/7/22/194826/857.

4. UNITE HERE! represented the merger of the major garment and textile union with the major union representing hotel and restaurant workers. The merger took place in 2004.

5. Jerry Tucker, "A New Labor Federation Claims Its Space: If Enthusiasm on Display Were Substance, CTW Could Claim a Good Start," *MR Zine*, http://mrzine.monthlyreview.org/tucker041005.html.

1. DUKIN' IT OUT

1. The term *Jacksonian Democracy* is an almost unbelievable misnomer. President Andrew Jackson posed as a friend of the white man and took on the interests of segments of the wealthy elite. Yet Jackson, who served in many respects as a model for what came to be known as right-wing populism, also advanced the ethnic cleansing of First Nations/Native Americans and was the author of the Trail of Tears that Native Americans marched from the Southeast into the West. He orchestrated attacks on Spanish-controlled Florida in order to

destroy the Seminoles and the liberated zones that they had created for runaway African slaves. See Chip Berlet and Matthew N. Lyons, *Right-Wing Populism in America: Too Close for Comfort* (New York: Guilford Press, 2000), 33–53.

2. Chip Smith, *The Cost of Privilege* (Fayetteville, N.C.: Camino Press, 2007), 11–21.

3. For an in-depth exploration of the issue of race, racism, and social control, see Theodore W. Allen, *The Invention of the White Race,* vol. 1, *Racial Oppression and Social Control* (London: Verso, 1994), and vol. 2, *The Origin of Racial Oppression in Anglo-America* (London: Verso, 1997).

4. See, for example, David R. Roediger, *The Wages of Whiteness: Race and the Making of the American Working Class* (London: Verso, 1991).

5. The terms *Global North* and *Global South* roughly correspond, respectively, to the countries of the advanced capitalist, or "Western," world (the United States, Canada, Japan, and the countries of Western Europe) and the regions of Africa, Asia, Latin America, and the Caribbean formerly known as the Third World. The former Soviet bloc of Eastern Europe, Russia, and the states of the moribund Commonwealth of Independent States are in a geopolitical twilight zone.

6. Sylvis was a complex character who recognized the need for collaboration between white and Black workers but was unprepared to engage this battle in the National Labor Union. See Philip S. Foner, *Organized Labor and the Black Worker, 1619–1973* (New York: Praeger, 1974), 19.

7. The exclusion of Asian workers became a rallying cry for white workers on the West Coast and led to the formation of political parties advancing this demand.

8. Craft unions organize workers according to skill, such as carpentry or plumbing.

9. Industrial unions represent workers in the entirety of an industry rather than organizing them by craft or trade.

10. The new regime of mass production using assembly lines is generally referred to as "Fordism."

11. Nick Salvatore, "Eugene V. Debs: From Trade Unionist to Socialist," in *Labor Leaders in America,* ed. Melvyn Dubofsky and Warren Van Tine (Urbana: University of Illinois Press, 1987), 107.

12. Ibid., 108.

13. Advocates of industrial unionism were more ambiguous in their statements about matters of gender and the full organizing of women.

14. John H. M. Laslett, "Samuel Gompers and the Rise of American Business Unionism," in Dubofsky and Van Tine, *Labor Leaders,* 84.

15. Ibid.

16. Ibid. Gompers's view was "nonideological" only in the formal sense. His position was very ideological in its full acceptance of the existence and inevitability of U.S. capitalism as a system. The nonideological notion was actually more akin to the philosophy of so-called American pragmatism in its rejection of formal theories and ideological constructs.

17. The philosophy of pursuing self-interest, elaborated in the nineteenth century, assigns meaning to things according to their observable practical con-

sequences. Essentially, the idea is whatever "works" is best. This position begs the question of what determines whether something "works."

18. By class character, we mean that the state fundamentally represents the interests of the dominant class and class fractions in a society. In such a state, individuals from the dominant class do not necessarily have to hold office, nor does the state have to look out for—in this case—individual capitalists. Rather, the job of the capitalist state is to look out for the interests of capitalism and to eliminate not only opposition but anything that seems to interfere with the normal workings of the capitalist system.

19. Laslett, "Samuel Gompers," p. 87.

20. Gompers's opposition to the Spanish-American War was most curious. Paul Buhle notes that Gompers opposed the war and U.S. empire in the late 1890s "because it invited the yellow race onto American shores." See Paul Buhle, *Taking Care of Business: Samuel Gompers, George Meany, Lane Kirkland and the Tragedy of American Labor* (New York: Monthly Review Press, 1999), 45. Buhle devotes a chapter to a fascinating examination of Gompers.

21. Ronald Takaki, *From Different Shores: Perspectives on Race and Ethnicity in America,* 2nd ed. (New York: Oxford University Press, 1994), 136.

22. Quoted in Elly Leary, "Crisis in the U.S. Labor Movement: The Roads Not Taken," *Monthly Review,* June 2005, www.monthlyreview.org/0605leary.htm.

2. THE NEW DEAL

1. The Populist candidate James B. Weaver won a million popular votes and twenty-two electoral votes for the presidency in 1892, and the party won nine seats in Congress. Eugene Debs drew 6 percent of the vote for president in 1912, and Socialists were elected to local and state offices throughout the United States in the years leading up to World War I.

2. Philip S. Foner, *History of the Labor Movement in the U.S.: The AFL in the Progressive Era, 1910–1915* (New York: International Publishers, 1980), 108–15.

3. Ibid., 129–30.

4. Melvyn Dubofsky and Warren Van Tine, eds., *Labor Leaders in America* (Urbana: University of Illinois Press, 1987), 134.

5. Craig Phelan, "William Green and the Ideal of Christian Cooperation," in Dubofsky and Van Tine, *Labor Leaders,* 135.

6. The theories of John M. Keynes (1883–1946) emphasized an increase in the money supply and an activist government role in the economy to promote the ability of consumers to purchase goods and thereby stimulate the economy. He was one of the first mainstream economists to challenge the idea of laissez-faire capitalism, in *The End of Laissez Faire* (1926). His work *General Theory of Employment, Interest and Money* (1936) provided much of the theoretical rationale for the New Deal.

7. The insurgency included the unemployment movement that had commenced shortly after the beginning of the Great Depression, as well as the workplace battles that culminated in the 1934 general strikes in the San Francisco Bay Area, Toledo, and Minneapolis, as well as the Great Textile Strike.

8. Nelson Lichtenstein, *State of the Union: A Century of American Labor* (Princeton, N.J.: Princeton University Press, 2002), 43.

9. *Corporatist,* in this context, refers to the theory of the unity of the government and various sectors of society. Normally, the concept carries the notion of "tripartism," the partnership of the government, business, and labor.

10. William Z. Foster, *History of the Communist Party of the United States* (New York: Greenwood Press, 1968), 306.

11. Because of Roosevelt's failing support after the CIO's victories in auto and big steel, Lewis dropped his support and vowed that he would resign as president of the CIO if Roosevelt won the election in 1940. Roosevelt won, and Phillip Murray replaced Lewis as CIO president.

12. Paul Buhle, *Taking Care of Business: Samuel Gompers, George Meany, Lane Kirkland and the Tragedy of American Labor* (New York: Monthly Review Press, 1999), 87.

13. Lichtenstein, *State of the Union,* 50.

14. Labor's Non-Partisan League in various locales had more on its agenda than drumming up support for Roosevelt. Former Communist Party leader Dorothy Healy has described the work of the LNPL in Southern California in the early 1940s. See Dorothy Healy and Maurice Isserman, *Dorothy Healy Remembers* (New York: Oxford University Press, 1990).

15. Steven Fraser, "Sidney Hillman: Labor's Machiavelli," in Dubofsky and Van Tine, *Labor Leaders,* 224.

16. Ibid., 232.

17. At any historical moment, one could identify a range of unionist positions that would qualify as Left, Center, and Right at the time. In the pre–Civil War period, for instance, the Left comprised unionists who took the lead in opposing slavery and ultimately called for the inclusion of African workers in the union movement. The leftists of the time were those at the forefront of opposing anti-Chinese racism and exclusion. Thus, the notion of a Left in the movement defines a tendency more than a specific organizational entity.

18. We mention the two forms of Marxism to identify some of the contending influences on the international and U.S. Left. In time, other variants on Marxism developed, particularly in the 1960s, which saw the emergence of Maoism, autonomous Marxism, and a form one could call neo-Trotskyism.

19. *Populism* is a political movement that, while blurring class distinctions, also advances the notion of the people against the rich. In the United States, Populism had its roots in the Jacksonian Democracy of the 1830s. However, it took on, at least at first, a more progressive orientation in the 1890s with the development of the People's (Populist) Party, which at first made significant efforts to unite white and Black farmers and workers. The Populist movement fell prey to racism, and the white segment of the movement was either crushed or absorbed into the Democratic Party at the time of the presidential candidacy of William Jennings Bryan. *Anarcho-syndicalism* is a tendency that emerged in Europe and spread to the United States in the late nineteenth century but came to influence the formation of organizations such as the IWW. Anarcho-syndicalism openly opposes capitalism and calls for replacing the capitalist state with a decentralized system of workers' control that uses the labor union as the means of organizing

the working class. Anarcho-syndicalists do not believe that the Left should participate in electoral politics, viewing electoral politics and political reforms as antithetical to the objectives of the working class.

20. We mention these parties not to discuss their relative merits but to identify some of the main Left players in the union movement.

21. This statement about commonalities between unions and leftist groups is general because it aims to include a broad array of socialist and leftist thinkers. The groups differed on strategy and tactics.

22. Judith Stepan-Norris and Maurice Zeitlin, *Left Out: Reds and America's Industrial Unions* (Cambridge: Cambridge University Press, 2003), 200, 187.

23. The capacity to carry out similar positions is not unique to leftists. Rightwing organizations such as the Alliance of Catholic Trade Unionists organized their work in much the same way.

24. Estimates indicate that nearly one hundred thousand members of the steel, metal, mining, and auto workers' unions were also members of the Communist Party (at least for a short time) during the period 1932–43. Roger Keeran, *The Communist Party and the Auto Workers Unions* (Bloomington: Indiana University Press, 1980), 17. This number does not include other socialists like Farrell Dobbs of the Socialist Workers Party, who led the militant Teamster local in Minneapolis, and Kermit Johnson and Genora Johnson (Dollinger), who played important roles in the Flint sit-down strikes. Dubofsky and Van Tine, *Labor Leaders*, 309; and Art Preis, *Labor's Giant Step: Twenty Years of the CIO* (New York: Pathfinder Press, 1964), 56–57.

25. For example, see Preis, *Labor's Giant Step*; Keeran, *Communist Party*; Harvey A. Levenstein, *Communism, Anticommunism, and the CIO* (Westport, Conn.: Greenwood Press, 1981); Lichtenstein, *State of the Union*; and Stepan-Norris and Zeitlin, *Left Out*.

26. Levenstein, *Communism, Anticommunism*, 164.

27. Ibid., 165.

28. Robert Michels, *Political Parties* (Glencoe, Ill.: Free Press, 1949 [1911]), 401. Seymour M. Lipset, Martin A. Trow, and James S. Coleman, *Union Democracy: The Internal Politics of the International Typographical Union* (New York: Free Press, 1980 [1962]), 239.

29. Lipset, Trow, and Coleman, *Union Democracy,* 248.

30. Stepan-Norris and Zeitlin, *Left Out,* 94.

3. THE COLD WAR ON LABOR

1. The term *social accord* referred to the notion that an implicit, if not explicit, arrangement existed between the unions, business, and government for the greater good. The idea originates in the view of eighteenth-century philosophers such as Jean-Jacques Rousseau and John Locke that an implicit partnership exists between the major classes of any society. Roosevelt's New Deal was based on the need for and existence of a social accord by which the three major elements of society—unions, government, and business—agreed to accept one another's existence. Needless to say, New Dealers could never gain such acceptance from business.

2. The public viewed the idea of the welfare state not in the narrow sense in which we in the United States have used the term historically—to suggest the state's provision of specific programs. Rather the view was that the government must protect the social welfare of the populace by creating a system of social services covering all citizens.

3. Beginning almost immediately after World War II, various commentators argued that the USSR wanted peaceful coexistence with the capitalist world. Edgar Snow's *The Pattern of Soviet Power* (New York: Random House, 1945) makes this argument quite explicitly. Between 1945 and 1947, the Soviet Union appeared willing to make compromises with the West in the interest of respecting spheres of influence. The lack of Soviet support for the Greek partisan leaders at the end of the war, Soviet leaders' pressure on Tito in the former Yugoslavia to compromise with the British, and the USSR's pullout from northern Iran are just three of the concessions the Soviets were willing to offer. These actions were largely ignored by the West or interpreted as signs of weakness. By 1947, the Soviet Union had concluded that a different path was necessary, at which point it began a major clampdown on its sphere of influence in Eastern Europe, staging absurd purge trials and placing significant limitations on political freedom.

4. Failure to sign this affidavit could cause a union to lose NLRA protection and certification of its collective-bargaining agreements. The requirement was eventually ruled unconstitutional in 1965.

5. Harvey A. Levenstein, *Communism, Anticommunism, and the CIO* (Westport, Conn.: Greenwood Press, 1981), 218.

6. An independent left-leaning labor federation was also thwarted by measures like the Communist Control Act of 1954, which could deprive "Communist-controlled" unions of NLRA protections (ibid., 314).

7. Taft-Hartley met with tremendous resistance, but after its passage, resistance to Red-baiting quickly collapsed among centrist union forces, and a certain calm overtook much of the union movement by the early 1950s, almost as if the Taft-Hartley attack had been an aberration.

8. The standard of living did double between 1940 and 1967.

9. The Treaty of Detroit was a national agreement between the Reuther-led UAW and General Motors that set the pattern for the rest of the auto industry, and because of Reuther's position in the union movement, the agreement influenced collective bargaining nationally as well. Nelson Lichtenstein, "Walter Reuther and the Rise of Labor-Liberalism," in *Labor Leaders in America,* ed. Melvyn Dubofsky and Warren Van Tine (Urbana: University of Illinois Press, 1987), 293. During the immediate postwar period, the popular expectation was that the United States would adopt some form of national health insurance. The emphasis by the UAW and other unions on employer-sponsored health care took energy away from this initiative.

10. Reuther's feints to the left—like his support for civil rights, his outrage at the failure of the AFL-CIO to endorse the 1963 civil rights march on Washington, his trade union militancy, and his proposal for the redistribution of wealth—presented opportunities for a left alignment, but his strategic unity with the virulent anticommunist Association of Catholic Trade Unionists, his use of Red-baiting to defeat his opposition at the expense of his members' wel-

fare, along with his anticommunist leadership within the CIO and the betrayal of the Mississippi Freedom Democratic Party in 1964, reveal the complexity of forging such a pragmatist-left alliance and the price of pragmatists' domination of such alliances.

11. Strikes like the 1997 United Parcel Service (UPS) strike are exceptions. The Teamsters strike against UPS raised a working-class-wide issue of full-time work, challenging UPS efforts to expand its use of part-time work. Jeremy Brecher, *Strike!* (Boston: South End Press, 1997), 358–62.

12. Various factors contributed to the collapse of Operation Dixie, not the least of which were racism and Red-baiting. See, for instance, Barbara S. Griffith, *The Crisis of American Labor: Operation Dixie and the Defeat of the CIO* (Philadelphia: Temple University Press, 1988).

13. Longtime Chicano activist Bert Corona touches on this abandonment of Southwest Chicanos in Mario T. Garcia, *Memories of Chicano History: The Life and Narrative of Bert Corona* (Berkeley: University of California Press, 1994).

14. Robert H. Zieger, "George Meany: Labor's Organization Man," in Dubofsky and Van Tine, *Labor Leaders*, 326.

15. Ibid., 337.

16. Under Sweeney, the AFL-CIO removed the specific bar to Communist membership (*Constitution of the AFL-CIO*, Article III, Section 7).

17. "Communism" eventually became anything the U.S. State Department declared it to be. Thus, despite the rhetoric, the AFL-CIO activities against Cheddi Jagan, prime minister of British Guiana in 1964, had less to do with whether Jagan was actually a communist than with his public and outspoken left-wing and nationalist politics. For a brief look at the U.S. and labor roles in overthrowing Jagan, see Gary N. Chaison and Tarique I. Nageer, "The Labour Movement/Evolution, Intervention, Stagnation, Transition: Guyana" (Spring 1998), http://members.tripod.com/~tnageer/Labour.html. An excellent collection of articles on the Caribbean labor movement and politics is Hilbourne Watson, "Guyana, Jamaica and the Cold War Project: The Transformation of Caribbean Labor," in *Caribbean Labor and Politics: Legacies of Cheddi Jagan and Michael Manley*, ed. Perry Mars and Alma H. Young (Detroit: Wayne State University Press, 2004), 89–125.

18. Business unionism has come to mean many things. In general, it is the sort of unionism that both treats the union as a business and emphasizes the need for the union (allegedly on behalf of the workers) and the employer to collaborate, at the expense of class struggle.

4. THE CIVIL RIGHTS MOVEMENTS, THE LEFT, AND LABOR

1. Though Meany did not place a premium on organizing, he still paid attention to any organizing that did take place.

2. Fernando Gapasin, "United Farm Workers," in *The Encyclopedia of Latinos and Latinas in the United States*, ed. Deena J. Gonzalez and Suzanne Oboler (New York: Oxford University Press, 2005).

3. Jacques Levy, *César Chávez: Autobiography of La Causa* (New York: W. W. Norton, 1975), cover.

4. Later, many leftists and activists were purged from the UFW.

5. Levy, *César Chávez*, back cover.

6. Socialist Farrell Dobbs pioneered leverage strategies in 1940 when he was a founder of the Teamsters Central States Drivers Council. Estelle James, "Jimmy Hoffa: Labor Hero or Labor's Own Foe," in *Labor Leaders in America*, ed. Melvyn Dubofsky and Warren Van Tine (Urbana: University of Illinois Press, 1987), 309.

7. See Philip S. Foner, *Organized Labor and the Black Worker, 1619–1973* (New York: Praeger Publishers, 1974), 333–54. Also, see a leftist critique by Harlem Fightback founder and longtime leader James Haughton, who helped form the Negro American Labor Council: "James Haughton on Racism in the House of Labor," interviewed by Janine Jackson, in *History Matters: The U.S. Survey Course on the Web*, http://historymatters.gmu.edu/d/7038/.

8. Many of the "construction workers" were actually business agents and other staff members, in addition to off-duty police officers dressed as construction workers.

9. Martin Halpern, *Unions, Radicals and Democratic Presidents: Seeking Social Change in the Twentieth Century* (Westport, Conn.: Praeger, 2003), 6–7. Individual leaders of AFL-CIO affiliates played important roles, but the movement as a whole remained basically disconnected.

10. The struggle of African American steelworkers for justice is excellently documented in the compelling book by Ruth Needleman, *Black Freedom Fighters in Steel: The Struggle for Democratic Unionism* (Ithaca, N.Y.: ILR Press/Cornell University Press, 2003). Several studies of the League of Revolutionary Black Workers are worth reviewing. The organization's own film, *Finally Got the News,* gives a sense of the times and the group's orientation (available at www.frif.com/new2003/fin.html). See also Dan Georgakas, *Detroit: I Do Mind Dying: A Study in Urban Revolution,* 2nd ed. (Boston: South End Press, 1998); and James A. Geschwender, *Class, Race and Worker Insurgency: The League of Revolutionary Black Workers* (New York: Cambridge University Press, 1977). From the African American Left, former Afrikan People's Party chairman A. Muhammad Ahmed offers an analysis entitled "The League of Revolutionary Black Workers (A Historical Study)," www.geocities.com/CapitolHill/Lobby/2379/lrbw.htm.

11. Our use of the term *traditional* is not the same as Warren R. Van Tine's in *The Making of the Labor Bureaucrat: Union Leadership in the United States, 1870–1920* (Amherst: University of Massachusetts Press, 1973).

12. Robert H. Zieger, "George Meany: Labor's Organization Man," in Dubofsky and Van Tine, *Labor Leaders,* 339.

13. Roger Keeran, *The Communist Party and the Auto Workers Unions* (Bloomington: Indiana University Press, 1980), 20.

5. WHOSE WELFARE MATTERS, ANYWAY?

1. An excellent work on the international economy and unions is Kim Moody's *Workers in a Lean World* (London: Verso, 1997). Moody offers an in-depth examination of the consequences of neoliberal globalization and changes in the production process for workers and their unions.

2. See Leo Panitch and Sam Gindin, "Global Capitalism and American Empire," in *Socialist Register 2004: The New Imperial Challenge,* ed. Leo Panitch and Colin Leys, 1–42 (New York: Monthly Review Press, 2003). Panitch and Gindin develop a provocative analysis not only of the postwar period but also of the relationships between the major capitalist states. Though we do not entirely agree with their conclusions, this analysis helps frame an understanding of the evolution of the neoliberal state.

3. Thomas Ferguson and Joel Rogers, *Right Turn: The Decline of the Democrats and the Future of American Politics* (New York: Hill and Wang, 1986).

4. "Volcker Asserts U.S. Must Trim Living Standard," *New York Times,* October 18, 1979. It's revealing that Volcker's announcement did not provoke a determined public counterattack by the AFL-CIO.

5. Initially, a very progressive national union of shipyard workers formed in the 1930s, largely in opposition to the AFL-craft approach to organizing shipyards. The union folded into the International Association of Machinists. A detailed history of the formation and early years of the national union is available in David Palmer, *Organizing the Shipyards: Union Strategy in Three Northeast Ports, 1933–1945* (Ithaca, N.Y.: ILR Press/Cornell University Press, 1998).

6. The Local 5 leadership did very little, but a rank-and-file campaign took on General Dynamics. One of the leaders of this campaign, a left-wing white welder, eventually ran for and won the presidency of Local 5. Unfortunately, he later resigned when he was undercut by his local's executive board, where he did not have majority support.

7. This recession was not planned, though the 1980–81 recession, named after Federal Reserve chair Paul Volcker, was largely orchestrated via a hike in interest rates. In using the term *discipline,* we seek to emphasize that within capitalism, the capitalists use recessions and depressions as a means of weakening the power of the working class and scaring off workers from making demands.

8. Arab oil producers launched the oil boycott in response to Western support of Israel in the so-called Yom Kippur War of 1973 between Egypt and Israel.

9. For one of the earliest and best analyses of deindustrialization, see Barry Bluestone and Bennett Harrison, *Deindustrialization of America: Plant Closings, Community Abandonment and the Dismantling of Basic Industry* (New York: Basic Books, 1982).

10. Through the FBI's Counter Intelligence Program (COINTELPRO) and other forms of repressive activity, key leaders of the Black Freedom Movement were killed, imprisoned, driven into exile, or driven insane. Similar actions were taken against leaders of the Puerto Rican, Chicano, Native American, and Asian American movements. See "Going Undercover/Criminalizing Dissent," *NOW,* www.pbs.org/now/politics/cointelpro.html.

11. The Chilean junta was advised by the protégés of U.S. economist Milton Friedman of the so-called Chicago School. For a brief and useful look at the Pinochet regime's implementation of Friedmanism, see Steve Kagas, "A Critique of the Chicago School of Economics, Chile: The Laboratory Test," www.huppi .com/kangaroo/L-chichile.htm. See also Naomi Klein, *The Shock Doctrine: The Rise of Disaster Capitalism* (New York: Metropolitan Books, 2007).

12. Perhaps *finale* would be a better term to describe the demise of the social accord. The social accord had been unraveling for some time, but with the PATCO strike, even the illusion of an accord vanished.

13. Stanley Aronowitz, *From the Ashes of the Old: American Labor and America's Future* (New York: Basic Books, 1998), 15.

14. Though class warfare had been well under way before the strike, particularly in the South and Southwest, Reagan nationalized the class war, and no ground was left untouched in its march from sea to sea.

15. One of the committee's more important suggestions, taken up by several unions, was to create an associate membership for workers unable to join or form a union. Though this recommendation seemed to open the door to innovative approaches toward union membership and expansion, few unions embraced it, and those that did were not terribly creative in defining the new brand of membership.

6. WHAT'S LEFT FOR US?

1. The Leadership Administration caucus was the "ruling party" of the United Auto Workers, for lack of a better term.

2. See "The Lincoln Hospital Offensive," Latino Education Network Service de los barrios de las Americas, http://palante.org/04LincolnOffensive.htm.

3. Philip S. Foner, *Organized Labor and the Black Worker, 1619–1973* (New York: Praeger, 1974), 409.

4. Exclusivity in collective bargaining has a complicated legal and political history. Per the National Labor Relations Act, a union is the exclusive representative of workers in a specific bargaining unit. Congress was particularly concerned about stability in the workplace and the establishment of industrial jurisprudence. Thus, an officially recognized union, whether recognized through a voluntary agreement by an employer or through an election, is chosen to represent all workers in that bargaining unit irrespective of their membership in the union (if membership is optional), race, gender, national origin, or religion. Contrary to labor-management relations in many other countries, where more than one union can represent the same types of workers in the same workplace, in the United States, only one union has that right. However, if there is not an officially recognized union, more than one union organizing committee can compete for the attention and support of the workers. The issue of exclusivity was made abundantly clear in the brilliant decision by Justice Thurgood Marshall in *Emporium Capwell Co. v. Western Addition Community Organization*, 420 U.S. 50 (1975), http://caselaw.lp.findlaw.com/scripts/getcase.pl?court = us&vol = 420&invol = 50. Nevertheless, the story does not end with this court decision. In the building trades, organizations such as Harlem Fightback were de facto hiring halls for Black and Latino workers who were largely excluded by the building trades unions. Also, in the extremely hostile environment in many fire departments after litigation opened the door to workers of color, the "Vulcans" operated as a de facto parallel union for Black workers who had no trust in the official union.

5. Vanessa Tait, *Poor Workers' Unions: Rebuilding Labor from Below* (Cambridge, Mass.: South End Press, 2005).

6. Under an agency shop agreement, an individual need not join a union that represents the bargaining unit but nevertheless pays a fee to help cover the union's costs for basic representation.

7. The leadership scenario we describe is common under typical circumstances. Obviously, when a union is dominated by the mob, as the Laborers International Union of North America and the International Longshoremen's Association allegedly have been at various times, its internal life and culture suffer even more, with a small clique using terror to retain control of the organization. Such mob domination, however, is nowhere near the norm in the union movement.

8. We qualify the term *apathy* to describe union members here because the word is subject to overuse, to the point of becoming a cliché. "Apathy" is often really a worker's sense of disconnection from the union, which can result from numerous sources.

9. One of us—Bill Fletcher, Jr.—was one of two individuals from outside the Mail Handlers Union brought in to help reorganize the union and develop the contract campaign. The other individual was Gene Bruskin, a former president of a school bus drivers' local union in Boston, who went on to work with the National Rainbow Coalition, the Food & Allied Service Trades (FAST) Department of the AFL-CIO (where he served as secretary-treasurer; FAST is now independent of the AFL-CIO), and the United Food and Commercial Workers union, where he directed the Smithfield (North Carolina) organizing campaign.

10. The pattern we describe is a slight variation on a point made by Richard Trumka, secretary-treasurer of the AFL-CIO and former president of the United Mine Workers, at an informal gathering of labor activists in 1990 in Cambridge, Massachusetts, convened by James Green, a professor at the University of Massachusetts–Boston.

7. ORGANIZING TO ORGANIZE THE UNORGANIZED

1. The information on central labor councils is based on data collected by Fernando Gapasin as the principal investigator (researcher) for the AFL-CIO's Union Cities program.

2. See the Jobs with Justice mission statement at www.jwj.org.

3. Discussion of an organizing model appeared as early as 1989, in Andy Banks and Jack Metzgar, "Participating in Management: Union Organizing on a New Terrain," *Labor Research Review* 14 (Fall 1989): 47. For more on the model, see Richard Hurd, "The Failure of Organizing, the New Unity Partnership and the Future of the Labor Movement," *Working USA,* September 2004; also available at www.aflcio.org/aboutus/ourfuture/upload/wusa_0021.pdf.

4. Rick Hurd has written several pieces with us on the organizing model. See, for example, Bill Fletcher, Jr., and Richard Hurd, "Overcoming Obstacles to Transformation: Challenges on the Way to a New Unionism," in *The Revival of the American Labor Movement?* ed. Lowell Turner, Harry Katz, and Richard

Hurd (Ithaca, N.Y.: ILR Press/Cornell University Press, 2000); Bill Fletcher, Jr., and Richard Hurd, "Beyond the Organizing Model: The Transformation Process in Local Unions," in *Organizing to Win,* ed. Kate Bronfenbrenner, Sheldon Friedman, Richard Hurd, Rudolph Oswald, and Ronald Seeber, 37–57 (Ithaca, N.Y.: ILR Press/Cornell University Press, 1998); Bill Fletcher, Jr., and Richard Hurd, "Political Will, Local Union Transformation and the Organizing Imperative," in *Which Direction for Organized Labor?* ed. Bruce Nissen, 191–216 (Detroit: Wayne State University Press, 1999).

5. The Justice for Janitors campaign was an SEIU effort to reorganize the janitorial industry, much of which had been lost to nonunion contractors in the 1980s when the industry changed its way of operating.

6. Trusteeship is a mechanism through which the international union can take over a local union for reasons such as malfeasance, theft, or a breakdown in constitutional order.

7. Zellers had been offended during the first round of negotiations that participants had not paid more attention to him. Such attention was, for all practical purposes, unnecessary. The goal was to determine whether the Reformistas were serious about trying to settle. Zellers had never indicated unwillingness to compromise.

8. One of the vice-presidents of the Los Angeles County Federation of Labor, who leads a large building trades local, has said that he is not interested in expanding his local because of what happened to SEIU Local 399.

9. John P. Kotter, "Leading Change: Why Transformation Efforts Fail," *Harvard Business Review,* March 1, 1995.

10. In using the term *semi-anarchist,* we mean a belief in spontaneity—a conviction that the masses will rise up spontaneously and bring about progressive change. This view also downplayed—ironically—the need for leadership, specifically leadership from among the rank-and-file workers. Thus, it downplayed grassroots worker and labor education and relied on the emergence of a "great leader" or leaders. In an interesting twist, anarchism can sometimes go full circle and promote hierarchical or patriarchal leadership.

11. Well before the trusteeship, a struggle had emerged between progressives within the local over the relationship between organizing and representation. The struggle was not about pursuing one over the other but about how to do both effectively.

12. Local 1877 president Mike Garcia, a longtime Chicano/labor activist, was appointed trustee. Eventually, he was put in charge of the building services section of Local 399. Garcia is a very progressive trade unionist and attempted to be inclusive in his oversight of the trusteeship. He paid special attention to the ethnic tensions popping up between African American and Latino leaders and staff.

13. Significant ethnic tensions arose within Local 399 precisely because of the restructuring of the janitorial industry as well as the failure—for whatever reason—of the Justice for Janitors campaign to determine how to approach this question of building a multiethnic union. Though organizing the increasingly Latino-dominated janitorial industry was essential, many Black workers felt that the union had cast them aside. Thus, a number of them resisted the attention being focused upon Latino workers.

8. THE NEW VOICE COALITION TAKES OFFICE

1. The 1974 coup in Ethiopia that overthrew Emperor Haile Selassie and replaced him with a military junta—the Dergue—might be a better example of a palace coup. The government takeover was an attempt to address a crisis ahead of a growing mass movement that stood in opposition to the emperor.

2. In contrast, central labor councils responded very favorably to Common Sense Economics and made a point of organizing train-the-trainer programs to develop personnel who could run various facets of the program. Some state federations of labor also embraced the program. Nevertheless, once a trainer was identified and prepared, deploying him or her was a major challenge. If a local union did not give a trainer sufficient free time to run aspects of Common Sense Economics, the training was for naught.

3. The New Left included activists from the domestic freedom movements, including the Black, Chicano, Asian, Puerto Rican, and Native American movements; women's movement; antiwar movement; welfare rights movement; and student movements; as well as revitalized versions of the communist (largely Maoist) and Trotskyist traditions. Established organizations like the Communist Party and the Socialist Workers Party also contributed cadre to the union movement. These leftist forces—both organizations and individuals—in the union movement helped build the antiracist caucus movements in the 1970s and prolabor democratic caucuses like the Teamsters for a Democratic Union and the UAW's New Directions. They were also instrumental in building progressive constituency groups like the Asian Pacific American Labor Alliance.

4. Two examples are the Brazilian CUT (Central Unica dos Trabalhadores) and the Congress of South African Trade Unions.

5. Fernando E. Gapasin, "The Los Angeles County Federation of Labor: A Model of Transformation or Traditional Unionism?" in *Central Labor Councils and the Revival of American Unionism,* ed. Immanuel Ness and Stuart Eimer, 82–98 (Armonk, N.Y.: M. E. Sharpe, 2001).

6. "Locked-Out Hunger-Striker Addresses AFL-CIO Leaders at N.Y. Convention," *News from the War Zone: Staley Workers' Solidarity Report* (October/November 1995), 2. Pepsi was a major client of Staley's, and many people saw the company as a driving force in the antiworker lockout.

7. Jerry Tucker, "Winning the Staley Struggle," October 30, 1995. Tucker ran afoul of the UAW Administrative Caucus because of his politics. He later sought the presidency of the UAW as the leader of the New Directions reform movement. Tucker was one of the chief architects of in-plant organizing, which calls for developing strategies and tactics workers can use to advance their objectives should a strike not be feasible or timely.

8. The United Steelworkers made a commitment during 2007 to build a global union along with allies in Germany. The details of this plan remain unclear at this writing. However, it appears to be an attempt to forge a transnational union partnership among unions in the Global North and is worth watching.

9. Miriam J. Wells, *Strawberry Fields: Politics, Class, and Work in California Agriculture* (Ithaca, N.Y.: Cornell University Press, 1996), 162–66.

10. The Chávez purges are a matter that few people wish to discuss, in part for fear of impugning the name and reputation of César Chávez. Nevertheless, the purges marked a painful period in the history of the UFW. Philip Vera Cruz, one of the founders and early leaders of the UFW (himself a Filipino), offers great insight into this experience in Craig Scharlin and Lilia V. Villanueva, *Philip Vera Cruz: A Personal History of Filipino Immigrants and the Farmworkers Movement* (Los Angeles: UCLA Labor Center, Institute of Industrial Relations & UCLA Asian American Studies Center, 1992).

11. Whether Bensinger's perception that he was being promoted out of the AFL-CIO was true would require further investigation. Nevertheless, his assumption was not illogical. The AFL-CIO, as well as its affiliates, commonly removes individuals by promoting them to meaningless positions. The stories about Bensinger's leaving are legendary. Sweeney's office gave incomplete information about the event, prompting speculation about what had transpired. Some leaders who had had their own complaints about Bensinger used this incident for political reasons, taking their own shots at Sweeney. The manner in which Sweeney's office handled the situation was so poor that it left a bad taste both within the AFL-CIO staff and with many of the affiliates.

12. Bensinger's CLC-based approach called for a multiunion, multisector organizing effort within a city. The Stamford, Connecticut, project became the best-known of these efforts. See Daniel HoSang, "All the Issues in Workers' Lives: Labor Confronts Race in Stamford," *NHI,* June 2000, http://www.nhi.org/online/issues/111/hosang.html. Another example of direct CLC organizing was the Downtown Organizing Project of the Santa Clara/San Benito Counties Labor Council. The labor council, led at that time by business manager Rick Sawyer (now international vice-president of UNITE HERE!), successfully organized the largest hotel in San Jose and eventually most of the restaurants in the downtown area. This example predated Sweeney's Union Cities program and served as a model for the use of labor councils to build political power and organize the unorganized.

13. *The global justice movement,* often called the "antiglobalization movement," comprises progressive critics of neoliberal globalization. Proponents of the global justice movement seek justice rather than the dominance of the interests of transnational capital.

14. For a useful critique of the AFL-CIO position and practice during the Seattle demonstrations, see Jeff Crosby, "Kids Are Alright," *New Labor Forum,* Spring/Summer 2000, 35–41.

15. For an excellent analysis of the World Trade Organization, see Lori Wallach and Michelle Sforza, *Whose Trade Organization? Corporate Globalization and the Erosion of Democracy* (Washington, D.C.: Public Citizen, 1999).

16. The AFL-CIO conducted hearings two years later in connection with immigrant rights and discrimination.

17. The results of the conference were overshadowed by the September 11, 2001, terrorist attacks.

18. In the late 1980s, the largest hotel in San Jose, California, was organized by the Santa Clara County Labor Council's Organizing Committee.

19. Fernando Gapasin and Howard Wial, "The Role of Central Labor Councils in Union Organizing in the 1990s," in *Organizing to Win: New Research on Union Strategies,* ed. Kate Bronfenbrenner, Sheldon Friedman, Richard W. Hurd, and Rudolph A. Oswald, 54–67 (Ithaca, N.Y.: ILR Press/ Cornell University Press, 1998).

9. DEVELOPING STRATEGY IN TIMES OF CHANGE

1. UNITE was particularly active in the South and Southwest. Formerly the textile workers union, UNITE merged with the Hotel Employees and Restaurant Employees International Union (HERE) in 2004 to form UNITE HERE! The union, which resulted from the merger of the Amalgamated Clothing and Textile Workers and the International Ladies Garment Workers Union, was known as the Union of Needle Trades, Industrial and Textile Employees. Later the union took the acronym UNITE as its official name.

2. The AFL-CIO supported two efforts at poultry-worker organizing. Richard Bensinger was particularly interested in expanding the poultry organizing. The United Food and Commercial Workers discussed a campaign in 1997 and 1998, but little came of the discussions. UNITE conducted some public-sector organizing, and SEIU conducted public-sector organizing in Georgia and a multiunion campaign in New Orleans.

3. A similar problem emerged some years earlier with the Los Angeles Manufacturing Action Project (LAMAP). The talk of the town during the 1995 AFL-CIO Convention, LAMAP was largely the brainchild of labor activist Peter Olney. The notion was to launch a multiunion effort to organize Los Angeles manufacturing. Though several unions committed to preliminary research, only the Teamsters under Ron Carey were willing to step forward and make a major commitment. Bensinger, representing the AFL-CIO at the time, took the position that the AFL-CIO could not advance funds if the affiliates were noncommittal. Olney insisted that if the AFL-CIO were to show its support for this project, the affiliates would likely step forward. Affiliates offered a host of excuses for not joining this project, and it eventually collapsed. On LAMAP, see Tom Gallagher, "Labor Report: Everybody Loved It, But . . . ," www.zmag.org/zmag/articles/nov98gallagher.htm.

4. The AFL-CIO designed a separate program for state federations— called Workers Voice—but this effort did not receive the same level of attention that Union Cities did. This lukewarm support was a source of tension because many state federations felt that the national AFL-CIO was going through the motions of interacting with them and that its real interest was in the central labor councils.

5. The presidents' paper was circulated but not published. The paper was highly controversial and received considerable attention at the AFL-CIO Convention. See www.d.umn.edu/~epeters5/MAPL5111/5111%20Articles/12-9-04 %20CLC%20advisory%20committee%20proposal.htm.

6. For more examples and detail on CLC renewal, see Immanuel Ness and Stuart Eimer, eds., *Central Labor Councils and the Revival of American Unionism: Organizing for Justice in Our Communities* (Armonk, N.Y.: M. E. Sharpe, 2001).

7. The New Alliance project had no relationship to the political party of the same name, which is now defunct. On the New Alliance, see Immanuel Ness, "From Dormancy to Activism: New Voice and the Revival of Labor Councils," in Ness and Eimer, *Central Labor Councils,* 24–32.

8. See the compelling analysis by International Brotherhood of Electrical Workers member and Cornell University professor Jeff Grabelsky in "A New Alliance in New York State: A Progress Report on the Labor Movement's Restructuring, Capacity Building and Programmatic Work," *Working USA,* March 2007.

9. Bennett Harrison, *Lean and Mean: The Changing Landscape of Corporate Power in the Age of Flexibility* (New York: Basic Books, 1994). Harrison died at the age of fifty-six in 1999, marking a great loss to the progressive movement.

10. Robert J. Thomas, *What Machines Can't Do: Politics and Technology in the Industrial Enterprise* (Berkeley: University of California Press, 1994), 178–84.

11. Debate has flourished since the early 1990s about the potential "end of work." Stanley Aronowitz, Jeremy Rifkin, and others have separately suggested that the introduction of new technologies signals the end of work as we know it. For an interesting collection of essays suggesting this proposition, see Jim Davis, Thomas A. Hirschl, and Michael Stack, eds., *Cutting Edge: Technology, Information Capitalism and Social Revolution* (London: Verso, 1997). Though we believe that this thesis has much to offer, we do not subscribe to the semi-apocalyptic vision that sometimes accompanies it.

12. Steven C. Pitts, "Organize . . . to Improve the Quality of Jobs in the Black Community: A Report on Jobs and Activism in the African American Community" (Berkeley: University of California Center for Labor Research and Education, May 2004).

13. The structurally unemployed, including informal workers such as street-corner vendors, make up an unregulated and untaxed sector of the economy.

14. Janny Scott, "Nearly Half of Black Men Found Jobless," *New York Times,* February 28, 2004.

15. See, for example, Gabor Steingart, "How Globalization Drives Down Western Wages," *Spiegel Online,* October 16, 2006, www.spiegel.de/international/0,1518,436976,00.html.

16. The problem was not one-sided. In organizing for a major meeting of community-based groups that were organizing the poor, the AFL-CIO received repeated inquiries about whether it would hand out financial support to organizations that agreed to participate.

10. GLOBALIZATION

1. Michael Hardt and Antonio Negri introduced the notion of globalization and empire into the mainstream in *Empire* (Cambridge, Mass.: Harvard University Press, 2000). An alternative and more nuanced left-wing version of the concept of empire appears in the writings of A. Sivanadan, editor of the respected British journal *Race & Class.* In a special issue in 1998 entitled "The Threat of Globalism," Sivanadan makes a distinction between globalization and globalism, with his definition of the former coming closest to the second definition we cite and his def-

inition of the latter being similar to our third definition. The notion of globalization as an epochal shift is also explicit in Roger Burbach and William Robinson, "The Fin De Siècle Debate: Globalization as Epochal Shift," *Science & Society* 63, no. 1 (Spring 1999): 10–69, www.globalpolicy.org/globaliz/define/findesie.htm. The definition we offer as version 3 is most consistent with our views.

2. Neoliberalism is the preferred form for the global reorganization of capital in that it strengthens the hand of capital in relation to other social forces, especially in relation to the working class. Nonetheless, some within the ruling circles disagree about how effective this form will be and whether the price will be too high, even for capital.

3. Ellen M. Wood, *The Origin of Capitalism* (London: Verso, 2002).

4. Protectionism is a popular strategy for fighting globalization among segments of the trade union leadership as well as among right-wing populists. It generally ignores the actual role the United States has played internationally, including the role of U.S.-based corporations. It also fails to take into account the need for economic development in the Global South. Protectionism lets capital off the hook. What is desperately needed is a progressive approach to reining in capital and pursuing economic development approaches in the Global North that are sustainable, environmentally friendly, and pro-people.

5. An excellent 1988 interview with Harrison reads as a timely piece on globalization and strategy. See "Fighting Capital Flight: An Interview with Bennett Harrison," *Multinational Monitor,* September 1988, http://multinational monitor.org/hyper/issues/1988/09/mmo988_05.html.

6. Jefferson Cowie offers a fascinating exposé of capital mobility in an examination of the U.S. corporation RCA. This example shows the impact of the class struggle on a corporation's growth and movement. At no point did RCA workers, whether unionized or not, develop a coherent strategy to address capital mobility and its impact on the workforce and community. See Jefferson Cowie, *Capital Moves: RCA's 70-Year Quest for Cheap Labor* (New York: New Press, 1999).

7. An organizing director of a non-service-sector union told Bill Fletcher, Jr., that organizing the sector represented by his union was impossible. He offered this explanation for abandoning organizing in this sector and looking to the public and service sectors for organizing prospects.

8. See, for instance, Zaragosa Vargas, *Labor Rights Are Civil Rights: Mexican American Workers in Twentieth-Century America* (Princeton, N.J.: Princeton University Press, 2005). Vargas discusses employers' use of migrant workers to undermine organizing efforts among Latinos and others in the Southwest from the 1920s through the 1950s.

9. For example, see Robert J. Thomas, *What Machines Can't Do: Politics and Technology in the Industrial Enterprise* (Berkeley: University of California Press, 1994).

10. Thatcher made this comment in a talk to *Women's Own* magazine on October 31, 1987.

11. Aimé Césaire, *Discourse on Colonialism* (New York: Monthly Review Press, 2000), 35–36.

12. A great deal of debate has centered on the nature of the neoliberal state. The attack on basic democratic rights and civil liberties has led many people to

262 / NOTES TO PAGES 95–97

believe that the United States is on the verge of becoming a fascist state. Drawing from the theoretician Nicos Poulantzas, we take issue with that specific characterization while agreeing with the concern behind it. Various forms of authoritarian capitalist states exist. Fascism is only one variety, normally associated with a mass and radical social movement that seeks to eliminate capitalist democracy. It is a form of right-wing populism that eventually aligns itself with a section of capital in an effort to change the terms of the power bloc that leads the capitalist society. We think that the situation in the United States and in the Global North as a whole differs from this scenario. See Nicos Poulantzas, *Fascism and Dictatorship* (London: Verso, 1979).

13. Two interesting articles in the November 2006 issue of *Monthly Review,* though they focus on the changes introduced under George W. Bush, offer useful perspectives on the evolution of the capitalist state: Michael Tigar, "The Twilight of Personal Liberty: Introduction to 'A Permanent State of Emergency'"; and Jean-Claude Paye, "A Permanent State of Emergency." Both writers call attention to the use of the so-called war against terrorism to alter the existing U.S. capitalist state.

14. Specifically, the so-called *Kentucky River* decisions move toward reclassifying any worker who has a modicum of responsibility as a supervisor and is therefore ineligible for unionization. See the lead case: *Oakwood Healthcare, Inc.,* Case 7-RC-22141, September 29, 2006, www.lawmemo.com/nlrb/oakwood.htm.

15. In other words, the transnational capitalist class is not at war—literally or figuratively—with the nation-state as such. Rather it uses the nation-state to advance its objectives. No analogous situation existed to that of the period of the U.S. Civil War, for instance, where a segment of the national capitalist class sought to build one national market and system of control in opposition to those in the South attempting to advance a different vision and economic and social structure. If a battle exists, it is more about how global capitalism should be led and who should lead it.

16. The Group of 8 comprises the eight strongest economies. Originally the Group of 7, or G-7, the group became G-8 with the inclusion of the Russian Federation.

17. U.S. foreign policy has always favored the use of international institutions when it is to the benefit of the United States. Particularly after World War II, segments of the ruling circles—specifically those advocating the "nationalist" position—made clear that they wanted no constraints on the nation's actions on the foreign stage. This battle between the "nationalists" and the "multilateralists" has gone on, in one form or another, since the beginning of the Cold War. The multilateralists do not want to see constraints on U.S. foreign policy, but they are keenly aware of and concerned about the nation's long-term relationships with its key allies.

18. See the website for the Project for a New American Century, specifically the organization's statement of principles: www.newamericancentury.org/statementofprinciples.htm.

19. See the September 2002 National Security Strategy Doctrine, www.white house.gov/nsc/nss.pdf.

11. COULD'A, WOULD'A, SHOULD'A

1. Fernando Gapasin and Howard Wial, "The Role of Central Labor Councils in Union Organizing in the 1990s," in *Organizing to Win: New Research on Union Strategies,* ed. Kate Bronfenbrenner, Sheldon Friedman, Richard W. Hurd, and Rudolph A. Oswald, 54–68 (Ithaca, N.Y.: ILR Press/Cornell University Press, 1998).

2. Some of the best labor councils are examined in Immanuel Ness and Stuart Eimer, eds., *Central Labor Councils and the Revival of American Unionism: Organizing for Justice in Our Communities* (Armonk, N.Y.: M. E. Sharpe, 2001).

3. Fernando E. Gapasin, "The Los Angeles County Federation of Labor: A Model of Transformation or Traditional Unionism?" in Ness and Eimer, *Central Labor Councils,* 81.

4. Ibid., 80.

5. This section covers some material also covered in ibid., 79–101.

6. Ibid., 83.

7. Fernando Gapasin, "The Los Angeles County Federation of Labor and UCLA Labor Center: Putting Organizing on the CLC Agenda," in *Working Together to Revitalize Labor in Our Communities: Case Studies of Labor Education–Central Labor Body Collaboration,* ed. Jill Kriesky, 85–90 (Orono: University and College Labor Education Association, University of Maine, 1998); Gapasin, "A Model of Transformation," 82–98; and Nelson Lichtenstein, *State of the Union: A Century of American Labor* (Princeton, N.J.: Princeton University Press, 2002), 262–69.

8. Ludlow stepped down in 2006 because of allegations of electoral improprieties. His departure was a loss to the movement given his strong progressive reputation.

9. Narro made this comment in a personal communication with Fernando Gapasin in 1998.

10. In Cincinnati, in the same period, the union addressed the question of immigrant rights in a different way. There, the labor council celebrated an Immigration and Naturalization Service raid on nonunion immigrant workers, to the chagrin and dismay of the "Union Summer" interns.

11. Dan Clawson, *The Next Upsurge: Labor and the New Social Movements* (Ithaca, N.Y.: ILR Press/Cornell University Press, 2003).

12. David Harvey, *The Limits of Capital* (London: Verso, 1982).

13. We recognize that some authors on the left challenge the view that globalization has progressed to the degree we suggest. For example, see Kim Moody, *Workers in a Lean World* (London: Verso, 1997); and Ellen Meiksins Wood, Peter Meiksins, and Michael D. Yates, *Rising from the Ashes? Labor in the Age of Global Capitalism* (New York: Monthly Review Press, 1998). They claim that foreign direct investment is relatively small in scope and limited mainly to other developed countries. However, limiting the discussion to direct investment misses the boat. The bulk of globalization is occurring through arm's-length transactions: contracting and licensing. A good proportion of the billions of

dollars' worth of products that flow into the United States each month are a product neither of foreign direct investment nor of independent exporters in other countries; instead, they result from U.S. corporations' efforts to arrange production offshore.

14. In other words, transnationals can control the production and consumption of resources and the dissemination of resources. Edna Bonacich and Jake B. Wilson conduct an in-depth exploration of these and related issues in *Getting the Goods: Ports, Labor, and the Logistics Revolution* (Ithaca, N.Y.: Cornell University Press, 2007).

15. An irony not lost on Peter Olney, LAMAP founder and current organizing director of the International Longshore and Warehouse Union, was the fact that LAMAP was the talk of the town at the October 1995 AFL-CIO Convention, popular with both slates of nominees. The expectation was that whoever won the AFL-CIO election would throw resources into this project. Circumstances did not work out that way. Unfortunately, because of several affiliates' unprincipled objections to supporting LAMAP, the new leadership offered disingenuous reasons why the project could not go forward.

16. One exception has been the UNITE for Dignity effort in southern Florida, initially a joint effort of UNITE and SEIU. This campaign was able to create organizing opportunities by taking a cross-sector geographic approach to organizing mainly Haitian workers.

17. The Los Angeles Labor/Community Strategy Center and the Bus Riders Union offer excellent examples of how to organize and mobilize workers across Los Angeles—in this case, around the community issue of mass public transportation—while integrating antiracist and anti-imperialist politics.

18. The discussion of LAMAP and sector organizing draws from Fernando Gapasin and Edna Bonacich, "The Strategic Challenge of Organizing Manufacturing Workers in the Global/Flexible Capitalism," in *Unions in a Globalized Environment: Changing Borders, Organizational Boundaries, and Social Roles,* ed. Bruce Nissen, 163–88 (Armonk, N.Y.: M. E. Sharpe, 2002).

19. Riley turned to other unions and organizations, but they largely ignored him or put him off.

20. Indeed, see the recently published book on the case by Suzan Erem and E. Paul Durrenberger, *On the Global Waterfront: The Fight to Free the Charleston 5* (New York: Monthly Review Press, 2008).

21. An important legal and tactical question arose during the campaign. The defense committee had prepared for actions on the first day of the trial, but some supporters wanted to go for a national, if not international, stay-away from work in the longshore industry. If they had proceeded, they could have stopped or significantly slowed commerce for a day. Some participants in the campaign were worried that the government might bring charges under the Racketeer Influenced and Corrupt Organizations Act if they took such an action. The national defense campaign never called for such an action, but this question was never resolved. Also of interest is the fact that the police conducted surveillance of the national defense campaign.

12. INTERNATIONAL AFFAIRS, GLOBALIZATION, AND 9/11

1. At the 2000 AFL-CIO Convention, the ICFTU showed a video documentary of its history that offered a montage of images from the beginning of the Cold War to the present. The video had no narration, but the images brought home the contradiction between the anticommunism of the 1940s, when the ICFTU originated, and the incorporation of Left-led national labor centers into the ICFTU in the 1990s.

2. Remarks by AFL-CIO president John J. Sweeney, ICFTU convention, April 4, 2000.

3. A concise summary of the Washington Consensus appears in the October 2007 issue of *Monthly Review,* in which it is defined as "a set of policies agreed upon by the U.S. Treasury, the IMF and World Bank that requires necessitous third-world borrowers to open their economies to foreign investment, curb inflation, cut back public expenditures, deregulate, and privatize. Imposed on third-world countries as in their alleged interest, they [the policies] close out alternative development options like giving first priority to serving human needs at home and, by a remarkable coincidence, seem to lavish benefits on foreign transnational corporations in the United States and elsewhere." Edward S. Herman and David Peterson, "The Dismantling of Yugoslavia: A Study in Inhumanitarian Intervention (and a Western Liberal-Left Intellectual and Moral Collapse)," *Monthly Review* 59, no. 5 (October 2007): 60.

4. The AFL-CIO Executive Council issued an official statement on the 9/11 attacks on November 8, 2001. See www.newecon.org/aflcioresolution11801 .html. The statement attempts to mix a condemnation of the terrorist attacks with a call for national defense and an appeal to the president and Congress to address the worsening situation for workers. While supporting a military response to the terrorist attacks (rather than the covert action or criminal justice approaches called for by many experts in terrorism), the statement attempts to warn against anti-Arab and anti-Muslim prejudices, as well as advocate development of a global justice agenda.

5. See www.aflcio.org/aboutus/thisistheaflcio/convention/2005/res_53.cfm.

6. For an article on the convention resolution and the work of U.S. Labor Against the War, see www.uslaboragainstwar.org/article.php?id = 8626.

7. However, two proposals related to U.S. foreign policy were quietly circulated within the AFL-CIO. One suggested that representatives of the Israeli labor federation, the Histadrut, and the Palestine General Federation of Trade Unions be invited to participate in an AFL-CIO Executive Council discussion of the Israeli/Palestinian conflict to enable the council to gain a better understanding of the conflict. (For more on Histadrut, see www.histadrut.org.il/serve/ Union/Folder_Template.asp?Folder_ID = 9999&ImgOn = 6&Curr_Folder = 233&inverse = 2&proj = &num = ; on the Palestinian federation, see www .pgftu.org/.) The second proposal suggested inviting leaders of several key national labor centers from the Global South to attend an Executive Council meeting to describe perceptions of the United States in the Global South. One

national labor center unofficially expressed interest in participating in such a discussion. However, both proposals went nowhere.

8. The leaders envisioned a form of international tripartism, for lack of a better term, that would engage labor, government, and business.

13. RESTLESSNESS IN THE RANKS

1. Shea went to the AFL-CIO to work with Donahue, who had been a close ally of Sweeney's before 1995. When Donahue took over after Kirkland's resignation, Shea became chief of staff of the AFL-CIO and, in effect, the person running Donahue's campaign for president of the AFL-CIO.

2. The protocol of the union movement frowns on recruiting individuals away from the union in which they are employed without the express permission of the principal officer of that union. This taboo does not apply to competing unions. Rather, an international or national union should not recruit someone from one of its locals, nor should the AFL-CIO recruit from its affiliates without permission. To ignore this protocol is an insult—and sometimes more.

3. *Core jurisdiction* is the core or traditional membership sector of one's organization. Thus, the core jurisdiction of the American Federation of State, County, and Municipal Employees is public-sector workers rather than autoworkers.

4. The complaints ranged from criticism of specific departments to criticism of individuals. Affiliates grew tired of staff presentations to the AFL-CIO Executive Council, for example, so much so that in the presplit debate, the American Federation of Teachers openly suggested that the council needed fewer presentations and more genuine discussion. Some affiliate presidents charged that AFL-CIO staff members were telling them what to do rather than working alongside them.

5. Sweeney's close relationship with former Teamster president Ron Carey was open. In the scandal that brought down Carey, allegations emerged that union leaders from other affiliates, as well as AFL-CIO secretary-treasurer Richard Trumka, had meddled in the internal affairs of the Teamsters. Though Trumka was never indicted and no evidence of his involvement surfaced, the new Teamsters leadership under James Hoffa, Jr., let its view be known that the national AFL-CIO had been involved in Teamster internal affairs. The Hoffa administration kept its distance from the AFL-CIO and made its skepticism of the Sweeney administration apparent.

6. The New Unity Partnership was the first public bloc of unions to challenge Sweeney, but it did so somewhat indirectly.

7. Class collaborationism is a view and practice built on the idea that unions and capitalists do not have contradictory interests and should thus eventually submerge differences and jointly pursue their interests. Gompers was the quintessential class collaborationist in that, though he believed that workers need unions and unions should strike hostile employers, he was convinced that the long-term interests of unions lay in getting along with capital and ignoring the reality of class struggle.

8. A "Left project," as we see it, would embrace the idea of a radical challenge to capitalism and seek to transform the current system and eventually eliminate oppressions.

9. SEIU had the most clearly articulated views on what the union movement needed/needs to do. Other unions associated with either the New Unity Partnership or, later, Change to Win tended to align themselves with these views or remain silent about differences. In some cases, as in Janice Fine's interview in the *Nation* with key people in the union movement, leaders within Change to Win have ignored obvious differences within the coalition.

10. The Change to Win Federation does not use the term *solidarity*. We understand that the organization based this decision on the results of focus groups by at least one affiliate, which revealed that U.S. workers do not understand the word *solidarity* but do understand the word *unity*. Thus, Change to Win has expunged the word *solidarity* from its lexicon. We will speak to this question later, but we hold that the choice is not just a semantic one.

14. CHANGE TO WIN

1. For Vavi's remarks on September 27, 2004, see www.cosatu.org.za/speeches/2004/zv20040927.htm.

2. The literature on this question of mergers, particularly on the Australian experience, has been in circulation for some years, which makes one wonder why no one presented it during the AFL-CIO debate. See, for example, Gerard Griffin, "Union Mergers in Australia: Top-Down Strategic Restructuring," in *Working Paper No. 80*, National Key Centre in Industrial Relations, Monash University, Melbourne, April 2002; Bernard Ebbinghaus, "Ever Larger Unions: Organizational Restructuring and Its Impact on Union Confederations," *Industrial Relations Journal* 34, no. 5 (2003); Magnus Sverke, Gary N. Chaison, and Anders Sjoberg, "Do Union Mergers Affect the Members? Short- and Long-Term Effects on Attitudes and Behavior," *Economic and Industrial Democracy* 25, no. 1 (2004). For more on the attack on Australian labor, see an October 2005 radio interview with Australian Labor Party leader Kim Beazley, www.alp.org.au/media/1005/riloo120.php.

3. Consider, for example, the debacle of the Southern California grocery workers' strike of 2004.

4. Edna Bonacich and Fernando Gapasin have written on these power dynamics in "The Strategic Challenge of Organizing Manufacturing Workers in the Global/Flexible Capitalism," in *Unions in a Globalized Environment: Changing Borders, Organizational Boundaries, and Social Roles,* ed. Bruce Nissen, 163–88 (Armonk, N.Y.: M. E. Sharpe, 2002). Bonacich also discusses the topic in her forthcoming book with Jake B. Wilson, *Getting the Goods: Ports, Labor, and the Logistics Revolution* (Ithaca, N.Y.: Cornell University Press, 2008).

5. Janice Fine, "Debating Labor's Future," *Nation*, August 1, 2005.

6. In an important article, labor activists and theoreticians Mark Erlich and Jeff Grabelsky examine the building trades industry and the problems facing the union movement in that sector. They point out that the nonunion sector has less "craft" identification than the union sector does, thus raising intriguing questions about forms of organization and approaches toward organizing. For such reasons, we believe that unions must embrace flexibility and experimentation in forms of organizing and organization. See "Standing at a Crossroads: The Building Trades in the Twenty-first Century," *Labor History,* November 2005.

7. This latter point is based on the quite reasonable conclusion that many global union federations are creatures of another era—in some cases co-opted by Cold War trade unionism—and have become inefficient bureaucracies. In practical terms, however, one must distinguish between the current leaderships of these global union federations and the institutions themselves.

8. A Wobbly was a member of the Industrial Workers of the World.

9. Paul Buhle, *Taking Care of Business: Samuel Gompers, George Meany, Lane Kirkland and the Tragedy of American Labor* (New York: Monthly Review Press, 1999), 77.

10. Though this line of thought may seem fanciful, when one views the domestic consolidation of several CTW unions and the elimination of practical local autonomy and democratic control, one must ask whether such a vision has international implications.

11. Kent Wong, "Interview with John Wilhelm," *New Labor Forum* (Spring 2005): 82–83.

12. Colin Powell is cut from a similar cloth, though his position on unions is unclear. Nevertheless, Powell has taken pro-choice and pro–affirmative action stands, and his positions have had no resonance in the Republican Party.

13. Before the convention, the AFL-CIO had been paralyzed and unable to take a stand on the war. During the 2004 elections, the leadership even told union campaigners not to take stands on foreign policy for fear of being divisive.

14. See the discussion on a possible alternative strategy in Danny Glover and Bill Fletcher, Jr., "Visualizing a Neo-Rainbow," *Nation*, February 14, 2005. A longer version of the same article is "The Case for a Neo-Rainbow Electoral Strategy," *Souls* 7, no. 2 (Spring 2005): 51–62.

15. Both of us have known Andy Stern for well over a decade and at various points have been close to him. We are among those who have been both surprised and unsettled by his ideological and political trajectory.

16. Jay Whitehead, "Is Outsourcing the New Union Movement?" *HRO Today*, April 2005.

17. Economic determinism is the philosophical view of the inevitability of certain economic processes over which humans can have little or no influence. It is a form of fatalism and assumes that the economy has its own laws, which are rarely, if ever, subject to human intervention.

18. Andrew Stern, "Union Split," interview by Ron Insana, *Street Signs*, CNBC, August 1, 2005.

19. Roberta Wood, "Change to Win Holds Founding Convention," September 29, 2005, www.pww.org/article/articleprint/7801/.

20. Andrew Stern, interview by Lesley Stahl, *60 Minutes*, CBS, May 14, 2006, www.cbsnews.com/stories/2006/05/12/60minutes/main1614451.shtml.

15. ANGER, COMPROMISE, AND THE PARALYSIS OF THE SWEENEY COALITION

1. "Sweeney response" is a shorthand way of describing the point of view of the AFL-CIO leadership and those aligned with it. The term does not, how-

ever, speak to or assume a consistency of views among the forces who opposed, and still oppose, the Change to Win coalition.

2. SEIU president Andy Stern issued two controversial statements. The first said, in effect, that a loss by presidential candidate John Kerry might not be terrible because it could trigger the sort of crisis necessary to transform the Democratic Party. This—supposedly—off-the-record comment created a stir in both parties' campaign circles as well as within organized labor. Stern later backed away from the statement, claiming that people had misunderstood his comments, which were nothing more than musings. The second break in the cease-fire was Stern's speech at the June 2004 SEIU convention, in which he declared that if the AFL-CIO did not change, SEIU would consider leaving the federation: "It is time and it is so long overdue that we join with our union allies and either transform the AFL-CIO—or build something stronger that can really change workers' lives" (speech delivered June 21, 2004, in San Francisco, www.labornet.org/news/0604/stern.htm).

3. *Winning for Working Families: Recommendations from the Officers of the AFL-CIO for Uniting and Strengthening the Union Movement,* April 2005, 3, www.workinglife.org/filebin/fol/Winning_Working_Families.pdf.

4. Some people argue that local debates did transpire, particularly under the sponsorship of central labor councils. This statement is both true and not so true. Yes, certain groups organized debates, but no one brought this issue to the members in a way that promoted genuine discussion—one relevant to the lives of the members. Certain positions on both sides did change as a result of the debate, but the core positions did not change. This tendency to hold fast to the fundamentals makes sense, in a perverse way, if the aim of the CTW process was to force Sweeney to step down so that a new group could step in and change the structure of the AFL-CIO. However, as we have said, at least some parties in this struggle had no intention of seeking a resolution because they favored a split, seeing it as the best course for the union movement.

5. SEIU and UNITE HERE! were and are two of the most active unions in organizing initiatives, a fact not lost on sections of the media.

6. *Winning for Working Families,* 2.

7. Though CTW forces were irritated by the notion that their ideas didn't differ much from those of the Sweeney team, independent commentators tended to draw this conclusion.

8. *Winning for Working Families,* 18–26.

16. LEFT BEHIND

1. The strategy of the United Food and Commercial Workers was similar to the approach the UAW has historically taken: identifying one company as the lead company for negotiations and then using that company to set a pattern.

2. The Elected Leader Task Force was a group of leaders that formed during the period of the Organizing Institute but continued into the Sweeney era and Bensinger's tenure as organizing director for the AFL-CIO. The task force brought together pro-organizing union leaders, largely from local unions but

also from the national and international unions, to explore solutions to the issues facing their unions. This approach was innovative and certainly built a bond among its participants.

3. The tensions between the two unions played out well after CTW split from the AFL-CIO, ironically, when SEIU president Andy Stern, to the surprise of most observers, embraced Wal-Mart as a partner in the fight for universal health care.

4. Constituency Groups were organizations that received support from the AFL-CIO. They included union members such as the A. Philip Randolph Institute, the Asian Pacific American Labor Alliance, the Coalition of Black Trade Unionists, the Coalition of Labor Union Women, the Labor Council for Latin American Advancement, and Pride At Work.

5. In fact, at a very late point in the process, Sweeney invited several foreign labor leaders to an Executive Council meeting. However, he reportedly had to cancel the invitations when at least two CTW leaders objected and suggested that the presence of foreign labor leaders would interfere with the time necessary for council members to talk with one another.

6. Longtime labor activist Harry Kelber made such a proposal.

7. At the May 2005 convention of the Coalition of Black Trade Unionists, the organization's leadership did not want the convention to go on record against a split. Leaders of the Asian Pacific American Labor Alliance were also reluctant to go on record against a split. In both cases, leaders were clearly aware of the potential damage of a split. However, they also didn't want to appear to be taking a side in the debate.

8. See Philip S. Foner's discussion of the emergence of Black union leadership in *Organized Labor and the Black Worker, 1619–1973* (New York: Praeger, 1974), 231–32.

9. The legendary A. Philip Randolph, leader of the Brotherhood of Sleeping Car Porters, had to fight against marginalization in the African American movement. See the discussion of this struggle in William Harris, *Keeping the Faith: A. Philip Randolph, Milton P. Webster and the Brotherhood of Sleeping Car Porters* (Urbana: University of Illinois Press, 1977).

17. THE NEED FOR SOCIAL JUSTICE UNIONISM

1. Several interesting experiments have taken place in labor-community work, including that of the Packinghouse Workers, which deployed its staff and members to build community-based organizations. Many consider the work of Saul Alinsky and the Back of the Yards Neighborhood Council to be the seminal work in linking labor and community. Though this work deideologized radical activity and substituted apparently neutral politics, it was nevertheless critically important in taking on entrenched forces in Chicago. Efforts to create links between a union and its community have also taken place in St. Louis. For an interesting look at the efforts by a St. Louis local of the Teamsters to implement a community-organizing approach, see R. Bussel, "'A Trade Union-Oriented War on the Slums': Harold Gibbons, Ernest Calloway and the St. Louis Teamsters in the 1960s," *Labor History* 44, no. 1 (February 2003). Looking at this

question from a different vantage point, however, one can identify the 1968 Memphis sanitation workers' strike or the 1969 Charleston, South Carolina, hospital strike as quintessential examples of a labor-community alliance.

2. *Community unionism* is an ambiguous term—no criticism is implied—that covers a variety of ways in which unions engage with the community and community-based organizations. See, for example, Amanda Tattersall, "Union-Community Coalitions and Community Unionism: Developing a Framework for the Role of Union-Community Relationships in Union Renewal," www.crimt .org/2eSite_renouveau/Samedi_PDF/Tattersall.pdf. See also Andy Banks, "The Power and Promise of Community Unionism," *Labor Research Review* 18 (1992): 17–32. This term can refer to either the intensity and scope of interaction with the community or the manner in which a union involves its members in the work and struggles of a community.

3. This group evolved into an independent organization and eventually changed its name to Neighborhood Assistance Corporation of America. See www.naca.com/index_flash.pbl.

4. Interestingly, Local 26 of HERE was unable to translate its significant success in contract campaigns into success in new organizing. When Bozzotto had a falling-out with the Massachusetts AFL-CIO, and later with many progressives in the greater Boston area, his influence declined and so did that of the local.

5. The campaign has some community advisors, but this arrangement is not the same as building a coalition or bloc.

6. The San Francisco Central Labor Council continues to use the Labor/ Neighbor approach.

7. We recommend Jennifer Gordon's instructive analysis in *Suburban Sweatshops: The Fight for Immigrant Rights* (Cambridge, Mass.: Harvard University Press, 2005), which addresses some of these questions. Though Gordon focuses particularly on the workers' centers and the immigrant-rights movement, she offers some lessons that have broader implications and are relevant to our thesis.

8. Jeremy Rifkin and Randy Barber, *The North Shall Rise Again: Pension, Politics and Power in the 1980s* (Boston: Beacon Press, 1978).

9. During the 1980s, Massachusetts conducted an interesting experiment under Governor Michael Dukakis called the Cooperative Regional Industrial Laboratory. This project, under the oversight of the state's secretary of labor, was something of a social democratic experiment in regional economic planning. State leaders never expanded the experiment statewide, though some activists in Boston's Black community contemplated using a version of the model for economic development in Boston. A variant of this approach appeared in the Dudley Street Neighborhood Initiative in Boston, which focused on community renewal. The achievements of the initiative were substantial (see www.dsni.org).

10. See Danny Glover and Bill Fletcher, Jr., "Visualizing a Neo-Rainbow," *Nation*, February 14, 2005.

11. Even in their most advanced conceptions, union political organizations are constituted by and for union members. In some cases, participants may be members of a specific union; in other cases, they may be members of different unions, coming from central labor councils, for example. We do not suggest doing away with these organizations. We simply point out their structural and

political limitations, particularly the difficulties they pose in establishing a social-political bloc.

One interesting AFLCIO project, Working America (www.workingamerica .org), seeks to combine a national-level project modeled on the Labor/ Neighbor program with an associate member program (pioneered in creative fashion by the CWA more than a decade ago). Led by Karen Nussbaum, former AFL-CIO director of the Working Women's Department and well-known as the founder of 9-to-5 (the organization of women office workers), Working America is an attempt to organize nonunion workers apart from a specific workplace. In some respects, it mirrors the American Association of Retired Persons (AARP). The project aims to reach workers who, for any number of reasons, are not in a union but wish to be part of the union movement. Some unions, such as SEIU, have union-specific programs along these lines (see, for example, www.purple ocean.org) that reach beyond their existing membership. Though these efforts help reframe the existing trade union movement, they are not equivalent to campaigns that seek to build a political-social bloc.

12. Steve Meacham of City Life/Vida Urbana, telephone conversation with Bill Fletcher, Jr., November 6, 2006.

13. Ruth Needleman describes the struggle within the United Steel Workers, led by African American workers in the National Ad Hoc Committee, in *Black Freedom Fighters in Steel: The Struggle for Democratic Unionism* (Ithaca, N.Y.: ILR Press/Cornell University Press, 2003).

14. This analysis draws from Nicos Poulantzas's notion of power. Power is not static and does not attach itself consistently to a specific position or institution; it is not separate from the person holding the position. Thus, during one person's tenure, the vice presidency of a union might be a figurehead position, whereas in someone else's hands, the position might suddenly acquire the power to get something done.

15. With this strategy, organizing workers into unions becomes a piece of a larger social justice partnership.

18. THE NEED FOR A GLOBAL OUTLOOK

1. For example, see Lawrence Mishel, Jared Bernstein, and Sylvia Allegretto, *The State of Working America 2004/2005*, Economic Policy Institute (Ithaca, N.Y.: ILR Press/Cornell University Press, 2005).

2. Jon Liss and David Staples, "New Folks on the Historic Bloc—Worker Centers and Municipal Socialism" (unpublished, 2003), available from Jon Liss at Tenants and Workers United, jliss@twsc.org.

3. See, for example, Rick Fantasia, *Cultures of Solidarity: Consciousness, Action, and Contemporary American Workers* (Berkeley: University of California Press, 1988), 226–45; Bill Fletcher, Jr., and Richard Hurd, "Beyond the Organizing Model: The Transformation Process in Local Unions," in *Organizing to Win,* ed. Kate Bronfenbrenner, Sheldon Friedman, Richard Hurd, Rudolph Oswald, and Ronald Seeber (Ithaca, N.Y.: ILR Press/Cornell University Press, 1998), 37–53; Bill Fletcher, Jr., and Richard Hurd, "Political Will, Local Union Transformation and the Organizing Imperative," in *Which Direction for Organized*

Labor? ed. Bruce Nissen, 191–216 (Detroit: Wayne State University Press, 1999); Michael Eisenscher, "Labor: Turning the Corner Will Take More Than Mobilization," in *The Transformation of U.S. Unions: Voices, Visions, and Strategies from the Grassroots,* ed Ray M. Tillman and Michael S. Cummings, 61–85 (Boulder, Colo.: Lynne Rienner, 1999); Bill Fletcher and Richard W. Hurd, "Is Organizing Enough? Race, Gender, and Union Culture," *New Labor Forum* 6 (Spring/ Summer 2000): 59–69; Bill Fletcher and Richard Hurd, "Overcoming Obstacles to Transformation: Challenges on the Way to a New Unionism," in *Rekindling the Movement: Labor's Quest for Relevance in the Twenty-first Century,* ed. Harry Katz, Lowell Turner, and Richard Hurd (Ithaca, N.Y.: ILR Press/Cornell University Press, 2001); and Paul Johnston, "Citizenship Movement Unionism: For the Defense of Local Communities in the Global Age," in *Unions in a Globalized Environment: Changing Borders, Organizational Boundaries, and Social Roles,* ed. Bruce Nissen, 236–63 (Armonk, N.Y.: M. E. Sharpe, 2002).

4. Altruistic solidarity is the sort of work most associated with the AFL-CIO–sponsored American Center for International Labor Solidarity (generally known as the Solidarity Center). Most of its funding comes from the U.S. government, a fact that is a source of great controversy in the U.S. union movement.

5. Abandonment of the term *solidarity* is not a matter of semantics for us. The term *unity* does not have an identical *political* meaning in discussions of international relations between movements.

6. The North American Free Trade Agreement, for instance, has been incredibly destructive in Mexico, undermining the agricultural sector and leading to the migration of hundreds of thousands of farmers and agricultural workers, first into the cities of Mexico and, often, later to the United States.

7. See Greg Albo, "The Old and New Economics of Imperialism," in *Socialist Register 2004: The New Imperial Challenge,* ed. Leo Panitch and Colin Leys, 88–113 (New York: Monthly Review Press, 2003).

8. Separate discussions of South-South relations have taken place among progressive forces in the Global South and have come to different conclusions.

9. *National populist* is a term advanced by the Egyptian theorist Samir Amin to describe movements in the Global South that were anti-imperialist but not socialist. Some of these movement, like the one in Algeria, grew out of national liberation wars; others, such as the one in India, resulted from significant independence movements; and still others, like those in Egypt and Libya, were the result of military insurrections. See "For Struggles Global and National: An Interview with Samir Amin," *ZNet,* January 31, 2003, www.zmag.org/content/showarticle.cfm?SectionID = 36&ItemID = 2934.

10. For example, the Mozambique Liberation Front (FRELIMO), after flirting with both the Soviet Union and China, fully embraced the Soviet bloc in the early 1980s. With the fall of the Soviet system, the FRELIMO leadership rushed quickly to embrace neoliberalism (by adopting free-market economics). In the process, FRELIMO cast off its trade union federation (OTM—the Portuguese acronym for the Organization of Mozambican Workers), which became a fully independent organization. This shift created major strategic challenges for the OTM, which had been used to a formal connection with the governing party. Nevertheless, the governing party was moving toward full acceptance of capitalism with no special

provisions for the workers. OTM is now attempting to define itself and its relationship to the project of national development.

11. This tension between social movements and governments is taking a most dramatic form in Zimbabwe, where a sharp struggle is under way between the Zimbabwe Congress of Trade Unions (ZCTU) and the government of President Robert Mugabe. Mugabe's administration charges that forces such as the ZCTU are betraying the Zimbabwe revolution by standing against him. In effect, the ZCTU says the same thing about Mugabe.

12. See, for example, Alma H. Young and Kristine B. Miranne, "Global Economic Crisis and Caribbean Women's Survival Strategies," in *Caribbean Labor and Politics: Legacies of Cheddi Jagan and Michael Manley,* ed. Perry Mars and Alma H. Young, 183–89 (Detroit: Wayne State University Press, 2004).

13. This antiwoman tendency also appears in other religious fundamentalisms.

14. Waterman has written a great deal on social movement unionism and offers suggestions similar to those in this book. See, for instance, Peter Waterman, "Needed: A New International Labour Movement for (and against) a Globalised, Networked Capitalism," *Global Solidarity Dialogue,* www.antenna .nl/~waterman/needed.html.

15. The Irish model that SEIU's Andy Stern finds so attractive has been actively promoted in South Africa. Much of the trade union movement, even when finding commonalities with the South African government, looks upon this model with a high degree of skepticism.

16. One example of such deadly consequences is the Chilean coup in 1973, where the progressive forces supporting the heroic president Salvador Allende underestimated the willingness of the political Right to use extralegal means to undermine democratic rule. They equally underestimated the force with which the Chilean state would react to the efforts of the Unidad Popular government of Allende to introduce change.

17. Alfonso Velásquez, member of the National Executive Committee of Colombia's largest trade union federation, CUT. Quoted in the U.S./Labor Education in the Americas Project, www.usleap.org/Colombia/ColombiaHome.html.

18. Consider, for example, the "Bamako Appeal," an international initiative that launched just before the World Social Forum/Africa in early 2006 in Mali. The document lays out the parameters for a redefined global justice movement, including ways to redefine the tasks of the labor movement. See www.forum tiersmonde.net/fren/Forums/FSM/fsm_bamako/appel_bamako_en.htm.

19. REALIZING SOCIAL JUSTICE UNIONISM

1. See, for instance, conservative commentator George Will's column "Searching for Labor's Role," *Washington Post,* December 29, 2005, for a remarkable embrace of "transformation" by a conservative. The terms under which SEIU's transformation have been unfolding are completely consistent not only with Gompers's view but with the sort of apolitical unionism that many conservatives would like to see emerge (if they are willing to accept any sort of unionism).

2. In fee-paying arrangements, individuals do not join the unions but pay an amount that allegedly covers the union's cost of pursuing collective-bargain-

ing rights. Our dismissal of the possibilities of top-down transformation speaks to the difference we have with SEIU and several other unions that have imposed changes from the top in a manner that we half-jokingly describe as *nonideological Stalinism*. In other words, they introduce dramatic changes in the structure of the union without first building a political consensus to justify the changes.

3. The membership of this local subsequently divided between SEIU and the American Federation of State, County, and Municipal Employees.

4. Clyde Summers, "The Kenneth M. Piper Lecture: Unions without Majority—a Black Hole?" *Chicago-Kent Law Review* 66 (1990): 531.

5. See Charles J. Morris, "Members-Only Collective Bargaining: A Back-to-Basics Approach to Union Organizing," in *Justice on the Job: Perspectives on the Erosion of Collective Bargaining in the United States,* ed. Richard N. Block, Sheldon Friedman, Michelle Kaminski, and Andy Levin (Kalamazoo, Mich.: W. E. Upjohn Institute for Employment Research, 2006). This book is a collection of articles on the plight of today's working class and possible ways to address workplace injustice.

6. Solidarity Charters are local agreements that permit central labor councils to include unions that are not affiliated with the AFL-CIO.

7. Even the UNITE HERE! merger has had difficulties melding different organizational cultures, despite the leaders' tending to agree about the general direction of the unified organization.

8. Judith Stepan-Norris and Maurice Zeitlin, *Left Out: Reds and America's Industrial Unions* (Cambridge: Cambridge University Press, 2003), especially 159–88.

9. Our use of the term *competitive* to describe the political atmosphere within unions differs from CTW advocates' use of the term. We are not speaking solely or mainly of *organizational* competition (for example, the competition between two auto dealerships) but rather *political* competition at the level of vision and direction. Some CTW advocates have suggested that the mere existence of competing labor organizations strengthens the union movement. This view has little historical support. Organizational competition has sometimes been one aspect of a more substantive competition, such as the competition between the AFL and the CIO in the 1930s and 1940s. In other cases, such as the United Farm Workers' competition with the Teamsters in the early 1970s, the competition was territorial and ideological and served the interests of the growers. This competition in no way helped the UFW grow. "Competition" is not an abstraction; it must be critically analyzed in each concrete circumstance.

10. See Peter Medoff and Holly Sklar, *Streets of Hope: The Fall and Rise of an Urban Neighborhood* (Boston: South End Press, 1994). "DSNI" was an innovative community organizing project.

11. See John S. Alquist's thought-provoking paper in which he asks whether democracy is possible within national labor centers: "Who Sits at the Table in the House of Labor? Rank-and-File Citizenship in Union Confederations" (paper presented at the Conference on Union Democracy Re-examined, University of Washington, February 24–24, 2006; modified June 8, 2006).

12. See, for example, Robert D. Putman, *Bowling Alone: The Collapse and Revival of American Community* (New York: Simon and Schuster, 2000), 48–64.

13. Ibid., 338.

14. The revision of labor laws is a strategic change needed for union revival. Dorothee Benz, "Sisyphus and the State," *Dissent*, Fall 2004, 78–83.

15. Fernando Gapasin and Edna Bonacich, "The Strategic Challenge of Organizing Manufacturing Workers in the Global/Flexible Capitalism," in *Unions in a Globalized Environment: Changing Borders, Organizational Boundaries, and Social Roles,* ed. Bruce Nissen (Armonk, N.Y.: M. E. Sharpe, 2002), 163–87.

16. Gabor Steingart, "A Casualty of Globalization: Death of the Unions," *Spiegel Online,* October 27, 2006, www.spiegel.de/international/0,1518, 445043,00.html.

17. Eduardo Cue, "The Hugo Factor: Venezuela's Firebrand President Seems Stronger Than Ever," *U.S. News and World Report,* January 30, 2006, 26–28.

APPENDIX B

1. Fernando Gapasin, "Race, Gender and Other Problems of Unity for the American Working Class, *Race, Gender and Class* 4, no. 1 (1996): 41–61; also, "Local Union Transformation: Analyzing Issues of Race, Gender, Class and Democracy," *Social Justice* 25, no. 3 (1999): 13–30.

2. Robert Asher and Charles Stephenson, eds., *Labor Divided: Race and Ethnicity in United States Labor Struggles, 1835–1960* (Albany: State University of New York Press, 1990); Dorothy Sue Cobble, "Remaking Unions for the New Majority," in *Women and Unions,* ed. Dorothy Sue Cobble, 3–24 (Ithaca, N.Y.: ILR Press/Cornell University Press, 1993).

3. Mike Davis, *Prisoners of the American Dream: Politics and Economy in the History of the U.S. Working Class* (London: Verso, 1986).

4. Richard Flacks, "Think Globally, Act Politically: Some Notes toward New Movement Strategy," in *Cultural Politics and Social Movements,* ed. Marcy Darnovsky, Barbara Leslie Epstein, and Richard Flacks, 251–63 (Philadelphia: Temple University Press, 1995).

5. Michael Omi and Howard Winant, *Racial Formation in the United States: From the 1960s to the 1990s,* 2nd ed. (New York: Routledge, 1994).

6. Richard J. Herrnstein and Charles Murray, *The Bell Curve: Intelligence and Class Structure in American Life* (New York: Free Press, 1994).

7. Omi and Winant, *Racial Formation.*

8. Ibid., 56.

9. On ethnicity theory, see Nathan Glazer, *Affirmative Discrimination: Ethnic Inequality and Public Policy* (New York: Basic Books, 1975). For a discussion of the limitations of the theory, see Edna Bonacich, "A Theory of Ethnic Antagonism: The Split Labor Market," *American Sociological Review* 37, no. 5 (1972): 547–59.

10. Howard Winant, "Race: Theory, Culture, and Politics in the United States Today," in Darnovsky, Epstein, and Flacks, *Cultural Politics,* 174–88.

11. Ruth Needleman, "Comments," in Cobble, *Women and Unions,* 406–13.

12. Cobble, *Women and Unions.*

13. The statistics in this paragraph come from Lois S. Gray, "The Route to the Top: Female Union Leaders and Union Policy," in Cobble, *Women and Unions,* 378–93.

14. Pamela Roby and Lynet Uttal, "Putting It All Together: The Dilemmas of Rank-and-File Union Leaders," in Cobble, *Women and Unions,* 363–77.

15. Roby and Uttal, "Putting It All Together"; Gray, "Route to the Top"; and Needleman, "Comments."

16. Alice H. Cook, Val R. Lorwin, and Arlene Kaplan Daniels, *The Most Difficult Revolution: Women in Trade Unions* (Ithaca, N.Y.: ILR Press/Cornell University Press, 1993).

17. Angela P. Harris, "Race and Essentialism in Feminist Legal Theory," in *Critical Race Theory: The Cutting Edge,* ed. Richard Delgado, 261–74 (Philadelphia: Temple University Press, 1995).

18. Paul Johnston, *Success While Others Fail: Social Movement Unionism and the Public Workplace* (Ithaca, N.Y.: ILR Press/Cornell University Press, 1994).

19. James D. Thompson, *Organizations in Action* (New York: McGraw-Hill, 1967).

20. Ruth Frankenberg, *The Social Construction of Whiteness: White Women, Race Matters* (Minneapolis: University of Minnesota Press, 1993).

21. Ibid.

22. Ibid. See also Chip Smith, *The Cost of Privilege* (Fayetteville, N.C.: Camino Press, 2007), 11–21.

23. David Roediger, *Towards the Abolition of Whiteness: Essays on Race, Politics, and Working Class History* (London: Verso, 1996), 1–17.

24. Smith, *Cost of Privilege,* 152–70, 227–30.

BIBLIOGRAPHY

AFL-CIO Constitution. Amended July 25–28, 2005. www.aflcio.org/aboutns/ thisistheaflcio/constitution/.

Ahmed, A. Muhammad. "The League of Revolutionary Black Workers (A Historical Study)." www.geocities.com/CapitolHill/Lobby/2379/lrbw.htm.

Albo, Greg. "The Old and New Economics of Imperialism." In *Socialist Register 2004: The New Imperial Challenge,* edited by Leo Panitch and Colin Leys, 88–113. New York: Monthly Review Press, 2003.

Allen, Theodore W. *The Invention of the White Race.* Vol. 1, *Racial Oppression and Social Control.* London: Verso, 1994.

———. *The Invention of the White Race.* Vol. 2, *The Origin of Racial Oppression in Anglo-America.* London: Verso, 1997.

Amin, Samir. Interview, *ZNet,* January 31, 2003. www.zmag.org/content/ showarticle.cfm?SectionID = 36&ItemID = 2934.

Asher, Robert, and Charles Stephenson, eds. *Labor Divided: Race and Ethnicity in United States Labor Struggles 1835–1960.* Albany: State University of New York Press, 1990.

Banks, Andy. "The Power and Promise of Community Unionism." *Labor Research Review* 18 (1992): 17–31.

Banks, Andy, and Jack Metzgar. "Participating in Management: Union Organizing on a New Terrain." *Labor Research Review* 14 (1989): 1–42.

Benz, Dorothee. "Sisyphus and the State." *Dissent,* Fall 2004.

Berlet, Chip, and Matthew N. Lyons. *Right-Wing Populism in America: Too Close for Comfort.* New York: Guilford Press, 2000.

Bluestone, Barry, and Bennett Harrison. *Deindustrialization of America: Plant Closings, Community Abandonment and the Dismantling of Basic Industry.* New York: Basic Books, 1982.

Bonacich, Edna. "A Theory of Ethnic Antagonism: The Split Labor Market." *American Sociological Review* 37, no. 5 (1972): 547–59.

———. "The Past, Present and Future in Split Labor Market Theory." In *Research in Race and Ethnic Relations,* edited by Cora Bagley Marrett and Cheryl Leggon, 20–62. Greenwich, Conn.: JAI Press, 1979.

Brecher, Jeremy. *Strike!* Boston: South End Press, 1997.

Bronfenbrenner, Kate, Sheldon Friedman, Richard Hurd, Rudolph Oswald, and Ronald Seeber, eds. *Organizing to Win.* Ithaca, N.Y.: ILR Press/Cornell University Press, 1998.

Buhle, Paul. *Taking Care of Business: Samuel Gompers, George Meany, Lane Kirkland and the Tragedy of American Labor.* New York: Monthly Review Press, 1999.

Burbach, Roger, and William Robinson. "The Fin de Siècle Debate: Globalization as Epochal Shift." *Science & Society* 63, no. 1 (Spring 1999): 10–39. www.globalpolicy.org/globaliz/define/findesie.htm.

Césaire, Aimé. *Discourse on Colonialism.* New York: Monthly Review Press, 2000.

Chaison, Gary N., and Tarique I. Nageer. "The Labour Movement/Evolution, Intervention, Stagnation, Transition: Guyana" (Spring 1998). http://members .tripod.com/~tnageer/Labour.html.

Clawson, Dan. *The Next Upsurge: Labor and the New Social Movements.* Ithaca, N.Y.: ILR Press/Cornell University Press, 2003.

Cobble, Dorothy Sue. *Women and Unions.* Ithaca, N.Y.: ILR Press/Cornell University Press, 1993.

———. "Remaking Unions for the New Majority." In Cobble, *Women and Unions,* 3–18.

Cook, Alice H., Val R. Lorwin, and Arlene Kaplan Daniels. *The Most Difficult Revolution: Women in Trade Unions.* Ithaca, N.Y.: ILR Press/Cornell University Press, 1992.

Cowie, Jefferson. *Capital Moves: RCA's 70-Year Quest for Cheap Labor.* New York: New Press, 1999.

Crosby, Jeff. "Kids Are Alright." *New Labor Forum* (Spring/Summer 2000): 35–41.

Cue, Eduardo. "The Hugo Factor: Venezuela's Firebrand President Seems Stronger Than Ever." *U.S. News and World Report,* January 30, 2006, 26–28.

Dannin, Ellen. *Taking Back the Workers' Law: How to Fight the Assault on Labor Rights.* Ithaca, N.Y.: ILR Press/Cornell University Press, 2006.

Darnovsky, Marcy, Barbara Leslie Epstein, and Richard Flacks, eds. *Cultural Politics and Social Movements.* Philadelphia: Temple University Press, 1995.

Davis, Jim, Thomas A. Hirschl, and Michael Stack, eds. *Cutting Edge: Technology, Information Capitalism and Social Revolution.* London: Verso, 1997.

Davis, Mike. *Prisoners of the American Dream: Politics and Economy in the History of the U.S. Working Class.* London: Verso, 1986.

Dubofsky, Melvyn, and Warren Van Tine, eds. *Labor Leaders in America.* Urbana: University of Illinois Press, 1987.

Dudley Street Neighborhood Initiative in Boston. www.dsni.org.

Ebbinghaus, Bernard. "Ever Larger Unions: Organizational Restructuring and Its Impact on Union Confederations." *Industrial Relations Journal* 34, no. 5 (2003).

Eisenscher, Michael. "Labor: Turning the Corner Will Take More Than Mobilization." In *The Transformation of U.S. Unions: Voices, Visions, and Strategies from the Grassroots,* edited by Ray M. Tillman and Michael S. Cummings, 61–86. Boulder, Colo.: Lynne Rienner, 1999.

Erem, Suzan, and E. Paul Durrenberger. *On the Global Waterfront: The Fight to Free the Charleston 5.* New York: Monthly Review Press, 2008.

Erlich, Mark, and Jeff Grabelsky. "Standing at a Crossroads: The Building Trades in the Twenty-first Century." *Labor History,* November 2005.

Fantasia, Rick. *Cultures of Solidarity: Consciousness, Action, and Contemporary American Workers.* Berkeley: University of California Press, 1988.

Ferguson, Thomas, and Joel Rogers. *Right Turn: The Decline of the Democrats and the Future of American Politics.* New York: Hill and Wang, 1986.

Finally Got the News. www.frif.com/new2003/fin.html.

Fine, Janice. "Debating Labor's Future." *Nation,* August 1, 2005.

Flacks, Richard. "Think Globally, Act Politically: Some Notes toward New Movement Strategy." In Darnovsky, Epstein, and Flacks, *Cultural Politics and Social Movements,* 251–63.

Fletcher, Bill, and Richard Hurd. "Beyond the Organizing Model: The Transformation Process in Local Unions." In Bronfenbrenner et al., *Organizing to Win,* 37–53.

———. "Political Will, Local Union Transformation and the Organizing Imperative." In *Which Direction for Organized Labor?* edited by Bruce Nissen, 191–216. Detroit: Wayne State University Press, 1999.

———. "Is Organizing Enough? Race, Gender, and Union Culture." *New Labor Forum* 6 (Spring/Summer 2000): 59–69.

———. "Overcoming Obstacles to Transformation: Challenges on the Way to a New Unionism." In *Rekindling the Movement: Labor's Quest for Relevance in the Twenty-first Century,* edited by Lowell Turner, Harry Katz, and Richard Hurd, 182–210. Ithaca, N.Y.: ILR Press/Cornell University Press, 2001.

Foner, Philip S. *Organized Labor and the Black Worker, 1619–1973.* New York: Praeger Publishers, 1974.

———. *History of the Labor Movement in the U.S.: The AFL in the Progressive Era, 1910–1915.* New York: International Publishers, 1980.

Foster, William Z. *History of the Communist Party of the United States.* New York: Greenwood Press, 1968.

Frankenberg, Ruth. *The Social Construction of Whiteness: White Women, Race Matters.* Minneapolis: University of Minnesota Press, 1993.

Fraser, Steven. "Sidney Hillman: Labor's Machiavelli." In Dubofsky, and Van Tine, *Labor Leaders in America,* 207–33.

Gallagher, Tom. "Labor Report: Everybody Loved it, But. . . ." www.zmag.org/zmag/articles/nov98gallagher.htm.

Gapasin, Fernando. "The Los Angeles County Federation of Labor and UCLA Labor Center: Putting Organizing on the CLC Agenda." In *Working Together to Revitalize Labor in Our Communities: Case Studies of Labor Education–Central Labor Body Collaboration,* edited by Jill Kriesky, 85–90. Orono: University of Maine, University and College Labor Education Association, 1998.

———. "The Los Angeles County Federation of Labor: A Model of Transformation or Traditional Unionism?" In *Central Labor Councils and the Revival of American Unionism,* edited by Immanuel Ness and Stuart Eimer, 82–98. Armonk, N.Y.: M. E. Sharpe, 2001.

———. "United Farm Workers." In *The Encyclopedia of Latinos and Latinas in the United States,* vol. 4, 259–61. New York: Oxford University Press, 2005.

Gapasin, Fernando, and Edna Bonacich. "The Strategic Challenge of Organizing Manufacturing Workers in the Global/Flexible Capitalism." In Nissen, *Unions in a Globalized Environment,* 163–88.

Gapasin, Fernando, and Howard Wial. "The Role of Central Labor Councils in Union Organizing in the 1990s." In Bronfenbrenner et. al., *Organizing to Win,* 54–67.

Garcia, Mario T. *Memories of Chicano History: The Life and Narrative of Bert Corona.* Berkeley: University of California Press, 1994.

Georgakas, Dan. *Detroit: I Do Mind Dying: A Study in Urban Revolution.* 2nd ed. Boston: South End Press, 1998.

Geschwender, James A. *Class, Race and Worker Insurgency: The League of Revolutionary Black Workers.* New York: Cambridge University Press, 1977.

Glazer, Nathan. *Affirmative Discrimination: Ethnic Inequality and Public Policy.* New York: Basic Books, 1975.

Glover, Danny, and Fletcher, Bill, Jr. "Visualizing a Neo-Rainbow." *Nation,* February 14, 2005. A longer version of this article is "The Case for a Neo-Rainbow Electoral Strategy." *Souls,* Spring 2005.

Gomez-Quinones, Juan. *Chicano Politics: Reality and Promise, 1940–1990.* Albuquerque: University of New Mexico Press, 1990.

Gordon, Jennifer. *Suburban Sweatshops: The Fight for Immigrant Rights.* Cambridge, Mass.: Harvard University Press, 2005.

Grabelsky, Jeff. "A New Alliance in New York State: A Progress Report on the Labor Movement's Restructuring, Capacity Building and Programmatic Work." *Working USA,* March 2007.

Gray, Lois. "The Route to the Top: Female Union Leaders and Union Policy." In Cobble, *Women and Unions,* 378–93.

Griffin, Gerard. "Union Mergers in Australia: Top-Down Strategic Restructuring." *Working Paper No. 80,* National Key Centre in Industrial Relations, Monash University, Melbourne, April 2002.

Griffith, Barbara S. *The Crisis of American Labor: Operation Dixie and the Defeat of the CIO.* Philadelphia: Temple University Press, 1988.

Halpern, Martin. *Unions, Radicals and Democratic Presidents: Seeking Social Change in the Twentieth Century.* Westport, Conn.: Praeger, 2003.

Hardt, Michael, and Antonio Negri. *Empire.* Cambridge, Mass.: Harvard University Press, 2000.

Harris, Angela P. "Race and Essentialism in Feminist Legal Theory." In *Critical Race Theory: The Cutting Edge,* edited by Richard Delgado, 261–74. Philadelphia: Temple University Press, 1995.

Harris, William. *Keeping the Faith: A. Philip Randolph, Milton P. Webster and the Brotherhood of Sleeping Car Porters.* Urbana: University of Illinois Press, 1977.

Harrison, Bennett. "Multinational Monitor." Interview, September 1988. http://multinationalmonitor.org/hyper/issues/1988/09/mm0988_05.html.

———. *Lean and Mean: The Changing Landscape of Corporate Power in the Age of Flexibility.* New York: Basic Books, 1994.

Harvey, David. *The Limits of Capital.* London: Verso, 1982.

Haughton, James. "Racism in the House of Labor." In *History Matters: The U.S. Survey Course on the Web.* http://historymatters.gmu.edu/d/7038/.

Healy, Dorothy, and Maurice Isserman. *Dorothy Healy Remembers.* New York: Oxford University Press, 1990.

Herrnstein, Richard J., and Charles Murray. *The Bell Curve: Intelligence and Class Structure in American Life.* New York: Free Press, 1994.

HoSang, Daniel. "All the Issues in Workers' Lives: Labor Confronts Race in Stamford." *NHI* (June 2000), .www.nhi.org/online/issues/111/hosang .html.

Hurd, Richard. "The Failure of Organizing, the New Unity Partnership and the Future of the Labor Movement." *Working USA,* September 2004. www .aflcio.org/aboutus/ourfuture/upload/wusa_0021.pdf.

James, Estelle. "Jimmy Hoffa: Labor Hero or Labor's Own Foe." In Dubofsky and Van Tine, *Labor Leaders in America,* 303–23.

Johnston, Paul. *Success While Others Fail: Social Movement Unionism and the Public Workplace.* Ithaca, N.Y.: ILR Press/Cornell University Press, 1994.

———. "Citizenship Movement Unionism: For the Defense of Local Communities in the Global Age." In Nissen, *Unions in a Globalized Environment,* 236–63.

Kagas, Steve. "A Critique of the Chicago School of Economics, Chile: The Laboratory Test." www.huppi.com/kangaroo/L-chichile.htm.

Keeran, Roger. *The Communist Party and the Auto Workers Unions.* Bloomington: Indiana University Press, 1980.

Klein, Naomi. *The Shock Doctrine: The Rise of Disaster Capitalism.* New York: Metropolitan Books, 2007.

Labor Community Strategy Center in Los Angeles. www. thestrategycenter.org.

Laslett, John H. M. "Samuel Gompers and the Rise of American Business Unionism." In Dubofsky and Van Tine, *Labor Leaders in America,* 62–88.

Levenstein, Harvey A. *Communism, Anticommunism, and the CIO.* Westport, Conn.: Greenwood Press, 1981.

Levy, Jacques. *César Chávez: Autobiography of La Causa.* New York: W. W. Norton, 1975.

Lichtenstein, Nelson. "Walter Reuther and the Rise of Labor-Liberalism." In Dubofsky and Van Tine, *Labor Leaders in America,* 280–302.

———. *State of the Union: A Century of American Labor.* Princeton, N.J.: Princeton University Press, 2002.

"The Lincoln Hospital Offensive." Latino Education Network Service de los barrios de las Americas. http://palante.org/04LincolnOffensive.htm.

Lipset, Seymour M., Martin A. Trow, and James S. Coleman. *Union Democracy: The Internal Politics of the International Typographical Union.* New York: Free Press, 1977 [1956].

Liss, Jon, and David Staples. "New Folks on the Historic Bloc—Worker Centers and Municipal Socialism." Unpublished manuscript, 2003. Available from Jon Liss at jliss@twsc.org.

Marcuse, Herbert. "Repressive Tolerance," 1965 essay. http://grace.evergreen .edu/~arunc/texts/frankfurt/marcuse/tolerance.pdf.

Mars, Perry, and Alma H. Young, eds. *Caribbean Labor and Politics: Legacies of Cheddi Jagan and Michael Manley.* Detroit: Wayne State University Press, 2004.

Marshall, Justice Thurgood. *Emporium Capwell Co. v Western Addition Community Organization*, 420 U.S. 50 (1975). http://caselaw.lp.findlaw.com/scripts/getcase.pl?court = us&vol = 420&invol = 50.

Michels, Robert. *Political Parties*. Glencoe, Ill.: Free Press, 1949 (1911).

Mishel, Lawrence, Jared Bernstein, and Sylvia Allegretto. *The State of Working America 2004/2005*. Economic Policy Institute. Ithaca, N.Y.: ILR Press/Cornell University Press, 2005.

Moody, Kim. *Workers in a Lean World*. London: Verso, 1997.

Morris, Charles J. "Members-Only Collective Bargaining: A Back-to-Basics Approach to Union Organizing." In *Justice on the Job: Perspectives on the Erosion of Collective Bargaining in the United States*, edited by Richard N. Block, Sheldon Friedman, Michelle Kaminski, and Andy Levin. Kalamazoo, Mich.: W. E. Upjohn Institute for Employment Research, 2006.

National Security Strategy Doctrine. September 2002. www.whitehouse.gov/nsc/nss.pdf.

Needleman, Ruth. "Comments." In Cobble, *Women and Unions*, 406–13.

———. *Black Freedom Fighters in Steel: The Struggle for Democratic Unionism*. Ithaca, N.Y.: ILR Press/Cornell University Press, 2003.

Ness, Immanuel, and Stuart Eimer, eds. *Central Labor Councils and the Revival of American Unionism: Organizing for Justice in Our Communities*. Armonk, N.Y.: M. E.Sharpe, 2001.

Nissen, Bruce, ed. *Unions in a Globalized Environment: Changing Borders, Organizational Boundaries, and Social Roles*. Armonk, N.Y.: M. E. Sharpe, 2002.

Omi, Michael, and Howard Winant. *Racial Formation in the United States: From the 1960s to the 1990s*. 2nd ed. New York: Routledge, 1994.

Palmer, David. *Organizing the Shipyards: Union Strategy in Three Northeast Ports, 1933–1945*. Ithaca, N.Y.: ILR Press/Cornell University Press, 1998.

Panitch, Leo, and Sam Gindin. "Global Capitalism and American Empire." In *Socialist Register 2004: The New Imperial Challenge*, edited by Leo Panitch and Colin Leys, 1–62. New York: Monthly Review Press, 2003.

Phelan, Craig. "William Green and the Ideal of Christian Cooperation." In Dubofsky and Van Tine, *Labor Leaders in America*, 134–59.

Poulantzas, Nicos. *Fascism and Dictatorship*. London: Verso, 1979.

Preis, Art. *Labor's Giant Step: Twenty Years of the CIO*. New York: Pathfinder Press, 1964.

Project for the New American Century. www.newamericancentury.org/statementofprinciples.htm.

Putman, Robert D. *Bowling Alone: The Collapse and Revival of American Community*. New York: Simon and Schuster, 2000.

Rifkin, Jeremy, and Randy Barber. *The North Shall Rise Again: Pension, Politics and Power in the 1980s*. Boston: Beacon Press, 1978.

Roby, Pamela, and Lynet Uttal. "Putting It All Together: The Dilemmas of Rank-and-File Union Leaders." In Cobble, *Women and Unions*, 363–77.

Roediger, David R. *The Wages of Whiteness: Race and the Making of the American Working Class*. London: Verso, 1991.

———. *Towards the Abolition of Whiteness: Essays on Race, Politics, and Working Class History*. London: Verso, 1996.

Salvatore, Nick. "Eugene V. Debs: From Trade Unionist to Socialist." In Dubofsky and Van Tine, *Labor Leaders in America*, 89–110.

Smith, Chip. *The Cost of Privilege*. Fayetteville, N.C.: Camino Press, 2007.

Snow, Edgar. *The Pattern of Soviet Power*. New York: Random House, 1945.

Stepan-Norris, Judith, and Maurice Zeitlin. *Left Out: Reds and America's Industrial Unions*. Cambridge: Cambridge University Press, 2003.

Sverke, Magnus, Gary N. Chaison, and Anders Sjoberg. "Do Union Mergers Affect the Members? Short- and Long-Term Effects on Attitudes and Behavior." *Economic and Industrial Democracy* 25, no. 1 (2004): 103–24.

Tait, Vanessa. *Poor Workers' Unions: Rebuilding Labor from Below*. Cambridge, Mass.: South End Press, 2005.

Takaki, Ronald. *From Different Shores: Perspectives on Race and Ethnicity in America*. 2nd ed. New York: Oxford University Press, 1994.

Tattersall, Amanda. "Union-Community Coalitions and Community Unionism: Developing a Framework for the Role of Union-Community Relationships in Union Renewal." www.crimt.org/2eSite_renouveau/Samedi_PDF/Tattersall.pdf.

Thomas, Robert J. *What Machines Can't Do: Politics and Technology in the Industrial Enterprise*. Berkeley: University of California Press, 1994.

Thompson, James D. *Organizations in Action*. New York: McGraw-Hill, 1967.

Van Tine, Warren R. *The Making of the Labor Bureaucrat: Union Leadership in the United States, 1870–1920*. Amherst: University of Massachusetts Press, 1973.

Vargas, Zaragosa. *Labor Rights Are Civil Rights: Mexican American Workers in Twentieth-Century America*. Princeton, N.J.: Princeton University Press, 2005.

Vavi, Zwelinzima, COSATU General Secretary. September 27, 2004, remarks. www.cosatu.org.za/speeches/2004/zv20040927.htm.

Wallach, Lori, and Michelle Sforza. *Whose Trade Organization? Corporate Globalization and the Erosion of Democracy*. Washington, D.C.: Public Citizen, 1999.

Waterman, Peter. "Needed: A New International Labour Movement for (and against) a Globalised, Networked Capitalism." *Global Solidarity Dialogue*. www.antenna.nl/~waterman/needed.html.

Watson, Hilbourne. "Guyana, Jamaica and the Cold War Project: The Transformation of Caribbean Labor." In Mars and Young, *Caribbean Labor and Politics*, 89–125.

Whitehead, Jay. "Is Outsourcing the New Union Movement?" *HRO Today*, April 2005.

Will, George. "Searching for Labor's Role." *Washington Post*, December 29, 2005.

Winant, Howard. "Race: Theory, Culture, and Politics in the United States Today." In Darnovsky et al., *Cultural Politics and Social Movements*, 174–88.

Winning for Working Families: Recommendations from the Officers of the AFL-CIO for Uniting and Strengthening the Union Movement, April 2005.

Wong, Kent. "Interview with John Wilhelm." *New Labor Forum*, Spring 2005.

Wood, Roberta. "Change to Win Holds Founding Convention." September 29, 2005. www.pww.org/article/articleprint/7801/.

Working America. www.workingamerica.org.

Young, Alma H., and Kristine B. Miranne. "Global Economic Crisis and Caribbean Women's Survival Strategies." In Mars and Young, *Caribbean Labor and Politics,* 183–89.

Zieger, Robert H. "George Meany: Labor's Organization Man." In Dubofsky and Van Tine, *Labor Leaders in America,* 324–49.

ACKNOWLEDGMENTS

There are many people we wish to acknowledge and thank. Countless people encouraged us to write this book, perceiving a need to expand the debate about the future of U.S. trade unionism and to link that debate to a renaissance of the labor movement. We wish, however, to offer a special acknowledgment to several people, none of whom should be held responsible for the content of this book. Each of them made this work stronger through the time they spent reviewing and commenting on the drafts.

Candice Cason cared enough about our project to tell us that regular folks might not get into the book unless we reorganized our presentation, and she then dedicated herself to weeks of work helping us to make our book more readable. JoAnn Sustrick, as a rank-and-file coconspirator of Fernando Gapasin in the fight for social justice and democracy in a local union, lent critical insight to history and constant enthusiasm for the project. Jerry Tucker shared his wealth of experience and his profound insights into the nature and character of working-class struggle in the United States and around the world—especially his firsthand experiences in the Staley strike and his excellent reporting of the 2005 AFL-CIO Convention. Elly Leary is past cochair of the United Auto Workers' New Directions Caucus, and our analysis benefited greatly from her experience in building a dissident movement within the bureaucratic UAW and developing strong rank-and-file leaders.

Jeff Crosby, whose thirty-plus years as a rank-and-file leader of a local union and central labor council helped him develop the model of "leadership development unionism," offered theoretical as well as practical help in developing our book. Jon Liss contributed by modeling how to carry out a struggle for municipal power for working people. The model of municipal socialism that he and David Staples have developed is an important theoretical contribution that strengthened our book. Fred Hirsch has been a living example for Fernando of what internationalism means in practice; he provided critical insight and encouraged both of us to write this book. Edna Bonacich, a coauthor of articles about building working-class movements in this era of global capitalism, lent theoretical insights that influence our argument.

Jeff Hermanson's excitement and passion for the struggle came through in his enthusiasm for this project. Gene Bruskin's critique of our manuscript drew from years of commitment to antiracist working-class struggle. Sam Gindin gave us the benefit of his insights, born of years as one of the chief theoreticians of progressive trade unionism in Canada. Cameron Barron took the time to methodically review our manuscript because he wanted to see it work. Bama Athreya's internationalism touches every project, with a bluntness that is always sobering. Michael Yates has been a constant source of theoretical clarity and an enthusiastic supporter of our efforts to theorize and write about our practice in the U.S. movements for social justice. We appreciate Kate Bronfenbrenner's thoughtful feedback and assistance in identifying a publisher. Steven Pitts has been there with his continuous support for this project. Jamala Rogers has been with us both in her tireless commitment to the struggle and in her encouragement to both of us to complete this journey. We thank Mario Castro for telling his story about his union.

Michael Funke, Kathryn Wood, and Barbara Rebenstorf inspired and informed parts of this book by their activism in the cause of social justice and their dedication to creating a form of community unionism through Jobs with Justice in central Oregon. Michael Funke was both generous and invaluable with his extensive library on labor history. Barbara Rebenstorf's logistical support, research assistance, proofreading, and critical comments about grammar helped to improve the quality of the book.

Our thanks also go to our peer reviewers, whose critique strengthened this work and helped us focus; to Colin Robinson, who recruited us to start this project and embark on this journey; and to Andy Hsiao, for his constructive criticism and support in making this project work.

We offer a special thanks to our editor, Steven Hiatt, whose knowledge of our subject, expertise as an editor, ability to work under tight deadlines, and collaborative and patient style of work brought the project to a collective conclusion.

A special thanks also to the University of California Press, which surprised and inspired us with its fervor for this project.

And, of course, we thank our families not only for supporting us in this endeavor but for putting up with us when we were pulling our hair out! We love each of you.

INDEX

ABOUT THE AUTHORS

Bill Fletcher, Jr., is a longtime Left activist in the labor and African American movements. He is a senior scholar with the Institute for Policy Studies in Washington, D.C., and a founding member of the Center for Labor Renewal. He served as the Belle Zeller Visiting Professor at Brooklyn College–City University of New York from 2005 to 2007 and was the president of TransAfrica Forum from 2002 to 2006. He was formerly the education director and later assistant to the president of the AFL-CIO. Before working for the AFL-CIO, he served at the Service Employees International Union, where he held several positions, the last being assistant to the president for the East and South. His labor activism began immediately after he graduated from Harvard College, when he helped organize unemployed workers. Later he secured employment as a welder at the General Dynamics–Quincy Shipbuilding Division, where he participated in efforts to reform Local 5 of the Industrial Union of Marine and Shipbuilding Workers of America. Following this work came various grassroots and staff activities centered on labor, including stints as an organizer for District 65 of the United Auto Workers in Massachusetts and on the national staff of the National Postal Mail Handlers Union in Washington, D.C. He was an adjunct instructor at the College of Public and Community Services/University of Massachusetts–Boston. He is a member of the Service Employees International Union and has been a member of the American Federation of Teachers, District 65-UAW, and the Industrial Union of Marine and Shipbuilding Workers of America. His writings have appeared in numerous books and publications. He writes regular commentaries for the National Newspaper Publishers Association and is on the editorial board of the *Black Commentator* (www.blackcommentator.com).

Fernando E. Gapasin, PhD, is a central labor council president, labor educator, author, and former professor of industrial relations and Chicana/Chicano studies at Pennsylvania State University and the University of California, Los Angeles. He was a visiting professor at the National Labor College at the George Meany Center. He was the principal researcher for the AFL-CIO Union Cities program. In his nearly forty years of activism in the U.S. union movement, Dr. Gapasin has served as an elected and appointed union representative in eleven unions in the private and public sectors. He was also the secretary and treasurer of the Santa Clara/San Benito Counties Labor Council (AFL-CIO) and a county commissioner during the 1980s. During Dr. Gapasin's tenure in the union movement, he has worked primarily with local unions and local labor movements. He has played many roles, from principal officer of local unions to rank-and-file insurgent. He has been a chief negotiator, grievance handler, arbitration advocate, and lead organizer. His numerous publications on the union movement, race, ethnicity, and gender are informed by his extensive experience in municipal and regional union movements.

Text:	Sabon
Display:	Franklin Gothic
Compositor:	BookComp, Inc.
Indexer:	Ruth Elwell
Printer and binder:	Sheridan Books, Inc.